Dedication

To Cheryl –
my favorite canoeing companion
and very best friend.

Boundary - Waters - Canoe Area

Volume 2: The Eastern Region

Robert Beymer

 WILDERNESS PRESS · BERKELEY, CA

The Boundary Waters Canoe Area Volume 2: Eastern Region

1st EDITION July 1979
2nd EDITION March 1986
3rd EDITION April 1991
4th EDITION September 2000
  2nd Printing August 2001
  3rd Printing April 2003
  4th Printing March 2006
  5th printing February 2008

Copyright © 1979, 1986, 1991, 2000 by Robert Beymer

Front cover photos copyright © 2000 by Robert Beymer
Interior photos, except where noted, by Robert Beymer
Maps: Roger Butler (foldout), Larry Van Dyke and Jaan Hitt
Cover and book design: Jaan Hitt

ISBN: 978-0-89997-238-1
UPC: 7-19609-97238-9

Manufactured in China

Published by: **Wilderness Press**
               1200 5th Street
               Berkeley, CA 94710
               (800) 443-7227; FAX (510) 558-1696
               info@wildernesspress.com
               www.wildernesspress.com

Visit our website for a complete listing of our books and for ordering information.

Cover photos: Gotter Lake, MN, Moose on South Brule River, MN,
                 Temperance Lake, MN *(front)*
Frontispiece: Bog Lake

SAFETY NOTICE: Although Wilderness Press and the author have made every attempt to ensure that the information in this book is accurate at press time, they are not responsible for any loss, damage, injury, or inconvenience that may occur to anyone while using this book. You are responsible for your own safety and health while in the wilderness. The fact that a trail is described in this book does not mean that it will be safe for you. Be aware that trail conditions can change from day to day. Always check local conditions and know your own limitations.

Library of Congress Cataloging-in-Publication Data
Beymer, Robert.
    The Boundary Waters Canoe area / Robert Beymer. -- 4th ed.
      p. cm.
    Includes index.
    Contents: v. 2. The eastern region
    ISBN 0-89997-238-1 (alk. paper)
      1. Canoes and canoeing--Minnesota--Boundary Waters Canoe Area--Guidebooks. 2. Boundary Waters Canoe Area (Minn.)--Guidebooks. I.   Title.
      GV7776.M62 B6815 2000
      917.76'7--dc21   00-033406

Boundary Waters Canoe Area Wilderness

VOLUME 2: EASTERN REGION

Acknowledgments

A book like this could never have been written without the help and encouragement of many people. Foremost are those with whom I have paddled during the past thirty years. While I stepped off portage trails, paused to take notes, backtracked on lakes to seek a desired photograph, or paddled and portaged out of the way to investigate some unknown territory, the patience of my companions was (and still is) certainly appreciated.

Long before the idea for this book ever entered my head, my father, the Scoutmaster, introduced me to the joys of camping experiences while my mother, the English teacher, always encouraged me to write about those experiences. Throughout the years since the publication of my first book in 1978, U.S. Forest Service personnel were quite helpful in answering my questions and supplying statistical data included in this and previous editions.

When finding the time for research could have been a serious obstacle, my employers (formerly the Eddie Bauer company and most recently the State of Minnesota) granted me summer leave to explore the Wilderness. Canoes were loaned for research trips at no charge by the Eddie Bauer company, Lowe Industries, Piragis Northwoods Company and Hill's Canoe Outfitting. The W.A. Fisher Company supplied the maps used for most of my research, while Chuckwagon Foods supplied the trail food at a discounted price for many of my earlier trips. Most of all, I thank my wife of over 22 years for her steadfast support and encouragement—and for not divorcing me when I spent $200 on my first electric typewriter at a time early in our life together when funds were extremely tight!

Preface

This book was written for the peripatetic paddler—the canoeist who wants to explore the BWCA Wilderness. Base-campers and easy-going anglers, however, should also find a good deal of useful information herein to help them plan their trips.

I have been canoeing in the Boundary Waters for more than 30 years. My introduction occurred in 1967, along with 14 other members of my Explorer Post from Indianola, Iowa, and I've dipped my paddle in the cool, clear waters of "canoe country" every summer since then. While guiding BWCA canoe trips for Camp Northland from 1969 through 1977, I saw the need for a published trail guide. None existed at that time. My trail notes at Camp Northland became the foundation for this book.

The BWCAW, with over 200,000 visitors each year, is the most heavily used wilderness in the nation. With over a million pristine acres of lakes, rivers and forests within its borders, however, the Boundary Waters should be large enough to accommodate its visitors. In 1976, less than one-third of the available quotas were actually used. Unfortunately, however, over two-thirds of the visitors to the Wilderness used less than 14% of the designated entry points. The result was (and still is) congestion at some of the most popular entry points. My book was written to help you discover the entry points and routes that suit your desires and will result in the highest quality wilderness experience possible.

Since publication of my first book in 1978, nearly 70,000 copies of both volumes have been sold to inquisitive paddlers. During the past 21 years, I have received feedback from friends and strangers alike. At my work with camping stores in the Twin Cities and in Ely, as well as at speaking engagements throughout the upper Midwest, I had opportunities to personally meet many of my readers—a valuable experience that presents itself to few writers. Because of the feedback received, and because of continuing research conducted from my current home near the Wilderness, there have been many changes made to these guidebooks in successive editions and printings. After 20 years in print and 5 revisions, it was time in 1998 to thoroughly update the books. So my wife, Cheryl, and I spent the entire summer of 1998 exploring the water routes—again—to ensure that the information contained in this book is accurate, informative and useful. That summer, we paddled 421 miles on 190 lakes and 20 rivers. We also hiked 191 miles on 250 portages and 4 hiking trails. Yes, it was tough work, but somebody's got to do it!

It may seem odd to the casual wilderness observer that frequent changes are necessary to update a guidebook like this one. "How can a wilderness change?" you might ask. Well, the BWCA Wilderness itself has changed very little over the past 20 years. Natural changes do occur, however, and readers need to know about them. Forest fires and windstorms occasionally alter the landscape. Beaver dams deteriorate and small lakes upstream literally dry up. Or new beaver dams are constructed, flooding portage trails.

More often, the changes that may significantly affect your visit are caused by decisions of Forest Service officials. During the past 30 years, I have witnessed many changes in the administration of the Boundary Waters. The ban against non-reusable food and beverage containers (cans and bottles) took effect in 1971. The visitor distribution (quota) system was started in 1976. Implementation of the BWCA Wilderness Act of 1978, which eliminated motorboats from most of the interior lakes, took effect on January 1, 1979. Since then, entry points have been eliminated, renamed, grouped together or separated for the purposes of quota restrictions. The use of trucks to transport motorboats from Lake Vermilion to Trout Lake and from Sucker Lake to Basswood Lake was banned by a court ruling in 1992, only to be reinstated by a congressional act in 1998. In 1995, a decision was made to restrict the number of people in a group to nine and the number of watercraft to four. Canoe rests on portage trails were also eliminated that year. These and many other changes did occur in the BWCA Wilderness.

Both my publisher and I want this guidebook to serve you, the paddler. We will continue to make changes in the future, reflecting new regulations, alterations to existing routes, and the wishes of our readers. I've tried to make this book interesting and useful. Above all, my goal has always been to impart accurate information. I believe that this attention to accuracy and to the concerns of our readers is why this book continues to be as popular today as it was when first published over 20 years ago.

This book was written for the canoe camper who is capable of taking care of himself or herself in a wilderness environment. It does not take you by the hand and lead you through the often-complicated mazes of lakes, streams and portages that characterize the BWCA Wilderness. It does not tell you when to turn right, when to veer left, or when and where to stop for lunch. You should already possess the · understanding and the basic skills that are essential for a canoe trip into a wilderness, particularly the ability to guide yourself along the suggested routes without detailed directions. This book also does not include such topics as how to paddle a canoe, how to carry your gear across portages, how to shoot rapids, or how to pack your gear. Many good "how to" books have been written about canoeing and camping in the Boundary Waters. This guide is a "where to" book.

If you need information about canoeing or camping techniques, or about other things related to the BWCA Wilderness, I suggest you read several of the books listed below and pick out what is appropriate to your needs.

- Books about canoeing or camping techniques:

   American Canoe Association, *Introduction to Paddling: Canoeing Basics for Lakes and Rivers*. Menasha Ridge Press, 1996.

   Bell, Patricia J., *Roughing It Elegantly: A Practical Guide to Canoe Camping*. Eden Prairie, MN: Cat's Paw Press, 1994.

   Drabik, Harry, *Harry Drabik's Guide to Wilderness Canoeing*. Minneapolis: Nodin Press, 1987.

   Furtman, Michael, *Canoe Country Camping: Wilderness Skills for the Boundary Waters and Quetico*. Duluth: Pfeifer-Hamilton, 1992.

   Jacobson, Cliff, three fine books from Merrilville, IN: ICS Books:

   > *Boundary Waters: Canoe Camping With Style*. 1995.
   > *The Basic Essentials of Canoeing*. 1997.
   > *The Basic Essentials of Camping*. 1988.

- Books about Boundary Waters wildlife:

   Heinselman, Myron, *The Boundary Waters Wilderness Ecosystem*. The University of Minnesota Press: Minneapolis, MN, 1996.

   Stensaas, Mark, **two indispensable books** from Duluth: Pfeifer-Hamilton:

   > *Canoe Country Flora: Plants and Trees of the North Woods and Boundary Waters*. 1996.
   > *Canoe Country Wildlife: A Field Guide to the Boundary Waters and Quetico*. 1992.

- A book about environmental protection of the BWCAW:

Proescholdt, Kevin, Rip Rapson and Myron Heinselman, *Troubled Waters: The Fight for the Boundary Waters Canoe Area Wilderness.* St. Cloud, MN: North Star Press, 1995.

♦ To capture the mood of canoeing in the Boundary Waters: Any of Sigurd F. Olson's vivid accounts (New York: Alfred A. Knopf), including:

Reflections from the North Country, 1976 (1997).

Listening Point, Random House, 1958 (1996).

The Singing Wilderness, Knopf, 1956 (1997).

Brandenburg, Jim, *Chased by the Light.* Minocqua, WI: Northword Press, 1998. Incredible photos with tantalizing text.

The Boundary Waters Journal, a fine magazine with exceptional photographs, published four times each year by the Boundary Waters Journal Publishing Co., 9396 Rocky Ledge Road, Ely, MN 55731.

♦ Books about other canoeing areas adjacent to the BWCA Wilderness:

Beymer, Robert, *A Paddler's Guide to Quetico Provincial Park.* Virginia, MN: W.A. Fisher Company, 1997.

Beymer, Robert, *Superior National Forest.* Seattle: The Mountaineers, 1989.

This book is a comprehensive guide, including all entry points that are used by canoeists in the eastern half of the Boundary Waters Canoe Area Wilderness, from Hog Creek to North Fowl Lake. Volume I deals with entry points in the western half of the BWCAW, from Crane Lake to Isabella Lake.

SPECIAL NOTICE ABOUT WIND DAMAGE

On July 4, 1999, after this book was written but before it went to press, a massive summer storm raced through the BWCA Wilderness. Straight-line winds estimated at between 80 and 100 mph severely damaged about 350,000 acres of woodlands. Another 150,000 acres also suffered damage, though not as severe. Nearly half of the Boundary Waters was affected by the storm, including much of the north-central and eastern parts of the Wilderness from Basswood Lake to the Tip of the Arrowhead. The primary path of the storm was 10-to-12 miles wide and 35-to-40 miles long. It was estimated by the Minnesota DNR that 80% of the trees blew down or snapped in that area. Forest Service crews reported trees stacked 6-to-8 deep, with some piles rising as high as 15 feet above the ground. Of course, that made scores of portages and campsites unusable immediately following the storm.

Soon after the storm, Forest Service officials reported that 800 campsites, 80 miles of portages and over 130 miles of hiking trails in the BWCAW were impacted by the storm. Some of the worst damage occurred along lakes that I describe in my book as among the most scenic in the Wilderness—including Knife, Kekekabic and Little Saganaga lakes in the central BWCAW, and parts of the Tip of the Arrowhead region. Eyewitness reports from paddlers caught in the storm included such descriptions as "phenomenal," "terrifying" and "devastating." Some biologists suggest that the storm could have been the biggest of its kind in 1,000 years. Certainly nothing like it has occurred during the recorded history of northeastern Minnesota.

Immediately after the storm swept through the region, helicopters were permitted in the BWCAW to facilitate evacuation of about 20 injured campers and to help survey all campsites and portages in the Wilderness for other parties in distress. To expedite clean-up of the debris, the Forest Service authorized the use of chainsaws and other motorized equipment through December 31, 2000. These were unprecedented decisions necessitated by an unprecedented natural catastrophe. If you hear chainsaws operating in the Boundary Waters during the summer of 2000, don't be alarmed or perturbed. They are being used to make the Wilderness more accessible and safer for you and other visitors in the most heavily used wilderness area in America.

Some of the descriptions in this book may serve to remind you of what the area looked like before the storm rather than what it looks like now. All of the photos in this book were taken prior to the storm of July 4, 1999. Some of the scenes illustrated by these photos may not appear the same to you as they did when the photos were taken. So,

Wind damaged area

what should you expect to see during your next visit to the BWCAW? In some parts of the Wilderness—the northwestern and south-central parts—you may not notice anything unusual. Even in the most affected parts of the Boundary Waters, the shorelines of the lakes were sometimes the least affected parts of the forest. So you may still see trees standing along the edges of the lakes on which you are paddling, while on higher ground between the lakes the devastation is nearly 100%. It may look like a massive timber clear-cut with the trees left on the ground to rot. The sight may bring tears to the eyes of visitors whose favorite destinations of the past have been altered nearly beyond recognition—and will remain so for decades. Some of the lake descriptions in this book may serve to remind you of what the area looked like before the storm, rather than what it looks like now.

For sure you can expect a ban on campfires in the affected parts of the Wilderness for several years. Five weeks after the storm, the Forest Service imposed campfire restrictions "in response to the heavy fuel buildup resulting from the storm." Only gas and propane stoves were allowed in the restricted areas. The sketch (following page) shows the only two parts of the BWCAW that were *not* severely affected by the storm and thus not included in the 1999 fire ban.

Beyond the immediate and obvious changes in appearance of the woodlands, there are less obvious results that have already occurred

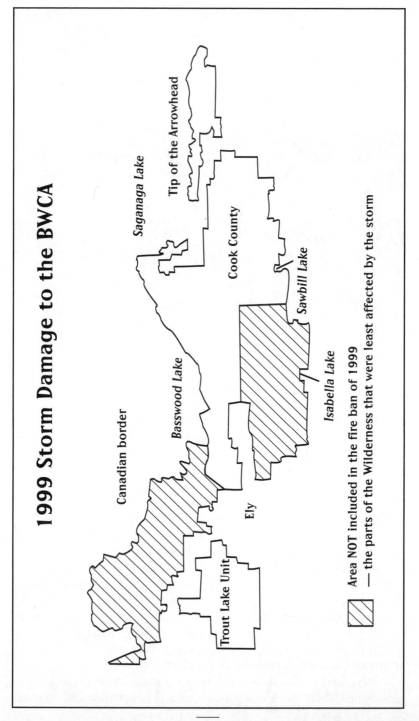

and long-term effects of the storm that can be predicted. Destroyed by the storm were many longtime nests of eagles and ospreys, as well as countless other birds that made their summer homes in the Boundary Waters. It's far too early to estimate other wildlife casualties of the storm. The long-term ecological effect may be similar to that of a massive forest fire. Indeed, fires ignited by lightning are likely to burn parts of the dead, downed forest. Roughly 80% of the forest covering half the Wilderness is now dead, and during a dry season this mangled pile of tinder could be virtually explosive for several years to come. The rest of the fallen forest will simply decay. Old forests will be replaced first by the lush new growth of small plants and shrubs and eventually by young forests. Animals like moose and deer, which thrive in open areas created by fires and clear-cuts, may proliferate—to the benefit of the wolf population. Other types of wildlife which benefit from older forests may now be absent from the storm-effected parts of the BWCAW. At this time, we can only speculate about the forthcoming changes to America's most popular wilderness.

A year after the storm, the Forest Service authorized prescribed burning of 75,000 acres of blown down forest. It began in the fall of 2001 and will continue for five to seven years at a rate of 5,000 to 20,000 acres per year. The primary goal of the project is to reduce the risk of wildfire that could put people at risk and threaten property adjacent to the Wilderness.

The USFS declares that its objective "is to accomplish this goal while being sensitive to ecological and wilderness values."

*The singing wilderness has to do with
the calling of the loons, northern lights,
and the great silences of a land lying
northwest of Lake Superior.
It is concerned with the simple joys,
the timelessness and perspective found
in a way of life that is close to the past.
I have heard the singing in many places,
but I seem to hear it best in the wilderness
lake country of the Quetico-Superior,
where travel is still by pack and canoe
over the ancient trails of the Indians and Voyageurs.*

— *Sigurd F. Olson*

Introduction to the BWCA Wilderness

THE BOUNDARY WATERS CANOE AREA WILDERNESS IS PARADISE FOR THE wilderness paddler. Stretching for nearly 200 miles along the Canadian border of northeastern Minnesota, this magnificent region offers more than 1,000 lakes, nearly 2,000 campsites, 160 miles of portage trails, and over 1,500 miles of canoe routes through some of the most beautiful country in the world. That's why over 200,000 people visit it each year and make it the most popular wilderness area in America. At over a million acres, it is the second largest unit of our National Wilderness Preservation system, containing the largest virgin forests remaining east of the Rocky Mountains.

History

The canoe routes on which you will paddle are the very same water trails used for hundreds of years by the Sioux and Chippewa Indians and by the French-Canadian Voyageurs. Jacques de Noyons, in about 1688, was probably the first white man to paddle through the lakes and streams that now compose the BWCAW. At that time, the Sioux may have still been the dominant Indians in the area. But by the time of the first fur traders in the 18th century, the Chippewa Indians had moved into the region from the east and had driven the Sioux farther west onto the plains. From then to about 1800, French-Canadian Voyageurs paddled their birch-bark canoes from the hinterlands of northwestern Canada to the shores of Lake Superior, transporting furs from trappers toward the European markets.

The populations of fur-bearing animals that had once flourished in the region were nearly depleted by the mid-1800s. The trappers moved on to more promising areas and the colorful Voyageur era came to an end.

After years of boundary disputes between the British and Americans, the two governments signed the Webster-Ashburton Treaty in 1842. It established the international boundary along the "customary" route of the fur traders. The Americans had argued that the customary route of the Voyageurs was along the Kaministikwia and Maligne rivers to the north. The British had claimed that the St. Louis River, far to the south, should constitute the boundary. The existing boundary was a compromise.

During the latter half of the 19th century, settlers moved into the area, including farmers, loggers and miners. Mineral prospectors first sought gold along the border region, and a short-lived gold rush did attract considerable attention to the area. Far more important to northeastern Minnesota, however, was the discovery of high-grade iron ore. Numerous mines sprung up at the present sites of Ely and Soudan and in the area southwest of those towns. After the railroad penetrated this part of the country, extensive logging and mining operations threatened to devastate the entire region.

The Superior National Forest was designated in 1909, and within it, in 1926, approximately one thousand acres were set aside as a primitive roadless area. This area was enlarged in the 1930s. In 1939 the wilderness area was re-designated as the Superior Roadless Primitive Area, establishing boundaries containing over one million acres. In 1958 the current name was adopted. The BWCA Wilderness Bill of 1978 established the current boundaries, containing 1,075,000 acres. It also prohibits logging, restricts mining operations and limits the use of motorboats to 24% of the total water area on just a few large perimeter lakes. The BWCAW is administered by the United States Forest Service, Department of Agriculture.

Thanks to the efforts of conservationists throughout the years, this beautiful region looks just as wild and enticing to visitors today as it did when De Noyons first viewed it.

Wildlife

Perhaps nothing represents the Boundary Waters to its visitors better than the eerie wail of the common loon, the Minnesota State Bird. But many other birds are equally at home here, including the bald eagle, the herring gull, the great blue heron, the osprey, the Canadian jay and several varieties of hawks and owls. The tranquilizing song of a white-throated sparrow is as much a part of the wilderness experience as is the scolding chirp of a red squirrel. In the BWCAW you will also find the last substantial population of timber wolves in the "lower forty-

Osprey nest on Ahmakose Lake

eight," as well as large populations of moose, white-tailed deer, black bears, beavers and red fox. Other less visible mammals include otters, lynx, fishers, mink, muskrats, martens, weasels, coyotes and a variety of squirrels. The more quietly you travel through the Wilderness, the greater are your chances of seeing these and other forms of wildlife along the way.

One creature of particular interest to most visitors is the magnificent moose. Where will you see moose? Just about anywhere! But they are most abundant in large open areas that have been cleared of dense forest. During the 1970s, there were two places in the Boundary Waters that contained two of the densest populations of moose in North America. One was in the vicinity of the Isabella Lake, Hog Creek and Kawishiwi Lake entry points—the south-central part of the Wilderness—where recent logging operations had cleared the forest. Another area was between the Moose River North and Little Indian Sioux River North entry points—the vast region north of the Echo Trail that had been burned by the Little Indian Sioux Fire of 1971. Both of these regions still contain good populations of moose, but they are not nearly as dense now that the forests have grown back. So where are moose most likely to be seen today? Expect to see them in and near large areas where the forest recently burned. The Gabbro Lake Fire, the White Feather Fire, the South Temperance Fire, the Winchell Lake Fire and the Saganaga Corridor Fire all resulted in clearing substantial parts of the forest during the 1990s, creating habitat that is quite favorable to moose and other wildlife. As the forest in these areas grows back to maturity, the moose will move on to other regions that recently burned. It's a natural cycle that is essential to sustaining the population of these burly beasts.

While traveling throughout the BWCAW, always treat the wildlife with respect. Remember, you are a visitor in the Wilderness but the wildlife are residents. You can help the wildlife stay wild and healthy by not feeding the creatures and not interfering with their normal routines. Don't paddle close to loons or try to imitate their calls, which are used for communication. Should you find yourself near any nesting birds, observe them from a distance. Human disturbance at a nest site may lead to nest abandonment and loss of eggs.

The predominant game fishes are northern pike, walleyes, smallmouth bass and lake trout. Black crappies and bluegills are also plentiful in many of the lakes. Even rainbow and brook trout have been stocked in some lakes.

Contrary to the perception of most paddlers, water covers only about 12% of the BWCA Wilderness. A coniferous forest of jack pine, Norway pine, white pine, tamarack, black spruce, white spruce, balsam fir and white cedar covers most of this region. There are also extensive stands of deciduous trees, including paper birch and quaking aspens. Very few dry land areas in the BWCAW are not forested. Bogs occupy the rest of the region that is not covered by lakes or forests.

Bears

Black bears are common throughout the BWCAW. Although they are not considered to be dangerous and are usually quite shy around campers, they may be pests when searching for food—your food.

Over the years bears have learned that canoe campers always travel with food packs and (unfortunately) often leave food scraps and garbage lying around their campsites. Where people most frequently camp, bears are most frequently a problem. Actually bears are not the problem, people are! Where campsites are kept clean and food packs are suspended properly, bears are not a problem. Nor are the smaller creatures that might otherwise depend on humans for their daily sustenance (chipmunks, mice and the like).

Seeing a bear on a canoe trip should be a treat, not a tragedy. Nevertheless, an unpleasant encounter with a bear could bring an abrupt end to your canoe trip—regardless of who caused the problem! There are no hard-and-fast rules to ensure protection from a bear. Bear behavior differs under different conditions. The bears you may encounter while visiting the BWCAW are wild animals and they *could* be dangerous. Always remember that! With a few precautions, however, you should have no problems with these fascinating and beautiful creatures.

◆ Avoid camping on the most popular lakes where there are numerous, frequently occupied campsites located relatively close together. A small island located well away from the shoreline and away from other islands offers a *degree* of safety. But don't let an island campsite lull you into a false sense of security. Bears are very good swimmers.

◆ When you are away from your campsite (even just fishing nearby) and at night, always hang your food pack off the ground. It should be at least 10 feet above the ground and 6 feet away from tree trunks and large limbs. Bears are good climbers, so the food must be a safe distance away from the trunk and from any limbs large enough to support a bear's weight.

◆ Never store food in your tent. And if food was spilled on your clothes, leave your clothes outside your tent at night.

◆ Keep a clean campsite. Thoroughly burn or safely bury all food scraps and leftover grease, or seal your garbage in an airtight plastic bag and carry it with your food pack. Do not dispose of leftovers in the latrine. Bears will find them and destroy the latrine in the process.

♦ Never get between a mother bear and her cub(s). If you see a cub, its mother is probably nearby. Female bears are extremely protective of their young.

♦ If a bear does wander into your campsite, don't panic! They are usually frightened off by loud noises. Try yelling or banging some pots together. Don't charge the bear; it may become defensive.

♦ If a stubborn bear does not back off or acts strangely, move to another campsite. It is extremely rare for a black bear to attack a human being; but it did happen to two campers in separate incidents (same bear) during the summer of 1987. Neither camper was seriously injured and the bear was later killed by authorities.

♦ Don't lose any sleep worrying about the sounds you hear outside your tent at night. In general, the noisiest critters are also the smallest—mice among the worst! (Moose are exceptions to this general rule.) Bears are extremely quiet, often stealthy creatures that can wander through a campsite in the black of night without arousing any attention from its human occupants. If

Snipe Lake campsite

you hear rustling leaves at night, chances are good that it's not caused by a black bear. Rest assured!

Finally, don't let a fear of black bears detract from your enjoyment of the BWCA Wilderness. Use good common sense, observe the tips above, and you should have no problem with bears—or any other wild animal.

Climate

For the canoeist in northern Minnesota, spring, summer and fall are essentially crowded into a span of five months—May through September. The ice is usually (though not always) off the lakes by the first week of May, but the trees are not fully leafed out until at least the middle of the month. That period, when the water levels are high and before the biting insects invade the Boundary Waters, is an excellent time to explore the tiny creeks that may later be too low for navigation. Be prepared, however, for weather cold enough to produce snow. Early June is often a wet, cool and gloomy time of year, usually plagued by hordes of mosquitoes, sand flies and ticks. The fishing is best then. July and August normally offer the best weather for campers and the worst for anglers (too warm for some fish species). As the summer progresses, the water levels of some shallow streams may become too low for navigating a loaded canoe, eliminating some excellent route possibilities. From late August through September, after the first frost, biting insects have nearly disappeared. This is a wonderful time to explore the Wilderness. But you must be prepared for extended periods of cool and rainy weather, or even snow. After September, contact local authorities for weather updates. It is not unusual for the lakes to ice over in October, and snow may accumulate on the ground. On the other hand, that month may also be mild and dry, with crisp nights that are ideal for sleeping.

Temperatures and rainfall vary, of course, throughout the BWCAW. The following statistics, recorded in International Falls, represent approximations for the western region of the Boundary Waters.

	May	June	July	Aug.	Sept.
Ave. temperature	51	60	66	63	53
Ave. low each day	38	48	53	51	41
Ave. high each day	63	72	78	76	64
Ave. precipitation	2.6"	3.9"	3.5"	3.6"	2.9"

Because of its close proximity to Lake Superior, the eastern part of the BWCA Wilderness sometimes exhibits extremely variable weather. While the lakes in the far-eastern region may be blanketed with a cool, misty fog from Lake Superior, nearby lakes to the northwest may be enjoying warm sunshine, thanks to the subtle yet significant effects of both Lake Superior and the Laurentian Divide. Consequently, no weather data from any one reporting station can accurately represent all of the Boundary Waters.

Geology

The rocks in this area are mostly Precambrian rocks covered by a thin veneer of glacial deposits. For approximately two billion years, during the Precambrian era, vast changes were generated by a large amount of diverse geologic activity that reshaped the landscape many times. Following long periods of erosion and igneous intrusions, the great ice sheets of the Pleistocene Epoch began to form nearly two million years ago. Ice scoured the Precambrian bedrock, gouging out the softer rocks and leaving behind irregular blankets of glacial debris. This created the topography that we see today.

The BWCA Wilderness contains some of the oldest exposed rock in the world, estimated to be as old as 2.7 billion years. It is part of the vast region known as the Canadian Shield, which underlies almost two million square miles of eastern Canada and the Lake Superior region of the United States. In Minnesota this belt of ancient exposed rock extends west from the area of Saganaga Lake on the international border through Ely and International Falls to the northwestern part of the state, where the old rocks disappear beneath younger sedimentary deposits. Included in this expanse of ancient rocks are the metavolcanic Ely Greenstone formation, the metasedimentary Knife Lake Group and great granitic batholiths like the Vermilion and the Saganaga batholiths.

A mountain-building period began about 2.6 billion years ago, during which the rocks became metamorphosed and strongly deformed, and the granites were intruded from below into the older rocks. The rocks that had been formed or altered deep within the earth's crust became exposed at the surface and were then subjected to erosion.

The geologic events that may have been the most economically significant to the state of Minnesota began with the encroachment of a broad arm of the ocean upon the eroded terrain. Inland seas covered what we now call the North Woods. Layers of sedimentary rocks were deposited at the bottom of that enormous sea. Called the Animikie

Group, these rocks lie in a belt extending westward along the border lakes from Lake Superior to just south of Saganaga Lake, and then reappearing in the Mesabi Range south of the BWCAW. The Animikie rocks include the Pokegama quartzite, the Biwabik iron formation and a sequence of shales and sandstones. Flint, too, is found in abundance in the vicinity of Gunflint Lake. Rich deposits of iron ore are scattered throughout northeastern Minnesota, upon which mining communities sprung up in the early 20th Century. Iron ore became the economic basis for many communities in northeastern Minnesota and it is still one of the most important industries for the state of Minnesota. The iron ore is so concentrated in some places that it will cause a compass needle to be deflected from magnetic north. Magnetic Lake, in fact, received its name because of just such a phenomenon.

Around 1.7 to 1.6 billion years ago, another period of mountain building occurred when the sedimentary rocks and other existing rocks were folded, faulted, metamorphosed and intruded by granitic magmas. Later an outpouring of lava in and around the area now occupied by Lake Superior created the major rock of the North Shore. After this volcanic activity subsided, stream erosion and deposition again became the dominant processes in the area.

The inland seas had long since disappeared and new mountains had risen on the continent when the great ice sheet of the Ice Age advanced from the north and began to cover northeastern Minnesota. It was the ice sheet that turned this mineral-rich region into the world's best canoe country. During four major periods of glaciation, the glaciers altered the landscape considerably. These periods began almost two million years ago. The last glacial advance and recession (the Wisconsin Glaciation) lasted from about 100,000 to 10,000 years ago. Evidence of the Ice Age is everywhere in the Boundary Waters today. Parallel grooves called striations are visible on many rock ledges that were scoured by the ice. Glacial debris from small pebbles to huge boulders is widespread. Here and there, you will see the large boulders, called erratics, that were left "stranded" when the glaciers melted.

Perhaps the greatest distinction of the border lakes area is the presence of exposed bedrock. This region is unlike the rest of the state, which is almost completely covered by glacial deposits. This domination of exposed bedrock in the Boundary Waters resulted in distinctive patterns of lakes and ridges, which reflect the underlying rock structures. In the eastern third of the region the lakes form a distinctive linear pattern. Long, narrow lakes give the terrain a notable east-west "grain." These lakes are set in two major types of rock formations. The lakes on the Duluth Gabbro formation, which is exposed over an area from Duluth north and east to the Canadian border, developed their particular pattern because alternating bands of less resistant rock and more resistant rock are oriented east-west. Erosion removed more of the less resistant rock, creating lake basins. In the area where the Rove Lake formation is exposed—along the international border from Gunflint Lake to Pigeon Point (the very tip of the Arrowhead)—the east-west linear pattern has a different cause. In this area intervening ridges separate the lakes. These ridges are the exposed edges of south-sloping layers of dark igneous rock that was intruded into sedimentary rocks after they were deposited. The north-facing slopes of the ridges are very steep and form escarpments 200-500 feet high. Huge piles of talus blocks cover the lower parts of many escarpments, the result of erosion by the advancing glaciers as they passed transversely over the ridges.

The lakes set in the Knife Lake group of rocks show a similar linear pattern, but the trend is northeast-to-southwest. In the rocks associated with the Ely Greenstone formation, the pattern is less regular and the depressions in the bedrock are not as deep. Thus shallower lakes are found there.

In the area underlain by the Saganaga Granite the story is a little different. Here the shapes of the lakes are dictated by cracks in the Precambrian rock. As the cracks were made wider by erosion, they became linear depressions that lakes could occupy. Many of the lakes lie in collections of linear depressions oriented in more than one direction, so that the lakes have zigzag shapes. An overhead view of the area reveals many jagged lakes interconnected by linear channels. Saganaga Lake itself is a good example.

Because of the glaciation of the Ice Age and the characteristic Precambrian rock of northeastern Minnesota, the Boundary Waters Canoe Area, with all of its interconnected lakes and streams, is one of the most extraordinary recreational wilderness areas in the world.

Fires

Under a Forest Service policy implemented in 1987, lightning-caused fires in the BWCA Wilderness are allowed to burn without suppression if the fires fall within certain prescribed limits. Those limiting considerations include location, risks to property and public safety, and weather factors. Natural fires that are not within prescribed limits and all human-caused fires are suppressed.

For centuries, large areas of the Wilderness burned from lightning-caused fires, which reduced fuel accumulations and created diverse wildlife habitats. The USFS fire policy is intended to partly restore fire to its natural role in the Wilderness, whenever it can occur within the limits of safety. The Forest Service informs the public about ongoing fires. Notices are posted at canoe landings, and field crews notify paddlers within the Wilderness about threatening blazes.

You may encounter natural fires in the BWCA Wilderness. Forest Service personnel may not be present at the fire site, although all fires are under some form of surveillance. If you choose to observe the fire, do so from a safe distance, and consider the following tips:

- Fires normally move in the same direction as the wind. Find a safe location away from the fire's path.
- Be careful while visiting a recently burned area. Ashes may remain hot for days, and there is always a danger of falling snags and tree limbs.
- Do not attempt to extinguish a prescribed fire. A natural fire is part of the Wilderness. It results in ecological changes that are consistent with Wilderness management.
- Fires may smolder and burn very slowly for days or even weeks without much increase in size. Then weather changes can cause dramatic and dangerous increases in fire size. Respect all fires as potentially dangerous.

Although wilderness fires result in positive benefits to the forest, fire can also be devastating. YOU HAVE A RESPONSIBILITY to prevent human-caused fires. The long-standing Smokey Bear message of fire prevention is still valid. Please be careful!

Safety

Risk is an integral part of a wilderness expedition. Risks associated with isolation, tough physical challenges, adverse weather conditions and lack of rapid communications are inherent in a visit to the BWCAW. At all times exercise caution, use common sense, and consider the following tips:

- Do not take chances to save time.
- Always wear a life preserver, even if you can swim. It is a law in Minnesota to have one wearable U.S. Coast Guard-approved personal flotation device (life jacket) readily accessible to each person in a canoe.
- Do not attempt canoe travel during a lightning storm or when there are large waves.
- Never stand in a canoe; keep your weight low and centered.
- If you should capsize, stay with the canoe; it won't sink.
- Use the portages. Do not run rapids unless you are confident

you can do it safely, and only after you have scouted them. Remember that water levels change considerably during the summer months. Rapids that may have been perfectly safe to run during your last trip in August could be a dangerous, raging torrent during your next trip in June (or vice versa). Canoeing mishaps occur every summer in the Boundary Waters. Some result in drowning. Many result in damaged canoes. Most result in spoiled trips.

◆ Carry a good first-aid kit and know how to use it. See to it that *every* member of your group knows CPR. Be alert for hypothermia, especially when any member of your group becomes wet.

◆ If a *serious* accident occurs, send one canoe for help immediately. Or use a heavy smoke signal to attract a Forest Service patrol plane. If you have a cellular phone with you, use it to get help *only* if an accident is life threatening! (Note: having a bear in your campsite is *not* a sufficient reason to summon assistance!) Evacuation by plane or other motorized vehicle is approved only when there are no other options available and a person needs the immediate services of a doctor. The local county sheriff authorizes all emergency searches, rescues and evacuations. *If an evacuation is necessary, you will be billed for the cost.*

◆ Boil or treat water before drinking. Even then, if algae are visible, don't drink the water. Although lake water may look pure, drinking it without first filtering, boiling or chemically treating it may cause illness. When using a filter or chemicals, be certain that they are designed to remove or kill *Giardia lamblia*, in particular—a nasty parasite that can cause a harsh intestinal illness.

◆ Before setting out on your trip, be sure that someone—Forest Service official, outfitter or friend—knows your itinerary and when you expect to return, with instructions to contact authorities if you are overdue. The Forest Service has no way of knowing when (or if) you exit the BWCAW.

Visiting a Wilderness

A wilderness, in contrast with those areas where man and his own works dominate the landscape, is hereby recognized as an area where the earth and its community of life are untrammeled by man, where man himself is a visitor who does not remain.

Using this definition, Congress passed the Wilderness Act of 1964 and created the National Wilderness Preservation System. Included as the only water-based wilderness, and the largest wilderness in the

Flying Lake portage

lower 48 states, the Boundary Waters is also the most heavily used wilderness in America. Many of the 200,000 annual visitors are not familiar with minimum-impact camping techniques and the need to protect the fragile wilderness from damage. Litter strewn along portages and left in fire grates; birch trees stripped of bark; red and white pines with carved initials; and fire-blackened areas resulting from campfires left burning are just some of the signs of abuse seen far too often in the BWCA Wilderness. Other problems caused by the large number of visitors may be less permanent but still inappropriate in a wilderness setting. Large, noisy groups shouting across a lake or singing boisterously around a campfire, and bright-colored equipment easily seen from across a lake detract from the feeling of quiet and solitude that wilderness visitors seek.

Wilderness areas are managed to protect and maintain the environment in its natural state for our enjoyment and for the enjoyment of generations to come. The responsibility for protecting these areas lies not only with professional managers, however. As a visitor, you and your group also share in this responsibility. You must realize that your place within the wilderness is not as a conqueror, but as a wise keeper and a good steward of this land and water. By ensuring a quality wilderness experience for yourself and others, you will be preserving the area for generations to come.

Regulations and Recommendations

In General...

+ Travel permits must be obtained before entering the BWCAW and must be in your possession while in the Wilderness. This applies to overnight use as well as daytime visits.
+ Party size is limited to 9 people, with a limit of 4 canoes per party. This applies to daytime travel as well as to campsite occupancy. Not only must two groups of 9 people each camp separately, they must also paddle separately.
+ Airplanes must not fly at an altitude below 4,000 feet while passing over the Boundary Waters.
+ Unauthorized use of metal detectors is strictly forbidden.
+ The use of firearms, while not illegal, is discouraged. There is no need for them in the Wilderness.
+ All federal, state and local laws must be obeyed. (Prior to your trip, call the Minnesota Department of Natural Resources for boating and fishing regulations: toll-free (888) 646-6367 or local (651) 296-6157.
+ Though dogs are not banned from the Wilderness, they are better off at home. Many dogs become barkers, even if they never bark at home, and barking is a disturbance to other campers. Other dogs may charge wild animals, including bears. They are also susceptible to attacks by timber wolves. If you choose to bring your dog, it must be kept on a leash at landings and on portages.

While traveling...

+ Motorized travel and mechanical portaging are permitted only on certain specified routes. Use of any other motorized or mechanical equipment of any type is not permitted within the Wilderness.
+ Watercraft, motors, mechanical devices or equipment not used in connection with the current visit may not be stored on or moored to National Forest land and left unattended.

+ If a portage is crowded, patiently wait on the water—away from the landing—for your turn. There should never be more than 9 people or 4 canoes together, even if they are not traveling in the same group.

+ Unload, move and reload as quickly as possible on portages. Don't stop for lunch or prolonged rest breaks where you might interfere with others along the trail.

+ Avoid dragging your canoe at portage landings and across the trails. Not only does it damage your canoe, but the noise may also be heard a great distance away.

While camping...

+ Camping is permitted only at Forest Service campsites that have steel fire grates and box latrines, and within certain designated Primitive Management Areas.

+ Camping is limited to a maximum of 14 consecutive days at one campsite.

+ Open campfires are permitted only within constructed fireplaces at developed campsites, or as specifically approved on the BWCAW travel permit.

+ Use dead, downed wood for campfires. The best place to look is back from the shore, away from campsites. Usually the driest wood is found on fallen trees that are leaning against other windfalls and not lying directly on the ground. The best firewood comes from dead, dry jack pine, white pine, spruce, tamarack, white cedar, aspen and ash. Paper birch is usually poor firewood when found lying on the ground, because it rots quickly. Red pine and balsam fir also make poor firewood. Do not cut live trees! Green wood from any tree burns very poorly, if at all. Damage to live trees (cutting, carving or peeling off the bark) is not only unsightly, but it also causes irreparable damage to the forest. It's also illegal. Carry some fire ribbon or other starting material to ignite fires in wet weather.

+ Fires must be drowned with water and be dead out before you leave a campsite—even if you just go fishing for awhile. Pour water over the fire while stirring the ashes. Then, if you feel any warmth in the ashes with your bare hand, douse the ashes again.

+ Non-burnable, disposable food and beverage containers (cans and bottles) are not permitted. Containers of fuel, insect repellent, medicine, and personal toiletry items, however, are permitted.

+ It is unlawful to cut live trees, shrubs or boughs, or to use moss or boughs for a bed. Digging trenches around tents, tarps or anywhere else is also not permitted. Trenching and using pine boughs for mattresses (once accepted practices but now illegal) inflict harm to the environment.

◆ Cord should be used instead of nails or wire.

◆ Demonstrate common courtesies. Leave clean campsites for those who follow. Preserve and respect the peace and solitude of the Wilderness. Sound carries far across open water—especially on a quiet evening. Keep noise to a minimum and you'll improve the quality of the wilderness experience for yourself and for others. You will also greatly improve your chance of seeing wildlife.

◆ Use Wilderness latrines. If no latrine is available, bury human waste in 6 to 8 inches of soil at least 150 feet from the shores of lakes and streams.

◆ Keep soap, dishwater and grease away from lakes and streams. Take your dishes and hot water back away from the lake to wash them. Rinse them well and dump all the soapy water at least 150 feet from the lake. Use biodegradable soap instead of detergents. Likewise, when you feel the urge to wash yourself, jump in the lake to get wet. Then soap up and rinse off at least 150 feet from the shore.

◆ Use the bottom of a canoe for a table, rather than constructing one from native materials.

◆ If your tent or tarp is bright-colored, set it up as far from the shore as possible, so that it cannot be seen by other campers across the lake.

◆ **Leave no trace!** That's the general rule for camping in any wilderness. When leaving a campsite, leave no trace of your presence there. Regarding leftovers, eat them, burn them or pack them out. If you burn them, do so in a *hot* fire. If you must bury leftovers or fish entrails, paddle along the shore away from campsites, go into the woods at least 150 feet from the water and bury them in 6 to 8 inches of soil. After a fire is dead out, sift through the ashes for twist ties, foil and other debris not completely burned. Pack them in your litterbag, along with any cigarette filters and other trash, and carry them out. Add to that any litter found on portages and at canoe landings. *Always leave an area cleaner than you found it.*

The Use of Modern Technology

To most people, the allure of a wilderness canoe trip is the opportunity to live simply and to travel much as the Voyageurs did over 200 years ago. While it is not illegal to take and use cellular phones, transistor radios or GPS devices, they really have no legitimate place in a wilderness setting.

Of course, some might argue that lightweight Kevlar canoes, ultralight nylon tents and camp stoves also do not belong in a wilderness. Perhaps they are right. Each of us must draw a line somewhere. Some folks need three trips across each portage to carry all their gear from lake to lake. Others can do it in just one trip. Most need two trips. Obviously, people have different requirements for comfort in the woods. Those of us with weak backs *need* lightweight canoes and other gear. Many use camp stoves not for their convenience but to mitigate the effect of their visit on the natural environment.

For some people, it is extremely hard to escape for a week in the wilderness, leaving all contact with their jobs and families, and with civilization in general. To not lose touch, however, is to deprive you of a truly unique experience that can only be found in a wilderness setting. While physically challenging, nothing is more mentally relaxing and emotionally recharging than *totally* escaping for several days from the evening news, the stock market reports, the family bills, the rush-hour traffic and the multitude of decisions that everyone makes during a daily routine. Listening to news reports on your radio or calling work from your cellular phone robs you of that experience. Indeed, even using your watch during a canoe trip should not be necessary. This is a time to enjoy the "natural rhythms." The sun will be your alarm clock. Your stomach will tell you when to eat. The sun will also tell you when it's time to make camp. When tired, you will sleep. Your only concerns should be basic—food, shelter and clothing. Since you will be carrying all three in your canoe, your only practical concerns are the weather (which dictates your clothing requirements) and finding a campsite at which to construct your shelter. (For some, catching fish may be another serious concern, if they brought no other food with them.)

Using a GPS (Global Positioning System) device, which is fascinating and remarkably accurate, deprives you of the traditional challenge of using a map and a compass to find your way. There is no disgrace to getting temporarily lost in the BWCA Wilderness. It happens to nearly everyone at one time or another. It surely must have happened to the Voyageurs, back when maps were mere approximations of the landscape. Accept the challenge. Leave modern technology at home and learn to explore the BWCA Wilderness much like the Voyageurs once did.

Primitive Management Areas

For small groups of visitors who desire a more primitive and secluded wilderness experience, there are 12 designated areas in the BWCAW that are managed like Quetico Provincial Park on the Canadian side of the border. PMAs occupy 124,000 acres of the least used parts of the Wilderness.

PMA access requires more effort and skill than do most parts of the BWCAW. The Forest Service does not maintain portage trails and campsites. Most lakes within the PMA must be reached by traveling cross-country or bushwhacking. To minimize damage to the environment, it is suggested that party size not exceed six people. Visitors may camp at any suitable location. Shallow latrines may be dug at sites that do not have box latrines, and campfires are permitted where there are no fire grates, as long as special care is paid to ensure that there are no environmental scars remaining after use. Camp stoves, however, are strongly recommended instead of open fires.

To enhance the opportunities for solitude, access to these areas is very limited. After obtaining a travel permit for the desired BWCAW entry point, you must also get special authorization from one of the USFS ranger stations where permits are picked up. Each PMA is divided into zones where only one group per night is allowed to camp. (There is no restriction on day-use activities by other groups, however.)

Reservations are not taken for the PMA visits. Authorizations are available only on a first-come-first-served basis. For more information about the specific locations of these remote areas, as well as the unique regulations that govern them, contact the Superior National Forest headquarters in Duluth or one of the USFS district offices listed in Chapter 2.

Provisions of the BWCA Wilderness Act

In the fall of 1978 Congress enacted legislation that drastically altered the regulations governing the Boundary Waters Canoe Area. The Wilderness may not *appear* any different now than it did before 1979, but it may *sound* different in places.

Before January 1, 1979, the BWCA was administered in accordance with the 1964 Wilderness Act. Logging was allowed in parts of the Wilderness and motorboats were permitted on 60% of the water surface area.

The BWCA Wilderness Act of 1978 added 20 small areas totaling 45,000 acres to the existing BWCA, and it established the current boundaries to include 1,075,000 acres. It also prohibited all logging, closed most of the interior motor routes, and restricted motorboats to 24% of the water surface area after 1999—mostly large perimeter lakes served directly by access roads or mechanical portages. A few lakes have no horsepower limits, but most are limited to either 10 or 25 horsepower, as follows:

+ No horsepower limits: Little Vermilion Lake, Loon River, Loon Lake, the southwestern end of Lac La Croix to Wilkins Bay, and on portions of lakes that lie partially outside the BWCAW (Fall, Moose, Snowbank, Sea Gull, Clearwater and East Bearskin lakes).

+ 25 horsepower limits: Trout Lake, Fall Lake, Moose Lake, Newfound Lake, Sucker Lake, Newton Lake, South Farm Lake, East Bearskin Lake, Snowbank Lake, Saganaga Lake east of American Point, and Basswood Lake (except that part lying northwest of Washington Island and north of Jackfish Bay to the Basswood River).

+ 10 horsepower limits: Sea Gull Lake east of Three mile Island, Clearwater Lake, North Fowl Lake, South Fowl Lake, and the Island River east of Forest Route 377.

Mining is also restricted and the Secretary of Agriculture has the authority to acquire mineral rights in the Wilderness and along three road corridors in a 222,000-acre Mining Protection Area. No other federal land controls are involved in the MPA.

Quotas were established for the daytime use of motorboats on the lakes where they are allowed. Resorts, cabin owners and their guests are exempt on their own lakes. Camping from motorboats is allowed for visitors with overnight camping permits. Towboats in excess of 25 horsepower are not permitted in the Wilderness.

Snowmobiles are prohibited in the BWCAW except for permanent use of the Crane Lake to Little Vermilion Lake winter portage to Canada and the Saganaga Lake winter route to Canada. The Secretary of Agriculture, however, is allowed to permit grooming by snowmobile of a limited number of cross-country ski trails near existing resorts.

Old and deteriorating dams within the Wilderness may be maintained only to protect wilderness values or public safety.

The federal government is given authority to enforce the motorboat and snowmobile regulations on state water. No other federal jurisdiction over state waters is asserted. The state is allowed to impose more stringent regulations.

Paddling Along the Canadian Border

Several of the BWCA Wilderness routes described in this book follow parts of the international boundary between the United States and Canada. It is important for visitors to respect Canadian property. While the Webster-Ashburton Treaty of 1842 permits use of the border lakes and their connecting portages by the citizens of both countries, it does not permit Americans to fish in Canadian waters without first securing an Ontario fishing license. Nor does it allow Americans to camp, picnic or even set foot on Canadian soil (except at portages connecting border lakes) without first being authorized by Canada Customs to enter the country. Furthermore, since Quetico Provincial Park borders much of the BWCAW on the north, you must also have authorization from the Ontario Ministry of Natural Resources to enter the Park after first clearing Customs. Don't stray out of the United States. Illegal entry into Canada is a serious matter.

A True Wilderness?

There are those purists who would not classify the BWCAW as a true wilderness. In one sense, they are right. Portage trails are regularly cleared of fallen trees and clogging brush. Regulations dictate that you must camp only on Forest Service campsites equipped with unmovable fire grates and box latrines. There are obvious signs all around you that other people have camped at the very same spot many, many times before.

There are also those who declare that one must paddle for weeks before feeling a true sense of "wilderness." Regarding the BWCAW, I must disagree. "Wilderness" is as much a state of mind as a physical condition. Seldom are more than one or two long portages necessary for visitors to feel a true sense of wilderness around them. The disquieting drone of motors fades into the past, and one enters a world of only natural sensations. Depending on your point of entry, it could take a day, or maybe two, to find your wilderness. On the other hand, it may be waiting only minutes from your launching site, scarcely more than a stone's throw from the road's end. Wherever you start, a magnificent wilderness it not far away in the Boundary Waters Canoe Area.

Wilderness involves emotions. A wilderness experience is an emotional experience. If a person cannot sense deep emotion while camped on the shores of some placid wilderness lake, hearing the cry of a loon, he will never understand the pleas of those who would save the Boundary Waters Canoe Area.

— *Charles Ericksen*

An organization that has worked diligently for years to protect and preserve the BWCA Wilderness is the **Friends of the Boundary Waters Wilderness**, 1313 Fifth Street SE, Suite 329, Minneapolis, MN 55414-4504. **Northeastern Minnesotans for Wilderness** is a regional grassroots organization that formed in the 1990s to represent people who believe that wilderness is good public policy and is worth defending: PO Box 625, Ely, MN 55731.

2

How to Plan a Wilderness Canoe Trip

Pre-Trip Planning

A SAFE, ENJOYABLE WILDERNESS EXPERIENCE STARTS AT HOME WITH CARE-ful planning. First, ask yourself and all members of your group if you really *want* a trip into the *Wilderness*—a place where you will find no running water, prepared shelters, predictable weather or easy travel. There are no signs to direct the way. You must know how to build a fire, administer first aid, read a map and use a compass. In an area that is unfamiliar and sometimes downright hostile, you must rely on your own resourcefulness for your comfort and perhaps for survival. You must be your own doctor, guide and entertainer—prepared for accidents, extended periods of rain, and obstacles such as large waves whipped up by strong winds.

Keep your group size small. Few campsites have tent pads for more than two or three tents. Some are barely large enough for one tent. If your group is large, plan to split up and travel separately. Better yet, plan completely different routes. You'll have more pictures and experiences to share when you get home. A small group has much less impact on the Wilderness and on other visitors. You will also have better opportunities to observe wildlife along the way.

Portaging to Unload Lake

Vacationing with a group of people is always challenging, because of variations in skills, interests and physical strengths. Get your group together ahead of time to plan the trip. Talk about what *each* person is looking for and expects on the trip. Decide as a group where and when to go, what equipment to take and what to eat. By considering these things ahead of time, the entire group will get a better idea of what to expect from the trip. There will be fewer surprises later to dampen spirits. Consider the positive aspects of a BWCAW canoe trip—sun-drenched afternoons on sky-blue lakes, gentle breezes, magnificent orange sunsets, fish striking at every cast, and a refreshing swim in a cool lake at day's end. Then consider the dreaded conditions that plague many canoe trips—hordes of hungry flying insects, fish with no appetite at all, long and muddy portage trails, prolonged periods of

cold rain, and gale-force winds that make canoe travel extremely difficult or impossible. Both trip scenarios are possible—indeed likely—at
one time or another. Hope for the best, but be psychologically and
physically prepared for the worst.

When planning your route, make sure you are not overly ambitious. Consider all members of the group, and plan to travel at the
speed of the least experienced or weakest paddler. It's a good idea to
plan a layover day for every three or four days of travel. You'll have
more time to fish or relax. If you encounter rough weather, you won't
have to worry about taking unnecessary chances just to stay on schedule.

Plan to make camp early enough in the day to assure finding an
available campsite. Most wilderness visitors are there for
solitude...quiet...to seek respite from the hustle and bustle of day-to-
day urban living. Each person wants the sensation of being the first and
only person in an area. To accomplish this objective, consider campsites that are off the main travel routes and in back bays. They are used
less often and offer a better opportunity for privacy. Firewood is usually more plentiful without having to search as hard for it. You will also
have a better chance of avoiding "problem bears" where few others
camp.

Respect for other Wilderness visitors starts before you ever leave
home. The first portage is no place to learn how to get a canoe up on
your shoulders. Practice picking up a canoe and other canoeing skills
before you start your trip. Know who is responsible for each pack, each
canoe and each piece of miscellaneous equipment *before* setting foot
on a portage trail. Accountability reduces the possibility of leaving
something behind. It also reduces the amount of time needed on each
portage, thus alleviating possible congestion on some of the trails.

Equipment, Clothing and Food

Equipment: When selecting equipment for your trip, choose environ-
mentally "natural" colored tents, packs and clothing to help you travel
and camp inconspicuously. Bright colors contribute to a crowded feeling. Carry a small stove and fuel to use when dry wood is hard to find.
Stoves heat more cleanly, quickly and evenly than campfires. Axes and
hatchets are not necessary (although a small hatchet is useful in an
emergency to prepare dry wood for burning). There is plenty of suitable firewood that can easily be broken or cut with a small camp saw.
See that at least one person in each canoe carries a map and a compass
and knows how to use both. Kept in a plastic case and tied to the

Chocolate cake baking in a reflector oven

canoe, the map is readily available for quick and frequent reference. Line your packs with large heavy plastic bags to keep all the contents dry. And, by all means, practice packing before you leave home. Remember that everything you pack will have to be carried on portages—by you.

Clothes: Clothing needs may vary somewhat from season to season, but always plan for extremes. Layering is the most efficient method to stay warm and dry. Lightweight cotton is comfortable in warm weather, while wool provides warmth on chilly days and at night, even when it's wet. Polypropylene and other synthetic garments that wick moisture away from your body are excellent choices for any temperature. Good raingear is essential, and it can also serve as a windbreaker on cool, windy days. Bring two pairs of footwear—boots or sturdy shoes for traveling and sneakers or moccasins for walking around the campsite. Wearing the latter at campsites is not only kind to your feet; it also causes less soil compaction damage to the campsite. Aqua Socks are also a good idea to wear while swimming, to protect your feet from sharp rocks. A pair of pants with zip-off legs is quite practical in the BWCA Wilderness, where temperatures may vary considerably from early morning to mid-afternoon.

Food: Since cans and bottles are not allowed in the Boundary Waters, some foods will have to be repacked in plastic bags or in other plastic, reusable containers. If possible, pack each meal's food together in a plastic bag to make meal preparation easier. Also line your food pack with a large and durable plastic liner to protect the contents from moisture. When sealed tightly at night, this may also help to contain the food's aroma from attracting animals. If you plan to catch fish, *don't ever count on fish* for your primary sustenance. Fish are good supplements to your diet, but if you depend on them, you are likely to be hungry.

If you don't have access to all the right stuff in your home town, you can find all the gear and clothing you'll ever need for a BWCAW canoe trip in the *Boundary Waters Catalog*, published by the Piragis Northwoods Company, 105 North Central Avenue, Ely, MN 55731. Call (800) 223-6565 or (218) 365-6745. Or access the catalog by Internet at http://www.piragis.com/catalog.

Choosing a Wilderness Route

Any group entering the BWCA Wilderness must have in its possession a travel permit, granting permission to enter through one of the 71 designated entry points. Thirty-four of those entry points are located in the eastern half of the Boundary Waters. Of those, 28 canoeing entry points are described in this book:

36 Hog Creek	52 Brant Lake
37 Kawishiwi Lake	54 Seagull Lake
38 Sawbill Lake	55 Saganaga Lake
39 Baker Lake	57 Magnetic Lake
40 Homer Lake	58 South Lake
41 Brule Lake	60 Duncan Lake
43 Bower Trout Lake	61 Daniels Lake
44 Ram Lake	62 Clearwater Lake
45 Morgan Lake	64 East Bearskin Lake
47 Lizz Lake & Swamp Lake	66 Crocodile River
48 Meeds Lake	68 Pine Lake
49 Skipper Lake & Portage Lake	69 John Lake
50 Cross Bay Lake	70 North Fowl Lake
51 Missing Link Lake	80 Larch Creek

Hikers use 6 other entry points (see Appendix V):

56 Kekekabic Trail (eastern end)	81 Border Route Trail West
59 Partridge Lake Trail	82 Border Route Trail Center
79 Eagle Mountain Trail	83 Border Route Trail East

Thirty-six entry points are found in the western half of the BWCAW, including 27 canoeing entry points that are described in

Volume I. One entry point (71) is for paddlers who enter the Boundary Waters from Canada.

The entry points included in this guide are grouped according to accessibility. Chapter 3 includes 6 entry points that are accessible from the Sawbill Trail. Chapter 4 includes 11 entry points that are accessible from and located *west* of the Gunflint Trail. Eleven entry points located *east* of the Gunflint Trail are described in Chapter 5. They are accessible from either the Gunflint Trail or the Arrowhead Trail.

Using statistical data and personal observations by the author, each entry point is briefly discussed. Statistics are from the summer of 1997, the most current data available when this book was written.

- **Seasonal Permits:** The number of overnight travel permits issued to groups using the entry point in 1997, including all modes of transportation.
- **Popularity Rank:** The relative popularity of the entry point, compared with all other BWCAW entry points (a total of 69 in 1997).
- **Daily Quota:** the maximum number of overnight travel permits that can be issued each day to groups using the entry point (as of 1999).

Further discussion includes the entry point's location, how to get there, public campgrounds nearby, amount of motorized use (if any) through the entry point, and other comments of interest to canoeists.

Following the discussion of an entry point are suggestions for two routes from that entry point. The first is a short route that can be completed by most groups in 2 to 4 days. The second is a longer route that takes 4 to 8 days. It is important to understand that this book is merely an accumulation of *suggestions*. It does not describe *all* possible routes through the BWCAW. Quite the contrary, the routes that you could take are virtually infinite in number. You may wish to follow only a part of one route, or you may wish to combine two or more routes. *Do not feel bound to the routes as they are described in this book.* You may follow them precisely as written, but you may also use the suggestions simply as a basis for planning your own route.

Introductory remarks about each route tell you: 1) the *minimum* number of days to allow; 2) the length of the route; 3) the number of different lakes, rivers and creeks encountered, as well as the number of portages en route; 4) the difficulty (easier, challenging, most rugged), 5) the maps needed for the route, and 6) general comments, including to whom the route should appeal. Then each route is broken down into suggested days, giving the sequence of lakes, streams and portages, followed by points of special interest.

Example: Day 2 (13 miles): Little Trout Lake, p. 376 rods, **Little Indian Sioux River**, p. 32 rods, **river**, p. 32 rods, **river**, p. 12 rods, **river**, rapids, **river**, rapids, **river**, p. 70 rods, **river**, p. 40 rods, **river**, p. 34 rods, **river**, p. 35 rods, **river**, p. 120 rods, **Otter Lake**. You will find this day to be a sharp contrast from the prior day of paddling on large lakes... etc.

Explanation: On the second day of this route, you will paddle across Little Trout Lake and then portage 376 rods to the Little Indian Sioux River. You will follow the river to Otter Lake, negotiating 8 portages and some rapids along the way. You will make camp on Otter Lake at a campsite that is marked by a red dot on the map. Comments about the day's route follow the outlined sequence of lakes, rivers and portages.

Most of the routes suggested are "loops"—they begin and end at (or within walking distance of) the same location. There is no need for car shuttles between two points. Other routes start at one entry point and end at another entry point far enough away to necessitate a shuttle. The name of each route indicates whether the trip is a "loop" (The Eddie Falls *Loop*) or requires a "shuttle"(The Three Rivers *Route*). If a shuttle is required, drop off your vehicle at the end of the route *prior* to starting the journey. That generally works better than scheduling a predetermined pick-up time at the end of your trip. If your parked vehicle is waiting for you, you won't be under any pressure to arrive at a particular time.

Of course, any route may be made more difficult by completing it in fewer days than recommended, or made easier by adding days. If fishing is a priority for your trip, you should consider adding at least one day for every three days suggested in this guide. For longer trips, you may also want to add layover days to your schedule. The longer you are tripping, the more likely you are to encounter strong wind, foul weather, sickness or injury that could slow your progress. (Always carry an extra day's supply of food, too, for just that reason.) Furthermore, after three or four days of rugged trekking, you may simply want to rest for a day before continuing.

About the author's biases: The difficulty ratings for the routes in this book are subjective. Difficulty is relative. A route that is "most rugged" to one party may be merely "challenging" to another group. An "easier" route to most paddlers may be "most rugged" to an inexperienced group of paddlers who really had no idea what they were getting into when they entered the BWCA Wilderness. Two major factors contribute to the difficulty ratings in this book: 1) the average distance paddled per day, and 2) the length, frequency, and difficulty of the portages. An "average" day in the BWCAW includes about 8 to10 miles of paddling, interrupted by 5 or 6 portages, measuring 50 to 100 rods in length. This should challenge most visitors. Anything less is usually rated "easier." Trips with a great deal more paddling and/or longer or more frequent portages are rated "most rugged." The ratings are based on my 30 years of Boundary Waters tripping and my experience with all age groups and experience levels.

Even more subjective is my opinion of what constitutes an interesting route and beautiful scenery. You may or may not agree, but it's background information that you may find useful in selecting your route. First, I prefer tiny creeks, narrow rivers and smaller lakes. Wind is less likely to be a problem and wildlife is often more visible. Such a route offers a much more intimate natural experience, in my opinion. Second, I like rocks and hills—lakes bordered by elevated terrain with exposed rock faces, and campsites with rock outcroppings on which to rest and contemplate the sunset and the moonrise. Almost every lake, swamp and bog in the Boundary Waters is beautiful in its own way. But to this author there is nothing more striking than a small or narrow lake surrounded by tall hills or ridges covered by a generous blend of pine, birch and aspen trees and trimmed with steep rock ledges or cliffs. Equally pleasing, however, is a tiny, meandering stream littered with lily pads and bordered by a tamarack bog. Why do these opinions matter to you? Because, if a route is described as having lovely scenery, you'll know what is meant by "lovely."

If fishing is your thing: General comments about the fishing potential for each suggested route are included. The serious angler will find more information about each lake in **Appendix IV**. All of the 243 BWCAW lakes in this book are listed alphabetically. Data about each lake were obtained from the Minnesota Department of Natural Resources, including overall size, littoral size (acreage of the lake that is less than 15 feet deep), maximum depth, and the game-fish species that are known to inhabit the lake.

About the use of rods: One rod equals 16½ feet. Since that is roughly the length of most canoes, it is the unit of linear measurement in canoe country. Both the Fisher maps and the McKenzie maps use this unit of measurement. Although the maps are topographic, the indicated number of rods tells little about the difficulty of the portages. Long trails may be quite easy, and short ones may be extremely rough. This guide will warn you about the rough ones. You may notice that the length of a portage on the maps sometimes differs from the length in this book. While traveling throughout the BWCA Wilderness, whenever I doubted the portage lengths shown on the maps, I did my own measurements. On the shorter portages, I counted my steps. A stopwatch was useful on the longer trails. Sometimes they are simply estimates based on my 30 years of experience walking across portages. Although there is no guarantee that my measurements are precise, there is no doubt in my mind that they are usually more accurate than those on the maps. You can decide for yourself. If you find an error, please let me know!

Maps

It would be nearly impossible to show detailed maps on the pages of this book. Instead, you will find a foldout map of the entire eastern region inside the back cover. Use this map to plan your trip. When actually taking your trip, however, I recommend using the water-resistant topographic maps published by the W. A. Fisher Company. Thirty-two "F-series" maps combine to cover all of the BWCA Wilderness and Canada's Quetico Provincial Park. The scale is 1½" to a mile, and there is sufficient overlap to provide smooth transitions from map to map. Designated USFS campsites are identified by red dots on the maps, which are updated annually. A disclaimer on each map reads *"This map is not intended for navigational use, and is not represented to be correct in every respect."* Nevertheless, these maps are published specifically for canoeists and are remarkably accurate and detailed.

The discussion of each route tells you which maps are needed. You can order them from:

W. A. Fisher Company
P.O. Box 1107
Virginia, MN 55792-1107
(218) 741-9544

Some routes are served better by McKenzie Maps, which are also topographic (scale 2" to 1 mile). They also provide excellent detail and use red dots to identify campsite locations. Some routes described in this book require as many as three Fisher maps but only one McKenzie map (and vice versa). When such is the case, it is pointed out in the introduction to the route. You can order them from:

McKenzie Maps
8479 Frye Road
Minong, WI 54859
(800) 749-2113

You can purchase both of these map series from an outfitter when you arrive in northeastern Minnesota. The maps are also available at many camping stores in the Twin Cities area, as well as in some other upper-Midwestern cities. You can also mail-order them by phone or e-mail from *Boundary Waters Catalog* (see the section *Equipment, Clothing and Food* earlier in this chapter).

When to Visit the Boundary Waters

What's the best time of year to schedule a BWCAW canoe trip? That depends on your group's priorities. (See *Climate* in Chapter 1.) If seeing animal wildlife ranks high on your list, *where* you travel may be more important than *when*. The same applies to those who seek quiet seclusion. But you can increase your chances of both viewing wildlife and not viewing other people by your choice of an entry date, as well as your choice of an entry point.

Over the past 30 years, there has been a substantial increase in the number of visitors to the BWCAW—the most heavily used wilderness in America. 19,732 overnight use permits were issued to visitors in 1982 from May 1 through September 30. That number grew to 27,319 permits in 1997—a 38% increase in 15 years. Visitation is now distributed fairly equally throughout the three summer months, but more and more people are enjoying the Boundary Waters in May and September. In 1997, the distribution of visitors was:

May	13%
June	23%
July	24%
August	26%
September	14%

You can increase your chance of avoiding other people and obtaining a BWCAW permit by considering the following:

- The busiest days for entry are Saturday, Sunday and Monday. If possible, start your trip on one of the other four days of the week.
- Memorial Day weekend, Independence Day weekend, Labor Day weekend and the month of August are the busiest times. In 1997, the 20 days of heaviest use all fell in the period from July 31 through August 30. If you can postpone your trip until September, you are bound to see far fewer people, virtually no biting insects, and a forest full of fall colors.
- Consider using an entry point that has traditionally ranked low in popularity. A majority of visitors use a very small minority of the entry points. For instance, *more overnight travel permits are issued for Moose Lake each summer than for the 40 least popular entry points combined!*

Obtaining Travel Permits

Any visitor in the Boundary Waters must have a BWCAW travel permit in possession. It allows you to enter the Wilderness only on the starting date and through the entry point specified on the permit. Once in the Wilderness, you are free to travel where you desire, as long as motor-use restrictions are not violated. This applies to daytime use as well as overnight use of the Wilderness, any time of the year.

There are two types of permit systems for BWCAW visitors. One is a self-issuing permit system for non-motorized daytime visits during the summer, as well as for all types of visits from October 1 through April 30, when there is no quota on the number of permits issued. This permit is free and does not require a reservation. The permits are available at most entry points. You simply fill out the form, leave the "official use copy" in the drop box there or return it to a Superior National Forest office, and keep the "visitor copy" with you at all times while in the BWCAW.

The other permit system is for overnight visitation as well as daytime motorboat use from May 1 through September 30. Entry quotas were established for overnight campers in order to reduce competition for the limited number of established campsites and to avoid unauthorized camping on undeveloped sites. The daily limit at each entry point (from as low as 1 to as many as 27) is based on the number of campsites available to visitors using the routes served by the entry point. The quotas pertain only to overnight campers during the 5-month canoeing season. There is a separate quota system for daytime use by visitors with motorboats. There are no limits on the number of BWCAW visitors after September 30 and before May 1.

Overnight User Fee

A fee is charged for camping in the Boundary Waters. Adults are charged **$10 per person per trip.** Youths under 18 and Golden Age or Golden Access Passport holders are charged $5 per person per trip. For visitors who plan to use the BWCA Wilderness more than four times during the same summer, seasonal fee cards may be obtained at a cost of $40 per adult or $20 for youth and Golden Age or Golden Access Passport holders. The Seasonal Fee Card may be purchased by mail or by phone from the BWCAW Reservation Center (see Reservations below), or in person after April 30 from any Superior National Forest District Office. This card fulfills the fee requirement for the entire season. But it does not eliminate the need for obtaining a BWCAW travel permit.

Most of the funds that are generated by the camping fees stay in the Boundary Waters. The funds allow the Forest Service to hire more employees to work in the Wilderness, maintaining and rehabilitating campsites and portage trails, educating visitors about low-impact camping techniques, assisting people in trouble, and expanding the hours of operation at the permit-issuing stations.

Reservations

All overnight travel permits are available through advance reservations for a nonrefundable processing fee of $12 per reservation (in 2002) plus a $20 deposit for your camping fee (in 2002). You don't have to make a reservation before arriving at the BWCA Wilderness. It is advisable, however, since quotas at many entry points do fill up early. A reservation assures you of a permit to enter the Wilderness on a specific day at a certain entry point.

Starting with the 1999 canoeing season, the BWCAW Reservation Center became part of the National Recreation Reservation Service (NRRS):

Mail: BWCAW Reservation Center
P.O. Box 462
Ballston Spa, NY 12020
Telephone Feb. 1–Sep. 30: (877) 550-6777 (toll free)
TDD telephone: (877) TDD-NRRS (toll free)
Fax: (518) 884-9951

Web site: www.bwcaw.org/ (good general information, including permit-issuing stations, recent changes, rules and regulations, an entry map, and contacts). Reservation requires login ID and password.

You may reserve a permit by mail, fax, phone or Internet. Reservation applications received by mail, fax or Internet through January 15 are then processed by lottery regardless of the order received. Applications received after January 15 are processed on a first-come-first-served basis. Telephone reservations are accepted starting February 1. Phone reservations are accepted only with the use of a valid American Express, Discover, MasterCard or VISA credit card during normal business hours (9:00 AM to 5:30 PM EST in 1999). Reservations may be made only at the BWCAW Reservation Center. Do not call the Superior National Forest headquarters or any of the District Offices to make reservations. Reservation requests must include the following information:

- Method of travel (paddle, hike or motorboat).
- Party size (maximum of 9 people).
- Number of watercraft (maximum of 4 boats).
- Name, address and phone number of the group leader.
- Names of up to three alternate group leaders who might

use the permit in the group leader's absence.
+ The desired entry point name and number.
+ The desired entry date.
+ The estimated exit date.
+ The planned exit point.
+ Whether or not the group is guided and, if so, the guide's name.
+ Location where the permit will be picked up.
+ Payment by check, money order or charge card (cash not accepted).

It is also a good idea to include an alternate entry date and an alternate entry point, in case your first choices are not available.

The reservation fee and the full amount of the camping fee for your party must be paid when you reserve your permit. Currently the total amount due when your reservation is made is $32 ($12 for the reservation and $20 for the camping fee). If your total fee is calculated to be less than $20 (i.e. for a single person or for a party with seasonal camping permits), you must still pay $20 plus the $12 processing fee when you make your reservation. The overpayment will be refunded after completion of your trip.

After making your reservation, the trip leader will receive a letter confirming that a BWCAW travel permit is reserved. Reservations made within the last 7 days before the trip will be processed, but no confirmation letter will be sent.

Picking Up Your Permit

An overnight travel permit must be picked up in person within 24 hours of the trip starting date at a designated USFS District Office or at an outfitter or business that is an official permit issuing station (cooperator). This face-to-face contact affords personnel at the issuing station an opportunity to inform visitors about BWCAW regulations, wilderness ethics and minimum-impact camping techniques. *Only the party leader or an alternate leader whose name appears on the application may pick up the permit.* Identification is required, and periodic checks may take place in the Wilderness. All cards (Golden Age, Golden Access or Seasonal Fee) must be presented when the permit is picked up to receive a discount. Otherwise, the full camping fee will be charged. Cooperators may charge an extra $2 fee for issuing each overnight permit. Office hours vary, so be sure to check with your permit pick-up location for its office hours. Also, if you don't have a reservation, you must pick up your permit at a time when the availability of permits can be confirmed by the BWCAW Reservation Center.

Any change to your permit, except group size, requires a new $12 reservation fee. Group size changes are made when the permit is picked up. If there are more than 2 people in your party , the cost difference will be collected then. Cash, checks and credit cards are accepted at all USFS District Offices. Only credit cards are accepted by non-Forest Service cooperators (outfitters or resorts). If the party size decreases, a refund will be made by the BWCAW Reservation Center after the trip.

Canceling a Permit Reservation

The entire camping fee will be refunded if your reservation is cancelled two or more days prior to the entry date. If the reservation is not cancelled in advance, or if you do not use the permit, you will forfeit the $20 deposit and the $12 reservation processing fee.

BWCAW Information

The BWCAW Reservation Center personnel are available *only* for making reservations and selling camping passes. For information about the BWCA Wilderness, contact the Superior National Forest headquarters or either of the Ranger District offices listed below. They can answer your questions but cannot process reservations. Normal business hours are 8:00 AM to 4:30 PM weekdays before May 1 and after September 30. During the summer permit-issuing season, the District offices are generally open from 6:00 AM to 8:00 PM. The hours do change from year to year, however, and they may vary from office to office. The Superior National Forest office in Duluth is open 8:00 AM to 4:30 PM on weekdays.

If you have access to the Internet, you'll find an excellent web site with Superior National Forest information, including the BWCA Wilderness, at:

www.superiornationalforest.org/bwcaw

It includes information about updates, rules, entry points and other web sites.

Superior National Forest
Attn: Forest Supervisor
8901 Grand Ave Place
Duluth, MN 55808-1102
(218) 626-4300

Entry Points	Closest District Ranger Station	Telephone Number
36-41	Tofte Ranger District Box 2159 Tofte, MN 55615	(218) 663-8060
43-83	Gunflint Ranger District P.O. Box 790 Grand Marais, MN 55604	(218) 387-1750

If you have not reserved a permit in advance, you may pick it up at any District Ranger office or cooperating business. It is advisable, however, to drop by one that is closest to your entry point. The personnel there are likely to be more familiar with your proposed route. They can alert you to high water or low water conditions, bear problem areas, suitable campsites, road conditions and other particulars.

National Forest Campgrounds

In the introduction to each entry point in this guidebook, the closest USFS campground is included for those who might want to camp near their starting point before their trip. You may reserve campsites up to 240 days in advance (360 days for group facilities) at 9 campgrounds on the Superior National Forest by calling the National Recreation Reservation Service (NRRS) at (877) 444-6777. Or you may use their Internet web site for reservations:

www.reserveusa.com/

In addition to the usual campsite fee, you will also be charged $9.00 (in 2002) for reservation processing. The service charge is the same whether you make your reservation by phone, by Internet, or in person at one of the NRRS field sites.

A Final Word

Believe it or not, these age-old routes *do change* from year to year. In fact, they may change several times each year. A deep navigable channel between lakes in early June may be shallow rock-strewn rapids that require a portage in August. A creek-side portage indicated as 35 rods on the map may turn out to be 135 rods when the creek dries up during a drought. Sometimes portages that were dry in June are flooded in August after beavers dam a stream adjacent to the trail. When a portage becomes too eroded from over-use, the Forest Service sometimes constructs a new trail, which is usually longer than the original. Likewise, trails through wet and muddy bogs may be elevated on boardwalks when there are funds available for trail maintenance. Or bypasses may be routed to higher and dryer ground.

On the other hand, occasionally an author's memory and notes fail him and a mistake is made. Or a typographical error occurs during publication that is overlooked during the proofing process. So, if you find inaccuracies in this book, or if you have any comments or suggestions to improve subsequent editions, please write the author (in care of the publisher). Thank you!

Important

The descriptions in this guidebook are necessarily cast in general terms. Neither the descriptions nor the maps can be assumed to be exact or to guarantee your arrival at any given point. You must undertake only those trips and trip segments that you know are within your competence. Given these cautions, you can have a wonderful time in the BWCA Wilderness.

Cooling off in Bearskin Lake

3

Entry from the Sawbill Trail

The Southeastern Area

ONLY 6 ENTRY POINTS SERVE THE SOUTHEASTERN PART OF THE BOUNDARY Waters Canoe Area Wilderness. Three of them, however, are among the 10 most popular entry points in all of the BWCAW—Sawbill, Brule and Kawishiwi lakes. The other three—Hog Creek, Baker Lake and Homer Lake—are far less popular, but visitation has increased markedly in recent years. All 6 offer quick and relatively easy access to a lovely part of the Boundary Waters, where scenic hills border crystalline waters and wildlife is often visible. This is one of the best areas in all of the BWCA Wilderness, in fact, in which to see bald eagles, ospreys and moose.

The Sawbill Trail (Cook County Road 2) originates at the tiny town of Tofte, on the shore of Lake Superior. Like most roads leading inland from the north shore of the lake, it has a hard surface for the first couple of miles during its ascent to an elevation high above Lake Superior. When the gradient levels off, the road turns to gravel and continues that way for the remainder of its 22-mile course to Sawbill Lake. Although it has its rough spots, the road is generally in excellent condition, with only a few sharp curves and steep grades. About the only sign of civilization along its entire course is at the end, where Sawbill Outfitters, a Forest Service Guard Station and Sawbill Campground are located along the south shore of Sawbill Lake.

The Tofte Ranger Station is the official place to pick up your permit. It is located on Highway 61 about a mile southwest of its junction with County Road 2. Or you can make prior arrangements to have your permit waiting for you at Sawbill Outfitters, if you're not planning to drive through Tofte en route to your entry point.

The village of Tofte is a small but upscale community with several lakeshore resorts and restaurants, a bakery and deli, a general store, a couple of gas stations and a few souvenir shops. You can purchase last-minute supplies at the general store in Tofte, as well as at Sawbill Outfitters. The closest business districts with bona fide supermarkets, however, are located far from these entry points, at either Silver Bay or Grand Marais (both on Highway 61).

Entry Point 36—Hog Creek

SEASONAL PERMITS: 422

POPULARITY RANK: 18th

DAILY QUOTA: 5

LOCATION: Hog Creek is located 20 airline miles northwest of Tofte, very near the center of the south boundary of the BWCA Wilderness. To get there from Highway 61 in Tofte, drive north on the Sawbill Trail for 17½ miles to its intersection with Cook County Road 3 (½-mile past the intersection of Forest Route 170). Turn left there and drive west on County Road 3 (which changes to Lake County Road 7) for 10 more miles on gravel to its junction with Forest Route 354. Turn right and proceed northbound on F.R. 354 for 2 miles to the Hog Creek parking lot on the west (left) side of the road. The final 2 miles are on a "single track road with turnouts." It is a good gravel road, but somewhat narrower than the county roads. (Note: County Roads 3 and 7 cross Hog Creek three times. Don't stop and launch onto the creek until you reach the entry point on Forest Route 354.)

Just before arriving at the creek (0.1 mile), you'll come to a spur road leading a short distance west to a parking lot that accommodates up to a dozen vehicles. A 15-rod portage trail leads downhill from the spur road, starting 20 rods from the north end of the parking lot.

DESCRIPTION: Hog Creek winds its way west for nearly 15 miles from Hog Lake to Perent Lake. Only the final 3 miles from F.R. 354 to Perent Lake are in the BWCA Wilderness. This is a fascinating way to enter the Boundary Waters for anyone who prefers the intimacy of tiny steams to the wide-open expanse of most lakes.

Over the years, Hog Creek has become more and more popular among canoeists. This may be attributed, in part, to the fact that motorboats were banned from this entry point in 1978. Prior to that year, most of the use was by people using motorboats. Back then, only 259 permits were issued and Hog Creek ranked 33rd among all entry points. Although the visitation has nearly doubled during the past 20 years, Hog Creek is still one of the easiest entry points for which to get a permit. With a quota of 5 parties per day, only 55% of the permits were actually used in 1997. And not many day-use permits were issued either. So, if you're looking for a quiet entry point into the winding wilderness of tiny streams and narrow rivers, Hog Creek may just be your gateway to paradise.

The Kawishiwi Lake Campground is a good, convenient place to spend the night before your canoe trip. It is located just 2.4 miles north of Hog Creek at the end of Forest Route 354, adjacent to the Kawishiwi Lake boat landing. There are only 5 campsites there and availability is on a first-come-first-served basis, so plan to arrive early to claim yours for the night. There is no camping fee at this "rustic" campground.

ROUTE #36-1: The Perent River Route

3 Days, 15 Miles, 3 Lakes, 1 Creek, 1 River, 15 Portages

DIFFICULTY: Easier

FISHER MAPS: F-4, F-5

INTRODUCTION: This fascinating route takes you along the south perimeter of the BWCAW from Hog Creek to Isabella Lake. From the parking lot at F.R. 354, you'll first meander 3 miles down Hog Creek to Perent Lake. After you paddle 3 more miles across that big lake, the Perent River will carry you west from Perent Lake to Isabella Lake. There you will exit the Boundary Waters and end your excursion at a parking lot just south of the lake, 32 miles by road from your origin (via County Road 7 and Forest Routes 369, 373 and 377).

Spread over 3 full days, this route is quite easy, even though you'll encounter 15 portages along the way. The longest carry is only 61 rods; most are less than 30 rods. All combined, the trails total less than 1½ miles—an average of just 28 rods per carry. Strong trippers could complete the route in just 2 days. Because of the scarcity of campsites on the Perent River, however, to paddle the route in just 2 days would require 1 long day covering 10 miles of travel by combining either days

41

1 and 2 or days 2 and 3 described below. Either way, you would cross most of the portages on just 1 of the 2 days. If you take 3 days, you can travel slowly enough to savor the experience.

Although this route may not appeal to dedicated anglers, there is some good fishing along the way. Perent and Isabella lakes are both known for their abundant populations of walleyes and northern pike. That's probably why most anglers are satisfied to stay on those 2 lakes and not explore the fascinating river in between. Motorboats are not permitted anywhere along this route.

Day 1 (5 miles): P. 15 rods, **Hog Creek,** p. 15 rods, **creek, Perent Lake.** Hog Creek is barely wide enough in places to carry a canoe, but there is always sufficient depth. You may feel as if you are on an African safari as you wind your way through the dense vegetation that borders the creek. In addition to the two15-rod portages near the road, small beaver dams may also occasionally require quick lift-overs.

There is a variety of bird life that is unique to this area. The only record of a nesting Wilson's Warbler in the state was made here. Other unique species include the Rusty Blackbird and the Virginia Rail, both of which were found nesting near Hog Creek. At least 1 pair of bald eagles has also nested in the Perent Lake area.

Perent Lake was named after a trapper who worked this area in the early part of the 20th Century. Beavers, muskrats, wolves and other fur-bearing animals trapped by Perent are still common in this region. Moose are also abundant, though not as commonly seen today as they were 20 years ago, when the adjacent area had been recently logged off.

Grab a good campsite near the center of Perent Lake for a 5-mile day of travel. There are many good campsites on the lake from which to choose. Then grease your fry pan and cast a line. Perent Lake is a good source of walleyes and large northern pike.

Day 2 (5 miles): Perent Lake, p. 61 rods, **Perent River,** p. 31 rods, **river,** p. 25 rods, **river,** p. 33 rods, **river, rapids, river,** p. 17 rods, **river,** p. 39 rods, **river, rapids, river,** p. 22 rods, **river,** p. 16 rods, **river.** The Perent River offers a lovely route for anyone who enjoys stream paddling. It descends only 64 feet during its 7-mile journey from Perent Lake to Isabella Lake. The Civilian Conservation Corps constructed most of the portages in this region during the late 1930s and the 1940s. These extremely well-made portages have survived the years with very little maintenance. They were built to a standard that would be very expensive, labor-intensive, and probably not possible today. The paths are easy to negotiate, and you'll be walking between towering ancient pines on some of the portages, stepping on terrain only recently vacated by moose, and over which bald eagles are frequently sited.

There are only 4 designated campsites along the Perent River. The first two are near the 10-mile point in your expedition. The first is located adjacent to the 16-rod portage. The portage intersects an old abandoned foot trail that was once part of the Pow Wow Hiking Trail. A wooden footbridge still spans the rapids there. **Day 3 (5 miles): Perent River, p.** 40 rods, **river,** p. 22 rods, **river,** p. 16 rods, **river, Boga Lake,** p. 26 rods, **Isabella Lake,** p. 35 rods. If your map shows a portage just after the second campsite, it should not be necessary. You should be able to paddle through the narrow channel just prior to the 40-rod portage. Be prepared for a slow and choppy crossing of Isabella Lake if there is a strong wind out of the west this day.

The parking lot just south of Isabella Lake where this route ends was once part of a large logging camp. From 1949 to 1964, 250 people called Forest Center their home. In addition to a sawmill there were 53 homes, a 2-room schoolhouse, a recreation center and a restaurant. There were also barracks and a mess hall for the lumbermen. Timber was hauled away by railroad. Most of Forest Center is now covered with a young growth of pine trees, but explorers may still find evidence of the logging era near the parking lot.

ROUTE #36-2: The Long Rivers Route

8 Days, 82 Miles, 21 Lakes, 3 Rivers, 1 Creek, 52 Portages

DIFFICULTY: Challenging

FISHER MAPS: F-3, F-4, F-5, F-10, F-11

INTRODUCTION: This fascinating loop essentially follows 2 long river systems all the way from Perent Lake to Kawishiwi Lake. From Forest Route 354, you will first meander down the narrow channel of Hog Creek to Perent Lake. From the west shore of Perent Lake, then, you will follow the Perent River west to Isabella Lake. The lovely Isabella River will continue to carry you west to the base of Bald Eagle Lake. From there you will point northwest and navigate the open waters of Bald Eagle, Gabbro and Little Gabbro lakes until you intersect the South Kawishiwi River. Up through the beautiful pools and rapids of the Kawishiwi River you will paddle, pull and carry your canoe northeast to Lake One. After paddling east across the popular "numbered lakes" and Hudson Lake you will enter island-studded Lake Insula. Continuing up the Kawishiwi River, you will pause to view a display of ancient Indian pictographs. At Malberg Lake, then, you will steer a southbound course to follow the lakes, ponds and creeks that compose the upper reaches of the Kawishiwi River until you reach its source at Kawishiwi Lake. From the parking lot at the south end of Kawishiwi Lake, it is a 2½-mile drive (or hike) on Forest Route 354 back to your origin at Hog Creek.

This route is a wonderful choice for paddlers who want to experience a little of everything that the BWCAW has to offer—tiny creeks, big rivers, lakes of all shapes and sizes, and some truly outstanding scenery throughout your journey. While there are many portages—averaging 6 or 7 each day—most are short, well maintained and quite easy to negotiate. Only 8 trails exceed 80 rods in length, and most are less than 40 rods long. The longest measures 190 rods, and it's downhill. So, even though this is one of the longer routes described in this book, it is not at all difficult. Nevertheless, if your group is inexperienced or physically weak, it might be a good idea to stretch the trip over at least 9 days.

Avid anglers may also want to add an extra day or two, to allow time to explore the waters for the walleyes and northern pike that are plentiful in most of the lakes along the route. Bald Eagle, Gabbro, Insula and Malberg lakes, in particular, have long been favorites among anglers.

If you start this route and find that you cannot complete the loop in the amount of time that you allowed, you'll have several places to "bail out" along the way. You will pass the Isabella Lake, Island River, Little Isabella River, Snake River, Little Gabbro Lake and Lake One entry points during the first 5 scheduled days of this route. You could also access this loop at any of those entry points, if Hog Creek is booked up on the day you want to start. A better option, however, is to reverse the route by starting at Kawishiwi Lake. Putting in at any of the other 6 entry points will require a 2½-mile portage between Kawishiwi Lake and Hog Creek. It's on the road that accesses both entry points, but it climbs over a big hill en route.

You will probably see the fewest people during the first half of the expedition, especially while traveling on the rivers. Isabella and Bald Eagle lakes, however, are popular destinations for anglers. The "numbered lakes" are nearly always busy. Lake One is the second most popular entry point in the BWCAW, and you aren't likely to escape from other people from there all the way to the route's end at Kawishiwi Lake, which is the 10th busiest entry point. Motorboats are banned from the entire loop.

Day 1 (10 miles): P. 15 rods, **Hog Creek,** p. 15 rods, **creek, Perent Lake,** p. 61 rods, **Perent River,** p. 31 rods, **river,** p. 25 rods, **river,** p. 33 rods, **river, rapids, river,** p. 17 rods, **river,** p. 39 rods, **river, rapids, river,** p. 22 rods, **river,** p. 16 rods, **river.** (See comments for Day 1, paragraphs 1-3, and Day 2, Route #36-1.)

Day 2 (10 miles): Perent River, p. 40 rods, **river,** p. 22 rods, **river,** p. 16 rods, **river, Boga Lake,** p. 26 rods, **Isabella Lake,** p. 28 rods, **Isabella River,** p. 15 rods, **river,** p. 110 rods, **river, Rice Lake.** (See comments for Day 3, Route #36-1). The 28-rod portage at the west end of Isabella Lake crosses the Pow Wow Hiking Trail. It's a seldom-used trail that loops through the isolated interior part of the BWCA Wilderness sandwiched between the Isabella River and Lake Three. A wooden bridge crosses the river just south of the intersection of the 2 trails.

In the vicinity of Rice Lake, you may see charred stumps on the north side of the Isabella River. They are the visible remnants of a wildfire that consumed over a thousand acres of forest in September of 1976.

Rice Lake is nearly surrounded by bog, and the lake itself is quite shallow. The 2 campsites there are a bit out of your way, but you'll be off the "beaten path" in a quiet location.

Day 3 (10 miles): Rice Lake, Isabella River, p. 10 rods, **river,** p. 27 rods, **river,** p. 27 rods, **river,** p. 40 rods, **river, rapids, river,** p. 33 rods, **river, rapids, river,** p. 190 rods, **river, Bald Eagle Lake.** You should make fairly good time paddling downstream on the scenic Isabella River. Though not extremely swift, the current is noticeable. Two or 3 of the shorter rapids may be safely shot if the water is sufficiently high. *Always scout them first and don't take chances!*

Don't worry about the 190-rod carry. It is mostly downhill and has a good, dry path. Don't try to avoid the portage by running the adjacent rapids. It's not safe. Help may not pass your way for quite some time, and it's a long walk back to your car.

Don't be confused by the appearance of the south end of Bald Eagle Lake. Both the Fisher and the McKenzie maps give the impression that Bald Eagle Lake extends all the way to the 190-rod portage on the Isabella River and the 10-rod portage on the Snake River. Wrong. What appears on the map to be the lower part of the lake (about 1 mile long) is actually a grassy bog through which both rivers flow and then merge.

The best campsites are located in the north end of Bald Eagle Lake. But, then, that's where most of the other people will be, too. For a 10-mile day, plan to camp near the south end of this big lake, south of the Gull Creek outlet. This is one of the best lakes in the area for catching northern pike. Walleyes and black crappies also inhabit the lake.

Day 4 (12 miles): Bald Eagle Lake, rapids, Gabbro Lake, Little Gabbro Lake, p. 122 rods, **South Kawishiwi River,** p. 28 rods, **river,** p. 18 rods, **river,** p. 12 rods, **river.** The short, swift rapids between Bald Eagle and Gabbro lakes can usually be easily run in your canoe. If you are not comfortable running the rapids, however, you should portage 5 rods across the northwest end of the rocky island around which the rapids pass. Along the northwest shore of Gabbro Lake and the north shore of Little Gabbro Lake, you may see the charred evidence of another forest fire. During the dry June of 1995, the Gabbro Lake Fire burned over 3,000 acres of forest across the region just north of Gabbro Lake and east of the South Kawishiwi River.

The 122-rod portage begins just upstream (west bank) from the site of an old, now nearly indistinguishable logging dam. It has a good path that descends much of the way to the river below. After reaching the South Kawishiwi River, you will be paddling upstream this day, but the current is seldom noticeable in the quiet pools between rapids. All of the portages along the river are quite easy. The longest trail (28 rods), however, does pass over a small but steep hill. With normal water conditions, you could eliminate all three of the portages by walking or lining your canoe up the shallow rapids.

Plan to camp near the confluence of the North and South Kawishiwi River branches, just beyond the final portage. There are some very nice campsites in that area, including a couple in the north branch of the river.

Day 5 (10 miles): Kawishiwi River, p. 8 rods, **river,** p. 40 rods, **river,** p. 20 rods, **river,** p. 25 rods, **Confusion Lake,** p. 41 rods, **Lake One,** p. 30 rods, **pond,** p. 40 rods, **Lake Two, Lake Three, Lake Four.** You'll be paddling on a very pretty part of the Kawishiwi River this day. Confusion Lake is also as attractive as it is confusing. The only portage that you might be able to eliminate by walking or lining your canoe through the rapids is at the 20-rod trail. Don't be tempted to bypass any of the other portages. The gradient is too great and the current is far too swift in the rapids. There is a small, scenic waterfall at the 8-rod portage.

You will surely see many other paddlers after entering Lake One. Most of them go no farther than the numbered lakes, so you may have considerable competition for campsites. Keep this day of travel short and claim your campsite early. For a little seclusion from the usual

"crowd," you could paddle into the narrow northeast bay of Lake Four, where you'll find three campsites that are well off the "beaten path."
Day 6 (12 miles): Lake Four, p. 25 rods, **Kawishiwi River,** p. 25 rods, **river,** p. 10 rods, **river, Hudson Lake,** p. 105 rods, **Lake Insula,** p. 18 rods, **Kawishiwi River, Alice Lake.** Like the previous 2 days, all of the portages this day are quite easy on well-maintained and well-traveled paths. In spite of the heavy traffic, moose are often seen throughout the area. Look for them in the shallow bays and creek inlets along the shoreline.

Island-studded Lake Insula may be confusing even to an experienced map-reader, particularly in the southwest end of the lake. Use your compass, if necessary, to follow a general heading, instead of trying to account for every little island you see.

Plan to camp at the south end of Alice Lake, where you'll find several nice campsites from which to choose. Then cast a line for the walleyes, northern pike and bluegills that occupy this large, open lake. In particular, it is considered to be a very good producer of walleyes.

Day 7 (9 miles): Alice Lake, p. 20 rods, **Kawishiwi River,** p. 90 rods, **river,** p. 20 rods, **river, River Lake, river,** p. 67 rods, **Malberg Lake,** p. 24 rods, **Koma Lake.** After completing the first portage, if you steer south, away from the main course of the river, you'll find a small display of Indian rock paintings along the west shore of the bay, about ½-mile from the portage.

If you're tired of freeze-dried foods by now and haven't had much luck finding fish during the previous 6 days, you'll be camped in a good place. Both Malberg and Koma lakes are known as very good walleye lakes. They also harbor northern pike.

Day 8 (9 miles): Koma Lake, p. 127 rods, **Kawishiwi River,** p. 48 rods, **river,** p. 19 rods, **Lake Polly,** p. 91 rods, **Townline Lake,** p. 181 rods, **Kawasachong Lake, Kawishiwi River,** p. 11 rods, **river,** p. 20 rods, **Square Lake, Kawishiwi River, Kawishiwi Lake.** Once again, you'll be travelling uphill this day, but none of the portages is difficult. The longest trail (181 rods) is the most challenging, as it climbs over 90 feet during the first 120 rods. The only place along the entire route where low water may be a problem is in the stretch of river between Kawasachong and Square lakes. Those short portages may stretch longer when the tiny river dries up. Don't worry though; you'll get through.

Entry Point 37—Kawishiwi Lake

SEASONAL PERMITS: 959

POPULARITY RANK: 10th

DAILY QUOTA: 9

LOCATION: Kawishiwi Lake is located 22 miles northwest of Tofte, very near the center of the southern boundary of the BWCA Wilderness. To get there from Highway 61 in Tofte, drive north on the Sawbill Trail for 17½ miles to its intersection with Cook County Road 3 (½-mile past the intersection of Forest Route 170). Turn left there and drive west on County Road 3 (which changes to Lake County Road 7) for 10 more miles on gravel to its junction with Forest Route 354. Turn right and proceed northbound on F.R. 354 for 4.4 miles to the Kawishiwi Lake landing at the road's end. F.R. 354 is a "single track road with turnouts." It is a good gravel road, but somewhat narrower than the county roads.

DESCRIPTION: A large parking lot on the opposite side of the road from the boat landing will accommodate nearly 2 dozen vehicles and, believe it or not, the lot is sometimes full.

In spite of its remote location, about midway between Ely and Lake Superior, the Kawishiwi Lake entry point is quite popular among canoeists. About 70% of its 9 daily permits are issued to visitors each summer. Although you may not need an advance reservation for a weekday visit, you will surely want to make a reservation for a weekend permit.

There are more than 40 designated BWCAW campsites from Kawishiwi Lake to Malberg Lake to accommodate the heavy use in this area. Much of the traffic goes no farther than Malberg Lake, which is a popular destination for walleye anglers.

In spite of the heavy traffic, moose are a common sight throughout the region. Some 20 years ago, soon after the adjacent area had been logged, the moose population was reputed to be among the densest of any in North America. With the new forest maturing, that is no longer the case, but there are still many moose in the area. So keep a watchful eye.

The Kawishiwi Lake Campground is a good place to spend the night before your trip. It lies adjacent to (just west of) the boat landing. There are only 5 campsites there and availability is on a first-come-first-served basis, so plan to arrive early to claim yours for the night. There is no camping fee at this "rustic" campground.

In addition to the 2 routes described below, you could also take a delightful 8-day loop from Kawishiwi Lake by reversing Route #36-2.

ROUTE #37-1: The Lady Lakes Route

3 Days, 24 Miles, 13 Lakes, 2 Rivers, 17 Portages

DIFFICULTY: Challenging

FISHER MAPS: F-5

INTRODUCTION: This is a delightful route that stays on smaller lakes and rivers. From Kawishiwi Lake, you will first head north on the lakes and streams that compose the upper flowage of the Kawishiwi River system. At Lake Polly, then, the route veers southeast and follows the Phoebe River to Hazel, Phoebe and Grace lakes. Another "lady lake" (Beth) will carry you farther east to Alton Lake. From there a short portage connects to Sawbill Lake, where you'll end at the public landing, 20 miles by road from your origin.

Most groups should have no problem completing the route in 3 days. Strong trippers could surely do it in just 2 days if they need only 1 trip across portages. For most paddlers, however, an average of 6 carries per day is plenty. While most portages are less than 60 rods long, 4 do exceed 100 rods. The longest measures 181 rods and you'll confront it right away.

While the water level should never be too low to prohibit travel on this route, you may encounter some problem areas along both the Kawishiwi and Phoebe rivers during drought years or late in the summer.

Don't expect to escape entirely from other people along this route. You'll be starting at the 10th busiest entry point and ending at the 3rd most popular entry point in the Boundary Waters. There are numerous campsites, but there is also plenty of competition for them. Start your days early, keep them short, and find your campsite as early in the afternoon as possible. You'll probably find the most seclusion while paddling on the Phoebe River. Motorboats are prohibited in this part of the Wilderness, except at the south end of Sawbill Lake.

Anglers should have plenty of time to wet their lines and they are likely to be well rewarded. Good populations of walleyes and northern pike inhabit most of the lakes along the route, and smallmouth bass may also be found in the last 2 lakes. The persistent angler may also pull lake trout from the cool, clear depths of Alton Lake.

Day 1 (7 miles): Kawishiwi Lake, Kawishiwi River, Square Lake, p. 20 rods, **Kawishiwi River,** p. 11 rods, **river, Kawasachong Lake,** p. 181 rods, **Townline Lake,** p. 91 rods, **Lake Polly.** Your first day will take you through the small lakes and streams that compose the upper part of the Kawishiwi River system. The portages are well used, generally downhill, and not difficult. Even the 181-rod trail leading north from Kawasachong Lake is mostly downhill and easy to negotiate. After a gentle climb during the first 60 rods, the path descends about 90 feet over the final 120 rods to the shore of Townline Lake. The only place along the entire route where low water may be a problem is in the stretch of river between Kawasachong and Square lakes. Those short portages may stretch longer when the tiny river shrinks. Don't worry though; you can always get through.

For a 7-mile day of travel, plan to camp at one of the sites in the north part of Lake Polly. Anglers should find good walleye fishing nearby. At dusk, keep a watchful eye for moose along the shoreline.

Be sure to hang your food pack properly this night. In frequently visited areas like this, bears are sometimes a nuisance. Rather intelligent animals, black bears learn to associate food with campers. And where campsites are plentiful, bears often "make the rounds" in search of easy food. If you keep a clean campsite and hang your food safely between trees at night and when you are away from the site during the day, however, the chances are slim that you will have any problems with these fascinating creatures.

Day 2 (8 miles): Lake Polly, p. 97 rods, **Phoebe River,** p. 16 rods, **river,** p. 92 rods, **river,** p. 25 rods, **river,** p. 59 rods, **Hazel Lake,** p. 140 rods, **Phoebe River, Knight Lake, Phoebe River, Phoebe Lake.** All 6 of the portages this day are generally uphill, as you gain a total of 144 feet from Lake Polly to Knight and Phoebe lakes, but the trails are normally dry and not difficult to cross. The most challenging is the final carry on a path that gains about 70 feet elevation during the first 90 rods.

The Phoebe River is a very scenic part of the route, where moose, beavers and mink abound. Although you'll be paddling upstream, the current is barely noticeable, except at the rapids where you'll portage.

You will probably encounter few other people between Polly and Phoebe lakes. On Phoebe Lake, however, you'll be joined by an influx of paddlers who entered the BWCAW at Sawbill Lake. Do your best to make camp early. There are several good sites near the west end of the lake.

Day 3 (9 miles): Phoebe Lake, Phoebe River, p. 85 rods, **river,** p. 5 rods, **river,** p. 15 rods, **river,** p. 15 rods, **Grace Lake,** p. 285 rods, **Beth Lake,** p. 140 rods, **Alton Lake,** p. 30 rods, **Sawbill Lake.** You'll continue your uphill journey from Phoebe Lake to Beth Lake, gaining a total of 116 feet elevation on the first 6 portages. But then, after climbing over the Laurentian Divide just east of Beth Lake, you'll descend about 85 feet to Sawbill Lake. The long portage from Grace to Beth Lake is not as bad as it looks on the map. It's not a difficult carry as you gradually ascend on a well-worn path that gains about 70 feet elevation en route. (An alternate route from Grace through Ella Lake to Beth may appear easier on the map, with shorter carries of 130 and 80 rods. But it's not. The 130-rod trail is quite rocky, with poor landings at both ends, and the shorter path may be wet and muddy. Perhaps the only reason to visit Ella Lake is to escape from other visitors in this area.)

In addition to the three short portages along the Phoebe River, you may also encounter a beaver dam or two along the way.

ROUTE #37-2: The Louse River Loop

   6 Days, 50 Miles, 25 Lakes, 4 Rivers, 45 Portages

DIFFICULTY: Most Rugged

FISHER MAPS: F-5, F-11, F-12

INTRODUCTION: This is a dandy route for anyone who enjoys frequent wildlife sightings and paddling on tiny rivers and smaller lakes—and for those who don't mind working hard to find their piece of Paradise. From Kawishiwi Lake, you will first head north on the lakes and streams that compose the upper flowage of the Kawishiwi River system. At Lake Polly, then, the route veers southeast and follows the Phoebe River to Hazel, Phoebe and Grace lakes. Another "lady lake" (Beth) will carry you farther east to Alton Lake. At that point, the route veers north along a chain of small lakes and streams to Mesaba Lake. You will then plot a westbound course by following the

Louse River flowage through the least visited part of the loop all the way to Malberg Lake. From there, you will follow the Kawishiwi River flowage south to your origin at Kawishiwi Lake.

This 6-day route is a challenge to even the most experienced trippers, and Northwoods neophytes should probably not take the route unless they can spare at least 7 full days. Although most of the portages are neither long nor difficult, the sheer number might frustrate those with little strength or experience. And there are a few long carries. By spreading the trip over 7 or 8 days, however, most groups could enjoy a pace that is not too grueling.

Don't expect to escape entirely from other people along most of this route. You'll be starting at the 10th busiest entry point and spending your third night close to the 3rd most popular entry point in the Boundary Waters (Sawbill Lake). There are numerous campsites in the popular areas, but there is also plenty of competition for them. Start your days early, keep them short, and find your campsite as early in the afternoon as possible. You'll probably find the most seclusion while paddling on the Phoebe and Louse rivers. Motorboats are prohibited from the entire loop.

Fishing is normally quite good throughout the loop. Walleyes and northern pike inhabit many of the lakes along the route, and pan fish are in some of the lakes. Lake trout also may be pulled from the depths of Alton Lake.

This route is most favorable during spring or early summer, when water levels are normally the highest. During late summer or dry years, you may find it to be a drag in places—literally. If in doubt, consult a USFS ranger in the Tofte District or the knowledgeable folks at Sawbill Outfitters before heading out.

Day 1 (7 miles): Kawishiwi Lake, Kawishiwi River, Square Lake, p. 20 rods, **Kawishiwi River,** p. 11 rods, **river, Kawasachong Lake,** p. 181 rods, **Townline Lake,** p. 91 rods, **Lake Polly.** (See comments for Day 1, Route #37-1.)

Day 2 (8 miles): Lake Polly, p. 97 rods, **Phoebe River,** p. 16 rods, **river,** p. 92 rods, **river,** p. 25 rods, **river,** p. 59 rods, **Hazel Lake,** p. 140 rods, **Phoebe River, Knight Lake, Phoebe River, Phoebe Lake.** (See comments for Day 2, Route #37-1.)

Day 3 (9 miles): Phoebe Lake, Phoebe River, p. 85 rods, **river,** p. 5 rods, **river,** p. 15 rods, **river,** p. 15 rods, **Grace Lake,** p. 285 rods, **Beth Lake,** p. 140 rods, **Alton Lake.** (See comments for Day 3, Route #37-1.) For a 9-mile day of travel, plan to camp at the north end of Alton Lake, and expect company. Sawbill Lake, the BWCAW's 3rd busiest entry point, is just a short portage away. Find your campsite early in the afternoon. Then try your luck at catching some of the lake trout, walleyes, smallmouth bass or northern pike that lurk beneath the surface of this deep, clear lake.

Day 4 (9 miles): Alton Lake, p. 10 rods, **Kelso Lake, Kelso River, Lujenida Lake,** p. 460 rods, **Zenith Lake,** p. 80 rods, **Duck Lake,** p. 3 rods, **Hug Lake,** p. 80 rods, **Mesaba Lake,** p. 20 rods, **Chaser Lake,** p. 7 rods, **pond,** p. 130 rods, **Dent Lake.** You'll want to get an early start again today. Although the distance traveled is only 9 miles, if you need 2 trips to get your gear across the portages, you'll be walking almost 5 additional miles on 8 portages measuring a total of 790 rods. Most of that walking is on the long trail connecting Lujenida and Zenith lakes. It is fairly level to slightly uphill for nearly 300 rods as the path closely parallels a creek flowage for the first half of the portage. If you prefer, you can break up the trek into three shorter segments with brief paddling interludes on 2 ponds. The final half-mile of trail gains over 100 feet in elevation as it passes over the Laurentian Divide before descending nearly that much to Zenith Lake. Fortunately the portage has a good, well-traveled path.

The next 2 quarter-mile portages are downhill, the first descending 86 feet from Zenith to Duck Lake, and the second dropping 57 feet from Hug Lake to Mesaba Lake. A beaver dam between Duck and Hug lakes makes the short portage there (3 rods) necessary. That dam maintains the water level on Duck Lake. Without it, the shallow lake is barely deep enough to cross in a heavily loaded canoe.

Short but rather steep climbs separate Mesaba and Chaser lakes and the small pond just west of Chaser Lake. The first half of the final carry of the day is over a hill, but the path then levels off en route to the narrow east end of Dent Lake.

There are just 2 campsites on Dent Lake. If you know (or suspect) that 2 groups are a short distance in front of you, you'd be wise to stop on Mesaba Lake and make camp early. Then, if blueberries are ripe, take time to explore the east shore of Mesaba Lake where the berries grow in abundance. There are no other campsites after Dent Lake until you reach Trail Lake, four portages away.

Day 5 (8 miles): Dent Lake, p. 45 rods, **Bug Lake,** p. 115 rods, **Louse River,** p. 50 rods, **river,** p. 130 rods, **Trail Lake,** p. 21 rods, **Louse River,** p. 56 rods, **river,** p. 41 rods, **river,** p. 20 rods, **river,** p. 100 rods, **river,** p. 60 rods, **Boze Lake,** p. 11 rods, **Louse River,** p. 21 rods, **river, Frond Lake, Louse River,** p. 15 rods, **Malberg Lake,** p. 24 rods, **Koma Lake.** For the most part, you'll be heading downhill this day as you follow the Louse River flowage to Malberg Lake, descending a total of 200 feet from Dent Lake. With 14 portages totaling 709 rods, however, don't expect an easy day. If 2 trips are needed on the portages, you'll be

Picking blueberries

walking over 6½ miles this day. Most of the carries are not difficult, but their frequency will slow your progress considerably. The first portage to Bug Lake, however, is marshy and rather tricky to negotiate. The 125-rod portage to Trail Lake is also a nasty one. It is steep in places, has tricky footing, and is challenging to even a seasoned tripper.

Crossing Bug Lake is no problem, as long as a beaver dam continues to maintain the water level there. If the dam breaks and beaver activity ceases, however, the lake may be barely deep enough for passage of a loaded canoe (as it once was).

You may encounter a beaver dam or two and occasional rocky shoals along the Louse River to further slow your progress. Large boulders may also obstruct passage frequently on the lower Louse River during low-water periods. If blueberries are in season, you may find them in abundance all along the Louse River. Picking them is a good way to rest between portages. If you are paddling late into the afternoon and you see a vacant campsite on Malberg Lake, grab it. Malberg and Koma lakes are popular destinations for anglers. Claim your campsite as early as possible. Anglers should have no problem finding walleyes and northern pike in the depths of either Malberg Lake or Koma Lake.

Day 6 (9 miles): Koma Lake, p. 127 rods, **Kawishiwi River,** p. 48 rods, **river,** p. 19 rods, **Lake Polly,** p. 91 rods, **Townline Lake,** p. 181 rods, **Kawasachong Lake, Kawishiwi River,** p. 11 rods, **river,** p. 20 rods, **Square Lake, Kawishiwi River, Kawishiwi Lake.** Contrary to the previous day, you will be traveling uphill on your final day in the Wilderness, but gaining only 87 feet all the way from Koma Lake to Kawishiwi Lake. But, with half the number of portages, this day should seem easy. After the first three carries along the Kawishiwi River (none of which is difficult), the remainder of the route should look familiar as you backtrack from Lake Polly to Kawishiwi Lake.

Entry Point 38—Sawbill Lake

SEASONAL PERMITS: 1,717

POPULARITY RANK: 3rd

DAILY QUOTA: 14

LOCATION: Sawbill Lake is located at the end of the Sawbill Trail, 23 miles north of Highway 61 in Tofte.

DESCRIPTION: In spite of its remote location, Sawbill Lake is the most popular entry point in the eastern region of the BWCA Wilderness. Even with a high quota of 14 overnight permits per day, the demand for them is often more than the supply. During the summer of 1997 80% of the available permits were issued. Don't wait too late to make a reservation, especially if you are planning to start your trip on a Friday, Saturday, Sunday or Monday. This entry point also ranks 4th among all entry points in the number of non-quota day-use permits issued, probably because of the large, popular campground at the south end of the lake. Motors are not permitted to enter the wilderness here, although they are permitted at the south end of Sawbill Lake, which lies outside the BWCAW.

With all its popularity, Sawbill Lake is still a good entry point from which to access several pristine wilderness areas that receive very light use and where motorboats are not permitted. To get there, however, you must be willing to cross many portages, some of which are long and exhausting. Moose, mink, beavers and black bears are common throughout much of the nearby region.

Adjacent to the public landing is the Sawbill Lake Campground—a convenient place to spend the night before your canoe trip. Sawbill Canoe Outfitters operates the campground, which has 50 campsites that are available on a first-come-first-served basis. A fee is charged for camping there. Sawbill Canoe Outfitters sells firewood, groceries, camping supplies, a sauna and hot showers, as well as complete and partial outfitting for canoe trips. You can also pick up your BWCAW permit there. So it is a good, convenient place to start and end your canoe trip.

In addition to the 2 routes described below, you may also enjoy a fine 3-day outing by reversing Route #37-1 and paddling from Sawbill Lake to Kawishiwi Lake via the "Lady Lakes" and the Phoebe River.

ROUTE #38-1: The Temperance River Loop

3 Days, 23 Miles, 12 Lakes, 1 River, 3 Creeks, 14 Portages

DIFFICULTY: Challenging

FISHER MAPS: F-5, F-6 (F-12 optional)

INTRODUCTION: This short loop offers an excellent introduction to the BWCA Wilderness for a group of strong paddlers, as well as a fine 3-day weekend route for any seasoned trippers. From the public landing, you will first paddle all the way to the north end of Sawbill Lake. Then you'll continue northbound on 3 small creeks and 2 small lakes to beautiful Cherokee Lake. From there, the route veers toward the southeast to the Temperance lakes and then follows the Temperance River flowage south to Kelly Lake. From there you will portage and paddle westward across the "fire lakes" and back to Sawbill Lake.

Along this lovely route you will cross the Laurentian Divide—the north-south continental divide—twice. The water north of the divide flows toward the Arctic Ocean while the water south of the divide eventually makes its way to the Atlantic Ocean. Although this "height of land" is topographically subtle, you will feel the strain while on the portages that cross the divide.

With a good variety of tiny streams and small to middle-sized lakes, this route should appeal to folks who prefer a variety of scenery. Don't expect to escape from other people anywhere along the route, but you'll probably see fewer people on the southbound east half of the loop.

Anglers may find northern pike in much of the water along this route. Walleyes, smallmouth bass and lake trout also inhabit some of the lakes.

Day 1 (9 miles): Sawbill Lake, p. 80 rods, **Ada Creek,** p. 80 rods, **Ada Lake, Skoop Creek,** p. 12 rods, **Skoop Lake,** p. 180 rods,

Cherokee Creek, Cherokee Lake. Plan an early departure this day to enable an early arrival at your campsite on Cherokee Lake, which is nearly as popular as it is beautiful. With a south breeze (or no wind at all), you should make good time to your first portage, at the north end of Sawbill Lake. That's half way to your destination—by far the easier half.

The first 2 quarter-mile portages along Ada Creek are not difficult. When the water level is low during a year of drought, as it was in 1998, Skoop Creek may nearly dry up. When that happens, you may have to carry your canoe and gear all the way from Ada Lake to Skoop Lake, which adds about 100 rods to the designated 12-rod portage. Then, after a brief rest on Skoop Lake, you'll confront your biggest challenge of the day—a half-mile carry across the Laurentian Divide. Fortunately, you'll be hiking on a good path that receives a considerable amount of use.

Cherokee Creek is a dependable waterway, even during drought years and late in the summer. You may want to return to the creek at dusk, after your campsite is set up for the night, to watch for the moose that are often seen along the banks of the creek.

There are many campsites on Cherokee Lake. But there is also a great deal of demand for them by visitors from at least three entry points. So don't delay in claiming your site for the night. Then take time to explore this lovely, island-studded lake. Lake trout and northern pike inhabit its depths. (Note: Without the F-12 map, you will be confined to the south end of Cherokee Lake. It's not wise to explore a lake of this size without a good map.)

Day 2 (6 miles): Cherokee Lake, p. 140 rods, **Sitka Lake,** p. 105 rods, **North Temperance Lake,** p. 55 rods, **South Temperance Lake,** p. 240 rods, **Temperance River,** p. 80 rods, **Weird Lake,** p. 12 rods, **Jack Lake.** Your first carry of the day will get your heart pumping fast. It is a hilly trail that rises over 90 feet in elevation before dropping to the north shore of Sitka Lake. The next trail also has its ups and downs, as it crosses the Laurentian Divide. After that carry, the remainder of the portages should seem easy as you move generally downhill from North Temperance Lake to Kelly Lake. Cherokee and Sitka lakes lie north of the divide; the rest of this loop is south of it.

The region lying east of South Temperance Lake was scarred by a large wildfire that burned 4,450 acres of timber in June of 1996. It was started by lightning and cost $1.5 million to fight. Unlike other "prescribed" natural fires that are allowed to burn in the Wilderness, The South Temperance Fire threatened areas lying outside the BWCAW and was, therefore, not allowed to burn freely.

Narrow lakes and shallow streams compose the Temperance River flowage that drains south from North Temperance Lake. Scenic hills rise as much as 250 feet above the water.

Anglers usually find the fishing in Jack Lake to be very good for walleyes and northern pike. If the 2 campsites there are occupied, proceed onward to Kelly Lake, where there are several more sites from which to choose. There should be some walleyes in Kelly Lake, too.

Day 3 (8 miles): Jack Lake, p. 65 rods, **Kelly Lake**, p. 230 rods, **Burnt Lake**, p. 90 rods, **Smoke Lake**, p. 100 rods, **Sawbill Lake.** Your downhill journey on the Temperance River flowage ends at Kelly Lake—abruptly. The long portage to Burnt Lake rises nearly 100 feet during the first 100 rods. After walking through a swampy area, you'll cross an old, abandoned logging road about midway across the portage. That carry should be the only serious challenge of the day.

ROUTE #38-2:	The Copper Pan Loop
	7 Days, 61 Miles, 38 Lakes, 3 Rivers, 5 Creeks, 49 Portages
DIFFICULTY:	Challenging
FISHER MAPS:	F-5, F-11, F-12
INTRODUCTION:	This loop combines an interesting variety of tiny creeks, larger rivers, and lakes of all shapes and sizes. From the public landing, you will first paddle all the way to the north end of Sawbill Lake. Then you'll continue northbound on 3 small creeks and 2 small lakes to beautiful Cherokee Lake. From there, you'll continue traveling north through Long Island Lake to Cross Bay Lake. At that point, the route veers west across a chain of lovely lakes leading to island-studded Little Saganaga Lake. You'll then pass through one of the least visited parts of this loop en route to the Kawishiwi River. The Kawishiwi River flowage will carry you south through a popular chain of lakes from Malberg to Lake Polly. At that point the route veers toward the southeast and follows the Phoebe River to the "Lady Lakes" and then on to Alton Lake. From there a short portage connects to Sawbill Lake and a short journey south will return you to your origin at the public landing.

This is a wonderful route for anyone who prefers paddling on smaller lakes and streams and who doesn't mind frequent portages along the way. But don't expect to completely escape from other people *anywhere* along this route. Your best chances of solitude are in the region between Little Saganaga and Malberg lakes and along the Phoebe River. Elsewhere, you'll be too close to one or more of the popular entry points that serve visitors to this region. Don't let that discourage you. This route is worth sharing. In spite of the human visitation, this is a good area in which to see wildlife, including a substantial population of moose. You might also hear timber wolves at night.

With an average of 7 portages per day, this loop is probably not well suited to a group of BWCAW neophytes, unless the route can be spread over more than 7 days. Only 13 of the 49 portages, however, are longer than 80 rods (¼ mile) and most are less than 50 rods. Two trails are longer than 200 rods.

Anglers will have plenty of opportunities to wet their lines, and the rewards are bountiful. Throughout the loop, walleyes and northern pike abound. And several of the lakes harbor good populations of lake trout or smallmouth bass.

Day 1 (9 miles): Sawbill Lake, p. 80 rods, **Ada Creek,** p. 80 rods, **Ada Lake, Skoop Creek,** p. 12 rods, **Skoop Lake,** p. 180 rods, **Cherokee Creek, Cherokee Lake.** (See comments for Day 1, Route #38-1.)

Day 2 (8 miles): Cherokee Lake, p. 13 rods, **Gordon Lake,** p. 28 rods, **Long Island River,** p. 5 rods, **river, Long Island Lake, Karl Lake,** p. 28 rods, **Lower George Lake,** p. 37 rods, **Rib Lake,** p. 56 rods, **Cross Bay Lake.** You may look back at this as one of the easiest days of your trip, as you descend about 80 feet from Cherokee Lake to Cross Bay Lake. This is good moose country, so keep a watchful eye along the way.

Like Cherokee Lake, Long Island is also a very popular lake that attracts visitors from several directions. Try to claim your campsite on Cross Bay Lake early in the afternoon. The lake is a fairly popular BWCAW entry point accessible from the Gunflint Trail to the north. If you prefer to get off the main route, continue onward to Snipe Lake. There you'll find some campsites situated in the quiet bays of that pretty little lake.

Day 3 (8 miles): Cross Bay Lake, p. 47 rods, **Snipe Lake,** p. 100 rods, **Copper Lake,** p. 69 rods, **Hubbub Lake,** p. 255 rods, **Tuscarora Lake,** p. 63 rods, **Owl Lake,** p. 55 rods, **Crooked Lake.** There is a short but rather steep climb on the first portage to Snipe Lake. The next trail (100 rods) also starts with a climb over a low hill and then skirts the edge of a swamp draining the northeast end of Copper Lake. The 69-rod portage is mostly downhill, after the first 15 rods. It was quite brushy in 1998, but trail crews were working the area nearby, so it may have been cleaned up since then.

The longest portage so far (and second longest of the whole route) crosses Howl Swamp en route to Hubbub Lake. Don't worry; it's actually not a swampy trail. Fortunately, there is a board walk across the swamp and the entire path is in fine condition. The first half of the trail is somewhat undulating, but there are no exhausting climbs. After dipping down to cross the swamp, the trail then levels off until the descent to Tuscarora Lake. The boardwalk was in need of repairs in 1998. Watch your step.

Tuscarora is a pretty lake, encircled by numerous rock outcrops and low cliffs, and surrounded by low hills. It has several nice campsites that are large enough to accommodate larger groups. If you are tired or running behind schedule, it's a good alternate destination to call "home" for the night.

The final 2 portages leading to and from Owl Lake are mostly downhill. Near the end of the final trail (55 rods) the path is littered with large boulders for about 10 rods where it crosses a small creek. The footing is tricky, so use caution, especially when the rocks are wet.

Crooked is a lovely lake with several nice campsites, some of which can accommodate larger groups with several tents. With time and patience, anglers will find lake trout in the deep, clear water nearby.

(If you already find yourself behind schedule when you arrive at Crooked Lake, you might consider taking one of two possible shortcuts. The most direct route to Sawbill Lake leads south from Crooked Lake through Mora, Hub and Mesaba lakes. This is *not* an easy shortcut, but any group should be able to cover the distance in 2 or 3 days. Or, if you are just a little behind schedule and prefer to continue on the main route, you could take a shortcut to Little Saganaga Lake on Day 4 via Tarry and Mora lakes. It's shorter and easier than the route described below.)

Day 4 (9 miles): Crooked Lake, p. 82 rods, **Gillis Lake,** p. 25 rods, **French Lake,** p. 33 rods, **Powell Lake,** p. 20 rods, **West Fern Lake,** p. 30 rods, **Virgin Lake,** p. 90 rods, **Little Saganaga Lake,** p. 19 rods, **creek,** p. 19 rods, **Elton Lake.** The portage from Crooked Lake has a rocky path and may be wet and muddy in a few places. Ten rods from the beginning of the trail, you will see the dilapidated remains of an old log cabin that was once used by a trapper. There is still an old dock (in disrepair, but usable) at the landing. After passing the old cabin, the trail skirts the edge of a pond for 23 rods. For those who prefer 2 short carries to a longer one, you can paddle across the pond and have carries of 13 rods and 46 rods at either end. It is probably quicker to simply portage the entire 82 rods, but the middle stretch that skirts close to the pond may be quite wet when the water level is high.

The chain of small lakes from French Lake to Virgin Lake doesn't entertain as many visitors as the parallel chain to the south (Mora, Tarry and Crooked). The portages are also not as well constructed or maintained. The paths are often littered with rocks and roots. The 90-rod portage from Virgin Lake may be one of the primary reasons why folks prefer the other route to Little Saganaga Lake. Fortunately, you'll be heading in the right direction—mostly downhill, and rather steep in a couple of places during the final 60 rods, after climbing the first 30 rods from Virgin Lake.

Little Saganaga, with its many islands and peninsulas, is a lovely lake and a popular destination for many BWCAW visitors. There are 2 dozen campsites on the lake to accommodate them. Expect to see people here.

An old rock-and-gravel dam maintains the water level in the creek connecting Little Saganaga and Elton lakes. After leaving Little Saganaga Lake, you will again be entering a part of the Wilderness that receives fairly light use during much of the summer.

Elton is another pretty lake, with rock outcrops along its shores. There are a couple of nice campsites near the middle of the lake. Northern pike is the only game fish you'll find there. The lake is known to harbor some big ones.

Day 5 (8 miles): Elton Lake, p. 55 rods, **Makwa Lake,** p. 60 rods, **pond,** p. 90 rods, **Panhandle Lake,** p. 50 rods, **Pan Lake,** p. 65 rods, **Anit Lake,** p. 18 rods, **creek, Kivaniva Lake,** p. 42 rods, **Kawishiwi River,** p. 48 rods, **Malberg Lake,** p. 24 rods, **Koma Lake.** Most of the portages this day have very good paths and there is very little change in elevation. Low water levels can cause problems at some of the portage landings.

The unnamed "pond" showing on the map between Pan and Anit lakes was no longer a pond in 1998. It had dried to a grassy bog with a tiny creek flowing through it. What were once a 20-rod portage and a 15-rod portage, separated by a small pond, are now a 65-rod portage. The beginning and end are on good, dry paths (the old portage trails). In the middle, however, you will be skirting the west edge of the bog on a soft, grassy path that may also be wet and muddy at times.

The next portage from Anit Lake can vary from 13 to 25 rods, depending on the water level in the creek draining into Kivaniva Lake. A large beaver dam maintains the water depth in Anit Lake. As long as it holds tight, water level should not be a problem in that lake.

A small beaver dam is also located in Kivaniva Lake, just after the first portage landing (42-rod trail to the Kawishiwi River). You can

Elton Lake

shorten the carry by 8 rods (to 34 rods) by lifting over the beaver dam and landing at a scenic spot across from a steep rock ledge. Regardless of the landing you choose, you'll be walking on an excellent path over a low hill.

You are bound to see more people again on Malberg and Koma lakes. Walleye fishing is usually very good in both lakes, and anglers flock there from Kawishiwi Lake—the 10th most popular entry point for the BWCAW. Try to claim your campsite early in the afternoon.

Day 6 (10 miles): Koma Lake, p. 127 rods, **Kawishiwi River,** p. 48 rods, **river,** p. 19 rods, **Lake Polly,** p. 97 rods, **Phoebe River,** p. 16 rods, **river,** p. 92 rods, **river,** p. 25 rods, **river,** p. 59 rods, **Hazel Lake,** p. 140 rods, **Phoebe River, Knight Lake, Phoebe River, Phoebe Lake.** Your first three portages bypass rapids in the Kawishiwi River. The trails are well used with good paths, and none is difficult—gaining only about 30 feet in elevation from Koma Lake to Lake Polly. (Also see comments for Day 2, Route #37-1.)

Day 7 (9 miles): Phoebe Lake, Phoebe River, p. 85 rods, **river,** p. 5 rods, **river,** p. 15 rods, **river,** p. 15 rods, **Grace Lake,** p. 285 rods, **Beth Lake,** p. 140 rods, **Alton Lake,** p. 30 rods, **Sawbill Lake.** (See comments for Day 3, Route #37-1.)

Entry Point 39—Baker Lake

SEASONAL PERMITS: 350

POPULARITY RANK: 23rd

DAILY QUOTA: 3

LOCATION: Baker Lake is 19 airline miles almost due north of Tofte. From US Highway 61, follow the Sawbill Trail 17 miles north to its intersection with Forest Route 170. Turn right and follow F.R. 170 northeast for 5 miles to the junction of Forest Route 1272 (just before the Temperance River bridge). Turn left there and drive ½ mile north to the public landing at Baker Lake. You will be using good gravel roads all the way from Tofte.

DESCRIPTION: A parking lot adjacent to the landing will accommodate up to 18 vehicles. The Baker Lake Campground lies just east of the boat landing and offers a good place to spend the night before your trip. There are only 5 rustic campsites and availability is on a first-come-first-served basis, so plan to arrive early to claim yours for the night. A camping fee is not charged. If the campground is full, it's only 3½ miles to the much larger Crescent Lake Campground (drive 2 miles east on F.R. 170 from the Baker Lake turnoff to the Crescent Lake turnoff leading south). A camping fee is charged there.

Baker is a small, shallow and weedy lake. If offers easy access to one of the more scenic parts of the BWCA Wilderness: the Temperance River flowage, where shallow lakes are surrounded by towering hills and connected by lovely rapids. With only three overnight groups per day allowed to enter the wilderness here, Baker Lake affords visitors a quieter alternative than nearby Sawbill Lake to access this region. Two-thirds of the available permits are issued each summer. Motors are not permitted.

ROUTE #39-1: The Weird Brule Route

2 Days, 15 Miles, 7 Lakes, 1 River, 1 Creek, 7 Portages

DIFFICULTY: Easier

FISHER MAPS: F-6

INTRODUCTION: This short route is a good introduction to the Boundary Waters Canoe Area. From the public landing, you will plot a northerly course up the Temperance River flowage from Baker Lake to South Temperance Lake, passing through several long and slender lakes along the way. Then, after one short portage, you will paddle east across Brule Lake to end at the public landing in the southeast corner of that huge lake, about 14 miles by road from your starting point.

You'll be paddling upstream on the Temperance River, but opposing current is found only at the rapids, which are bypassed on portage trails. Wind is much more of a factor than water current along this route—especially on big Brule Lake. Although there are 6 portages during the first day, including one measuring ¾ of a mile, none is difficult—including the long one. Even a group of novice paddlers should consider this an "easier" route.

Anglers will find walleyes and northern pike along much of the Temperance River flowage, as well as smallmouth bass in South Temperance and Brule lakes. With only 15 miles to travel in 2 days, there should be plenty of time to search for them.

Day 1 (8 miles): Baker Lake, p. 15 rods, **Temperance River, Peterson Lake,** p. 3 rods, **Kelly Lake,** p. 65 rods, **Jack Lake,** p. 12 rods, **Weird Lake,** p. 80 rods, **Temperance River,** p. 240 rods, **South Temperance Lake.** This is a scenic part of the BWCA Wilderness. Narrow lakes and shallow streams compose the Temperance River flowage that drains south from North Temperance Lake through Baker Lake en route to its ultimate rendezvous with Lake Superior. Hills rise high above the river valley—as much as 250 feet above Kelly and Jack lakes. You will be traveling uphill, but gaining less than 90 feet elevation throughout the day.

Under normal or high water conditions you may be able to avoid the first 2 portages by pulling or paddling your canoe up the shallow rapids connecting Baker, Peterson and Kelly lakes. In fact, when the water is high enough, you can easily paddle right through the channel connecting Peterson and Kelly lakes. On the other hand, when the

Temperance River—Baker to Peterson Lake

water is quite low (as it was during the dry summers of 1997 and 1998), you may encounter a challenge right away. The first portage from Baker Lake may stretch to nearly 40 rods on a rocky, brushy path along the river's edge until you reach Peterson Lake.

As you would expect, the only real challenge of the day is the final carry to South Temperance Lake. It gains about 60 feet elevation across the ¾-mile course on a good path that is well maintained and well used.

There may be competition for the limited number of campsites on South Temperance Lake, so don't delay in claiming yours for the night. Then, take time to explore the irregular shoreline. Anglers should find good fishing for smallmouth bass in this lake, which also harbors walleyes and northern pike.

The region lying east of South Temperance Lake was scarred by a large wildfire that burned 4,450 acres of timber in June of 1996. It was started by lightning and cost $1.5 million to fight. Unlike other "prescribed" natural fires that are allowed to burn in the Wilderness, the South Temperance Fire threatened areas lying outside the BWCAW and was, therefore, not allowed to burn freely.

Day 2 (7 miles): South Temperance Lake, creek, p. 10 rods, **Brule Lake.** If there is a light breeze from the west or no wind at all, this day should be quite easy as you cross big Brule Lake. If the wind is strong from any direction, however, brace yourself. A strong head wind is always a retarding menace, but also beware the strong *tail* wind.

When starting across a wide-open expanse of water with a strong wind at your back, the lake ahead of you may appear relatively calm and quite safe. As you proceed farther and farther out from the lee side of a sheltering shoreline, however, the waves grow higher and higher. Suddenly you may find your canoe in rougher water than you can handle, resulting in either a swamped or a capsized canoe. Wind can be either a friend or a foe, depending on how much respect you have for it and how much good judgment you demonstrate in its presence. It is always best to paddle close to the shoreline of a large lake. Not only is it safer, it is also far more interesting. That's where the wildlife resides.

ROUTE #39-2: The Jack Frost Loop

> 8 Days, 62 Miles, 38 Lakes, 5 Rivers, 61 Portages

DIFFICULTY: Most Rugged

FISHER MAPS: F-5, F-6, F-11, F-12

INTRODUCTION: This high-quality wilderness route combines an interesting variety of tiny creeks, larger rivers, and lakes of all shapes and sizes. From the public landing it first leads you north from Baker to North Temperance Lake, following the Temperance River flowage to the Laurentian Divide. From there, you will continue northbound to Cherokee and Gordon lakes and then west to Frost Lake. From there you will paddle down the remote and wild Frost River system of pools, creeks and elongated lakes to Mora Lake. After portaging west to cross island-studded Little Saganaga Lake, you will proceed southwest across a chain of smaller lakes leading to the Kawishiwi River. The Kawishiwi River flowage will carry you south through a popular chain of lakes from Malberg to Lake Polly. At that point the route veers toward the southeast and follows the Phoebe River to the "Lady Lakes." Then you'll proceed farther east to cross Alton, Sawbill and the "fire lakes" en route to Kelly Lake. A short journey south will return you to your origin at the Baker Lake public landing.

Fine scenery and bountiful wildlife characterize much of this varied loop. On your third day, in particular, you will be in one of the most pristine and seldom visited parts of the BWCA Wilderness: the Frost River. In this isolated region moose demonstrate little or no fear of your intrusion.

Motors are not allowed on any part of the route, and much of the loop entertains relatively few visitors during all but the peak summer periods. Even then, only in the vicinities of Cherokee, Little Saganaga, Polly and Sawbill lakes are you likely to encounter many other people.

Anglers will have good opportunities to catch most of the common game fish in the Boundary Waters. Walleyes and northern pike inhabit many of the lakes. Bluegills and smallmouth bass are also found in some of the lakes. The serious angler may also want to search the depths of Cherokee, Frost and Little Saganaga lakes for elusive lake trout.

With an average of nearly 8 portages per day, few would argue that this route deserves a "most rugged" rating. Fortunately, though, most of the carries are short. Only three are longer than half a mile; the longest is 285 rods. Nevertheless, this route is recommended only for those trippers who are willing to work hard for a high-quality wilderness experience.

Day 1 (8 miles): Baker Lake, p. 15 rods, **Temperance River, Peterson Lake,** p. 3 rods, **Kelly Lake,** p. 65 rods, **Jack Lake,** p. 12 rods, **Weird Lake,** p. 80 rods, **Temperance River,** p. 240 rods, **South Temperance Lake.** (See comments for Day 1, Route #39-1.)

Day 2 (8 miles): South Temperance Lake, p. 55 rods, **North Temperance Lake,** p. 105 rods, **Sitka Lake,** p. 140 rods, **Cherokee Lake,** p. 13 rods, **Gordon Lake,** p. 140 rods, **Unload Lake, creek, Frost Lake.** Portaging will have its ups and downs this day, as you pass over the Laurentian Divide. South of Sitka Lake, water flows eventually to the Atlantic Ocean. On the north side of the Divide, the water ultimately drains into the Arctic Ocean. The most exhausting carry of the day is on your first hilly 140-rod portage connecting Sitka and Cherokee lakes.

Beautiful Cherokee Lake attracts many visitors from both the Sawbill Lake and Brule Lake entry points. Expect to share this lovely setting with other people.

The second 140-rod trail leading west from Gordon Lake climbs over a fairly steep hill, but then levels off on a good, smooth path to Unload Lake. The shallow creek joining Unload and Frost lakes may be blocked by a beaver dam that requires a lift-over. Or you can bypass the creek on a 40-rod portage to Frost Lake. It is a rough path that is not often used. But it may be necessary during late summer or an unusually dry year, when the connecting creek is too shallow for a loaded canoe.

Little Saganaga Lake

There are a couple of excellent campsites on the north shore of Frost Lake. Three other sites are also available. There are some fine sand beaches along the north shore of the lake, while some small cliffs adorn the south shore of this interesting lake. Watch for moose along the sandy shoreline at dawn and dusk.

Day 3 (7 miles): Frost Lake, p. 130 rods, **Frost River, Octopus Lake,** p. 18 rods, **Frost River,** p. 25 rods, **river,** p. 5 rods, **river,** p. 30 rods, **Chase Lake,** p. 20 rods, **Pencil Lake,** p. 60 rods, **Frost River,** p. 10 rods, **river,** p. 5 rods, **river,** p. 12 rods, **river,** p. 20 rods, **river, Afton Lake.** You are in for one long, exhausting day—and maybe worse if the only campsite on Afton Lake is already taken. But, if you are ready for a challenge, it's worth the effort. One hot and sunny day in August, my wife and I paddled, portaged and tugged on our canoe for over 9 hours. En route, we saw 4 moose, 2 great blue herons, countless aquatic birds and more blueberries than we had ever seen before. There are no designated USFS campsites between Frost and Afton lakes. Try to get an early start, and don't be too disappointed (or unprepared) if you find it necessary to proceed all the way to Mora Lake to find a vacant campsite (or on to Little Saganaga Lake to find a *good* campsite.)

If you find yourself behind schedule at Chase Lake, there is 1 site just off the route in Bologna Lake, south of Chase Lake, where you can seek refuge. (In fact, you might want to *plan* to camp there and spread this part of the route over 2 days to afford an opportunity to travel slower and savor the experience.)

Octopus is a pretty little lake, with some exposed rock along the shore. Your map may show a 15-rod portage just before entering the lake. It should not be necessary when you paddle or walk your canoe down the shallow, rocky river. The second portage after Octopus Lake (25 rods) is plagued with large boulders that make walking both difficult and treacherous—especially at the put-in after the portage. The next short carry (5 rods) bypasses a scenic little waterfall.

Most of the portages this day are rocky, not well marked, and steep in places. They also receive light use. But then, they are also short and not too tiring (except for their frequency). In addition to the portages mentioned, you may encounter numerous obstacles that require lift-overs—5 or 6 beaver dams, sunken logs, and an assortment of boulders, sandbars and mud. These are particularly a problem during dry periods. In fact, in August or during a drought year, you may do as much pulling and lifting as paddling, even when there are no portages designated. Watch out, especially, for the stretch after the 60-rod portage from Pencil Lake. The last time we were there, my wife walked along the river's grassy bank, while I solo paddled the canoe, stepping out frequently to get past sandbars and sunken logs. It is very slow progress until after the next portage (10 rods).

Day 4 (8 miles): Afton Lake, p. 20 rods, **Frost River, rapids, Fente Lake,** p. 15 rods, **Whipped Lake,** p. 100 rods, **Mora Lake,** p. 45 rods, **Little Saganaga Lake,** p. 19 rods, **creek,** p. 19 rods, **Elton Lake.** You are in for a challenge right away this day. The 20-rod trail that leads northwest from Afton Lake is *very steep*, both up and down. Use extreme caution! After that thriller, however, this day will seem easy compared to the previous day, with portages spaced more evenly along the route.

The rapids flowing into Fente Lake may require a lift-over, unless the water level is quite high. The long trail connecting Whipped and Mora lakes (100 rods) has an excellent path on a gentle slope over a low hill. Mora is a pretty lake, bordered by mixed forest habitat with some exposed rock along the shore.

The 45-rod portage connecting Mora and Little Saganaga lakes follows close to some lovely rapids. This good trail is one of the prettiest portages in the BWCAW. Little Saganaga, with its many islands and peninsulas, is a lovely lake and a popular destination for many BWCAW visitors. There are 2 dozen campsites on the lake to accommodate them. Expect to see people here.

An old rock-and-gravel dam maintains the water level in the creek connecting Elton and Little Saganaga lakes. After leaving Little Saganaga Lake, you will again be entering a part of the Wilderness that receives fairly light use during much of the summer.

Elton is another pretty lake, with rock outcrops along its shores. There are a couple of nice campsites near the middle of the lake. Northern pike is the only game fish you'll find there. The lake is known to harbor some big ones.

Day 5 (8 miles): Elton Lake, p. 55 rods, **Makwa Lake,** p. 60 rods, **pond,** p. 90 rods, **Panhandle Lake,** p. 50 rods, **Pan Lake,** p. 65 rods, **Anit Lake,** p. 18 rods, **creek, Kivaniva Lake,** p. 42 rods, **Kawishiwi River,** p. 48 rods, **Malberg Lake,** p. 24 rods, **Koma Lake.** (See comments for Day 5, Route #38-2.)

Day 6 (7 miles): Koma Lake, p. 127 rods, **Kawishiwi River,** p. 48 rods, **river,** p. 19 rods, **Lake Polly,** p. 97 rods, **Phoebe River,** p. 16 rods, **river,** p. 92 rods, **river,** p. 25 rods, **river,** p. 59 rods, **Hazel Lake.** After the first 3 portages, which descend along the Kawishiwi River flowage, the remaining 5 portages this day are generally uphill, as you gain a total of 93 feet elevation from Lake Polly to Hazel Lake. None of the carries, however, is very difficult, and they are in a very scenic part of the route, where moose, beavers and mink abound. You probably won't see many people along the Phoebe River.

Nevertheless, you should still plan to make camp as early as possible. Phoebe Lake is a popular destination for paddlers starting at the Sawbill Lake entry point, and some people continue on to Hazel Lake. Anglers should find plenty of northern pike there.

Day 7 (9 miles): Hazel Lake, p. 140 rods, **Phoebe River, Knight Lake, Phoebe River, Phoebe Lake, Phoebe River,** p. 85 rods, **river,** p. 5 rods, **river,** p. 15 rods, **river,** p. 15 rods, **Grace Lake,** p. 285 rods, **Beth Lake,** p. 140 rods, **Alton Lake.** The day starts with a heart-pumping portage, as you gain about 70 feet elevation during the first 90 rods from Hazel Lake. (Also see comments for Day 3, Route #37-1.) Plan to camp near the middle of Alton Lake for a 9-mile day of travel.

Day 8 (7 miles): Alton Lake, p. 30 rods, **Sawbill Lake,** p. 100 rods, **Smoke Lake,** p. 90 rods, **Burnt Lake,** p. 230 rods, **Kelly Lake,** p. 3 rods, **Peterson Lake, Temperance River,** p. 15 rods, **Baker Lake.** You may see or hear motorboats in the south end of Sawbill Lake, the only part of the lake where they are permitted. And you'll surely see other canoeists on Sawbill—the 3rd most popular entry point for the BWCA Wilderness. After you portage to Smoke Lake, however, most of the traffic will be left behind.

The only exhausting portage of the day is also the longest (230 rods). The trail climbs nearly 70 feet above Burnt Lake before leveling off and then descending nearly 100 feet to Kelly Lake. About midway across the portage, the trail crosses an old abandoned logging road just before entering a swampy area.

Entry Point 40—Homer Lake

SEASONAL PERMITS: 208

POPULARITY RANK: 31st

DAILY QUOTA: 2

LOCATION: Homer Lake is 23 airline miles northeast of Tofte and 17 miles northeast of the Sawbill Trail via Forest Routes 170 and 326. These are good gravel roads, but there is another route that involves less driving on gravel. The Caribou Trail is a more winding and hilly road than the Sawbill Trail, but it offers a more direct route to Homer Lake from US Highway 61 at Lake Superior. Designated as County Road 4, the Caribou Trail begins 1 mile northeast of "downtown" Lutsen (10 miles northeast of Tofte). Drive north on the good gravel road (blacktop at first) for 18 miles from Highway 61 to Forest Route 170. Turn left at the **T** intersection where the Caribou Trail ends and follow F.R. 170 for 1½ miles west to its junction with F.R. 326. Turn right and follow the Brule Lake Road (F.R. 326) 4 miles north to the Homer Lake turnoff (Forest Route 1282) on the left.

DESCRIPTION: Camping is not allowed at the Homer Lake boat landing. A good place to spend the night before your trip, however, is not far away. The Crescent Lake Campground is 10 miles by road southwest of Homer Lake (¼ mile south of F.R. 170 at a point 6 miles southwest of the Brule Lake Road turnoff). A fee is charged for camping at any of 33 designated campsites, all of which are available on a first-come-first-served basis. There is also a campsite available for large groups.

The east ⅔ of Homer Lake is open to motorized watercraft. The west end of the lake and the interior lakes to which it leads, however, are "paddle only." Homer provides easy access to a lightly used part of the BWCA Wilderness where good fishing for walleyes and northern pike attracts weekend anglers but few other people. Though not a busy entry point, with a quota of only 2 permits each day, a reservation is often needed—especially if your trip starts on a weekend. About ⅔ of the available permits are issued to visitors each summer.

Bordered by a low ridge covered with spruce and balsam fir, Homer Lake, itself, is not a particularly attractive lake. There was extensive wind damage to the forest at the west end of the lake, caused by a storm during the fall of 1986. And submerged rocks are a hazard to motorboat anglers using the east part of the lake. In June of 1996, the South Temperance Fire burned 4,750 acres of forest just west of Homer Lake, up to the southwest shore of Brule Lake and west to the Temperance River. This area affords visitors a unique opportunity to see first-hand how quickly the forest rejuvenates itself after the devastation of a forest fire. Furthermore, the burned area also provides good feeding habitat for a thriving moose population.

In spite of the scenic setbacks caused by natural forces, Homer Lake does provide access to the same lovely part of the BWCAW that is also served by the more popular Brule Lake entry point. Scenic shorelines of pine and spruce are highlighted by rocky cliffs and outcroppings and surrounded by impressive hills. The immediate vicinity of Homer Lake is usually a very quiet place to spend a weekend, or a good start for a delightful longer itinerary that extends north through Brule Lake.

ROUTE #40-1: The Juno Lake Loop

        2 Days, 11 Miles, 4 Lakes, 1 River, 4 Portages

DIFFICULTY: Easier

FISHER MAPS: F-6

INTRODUCTION: This short, peaceful route will take you from the public landing west through Homer Lake and down the Vern River to Vern Lake. You will then follow this long, narrow lake northwest to Juno Lake, which in turn leads northeast to Brule Lake. The canoeing ends at the Brule Lake landing, less than 2 miles by road north of your origin. From there it's an easy walk (without gear) back to your car, if you did not already shuttle a vehicle to the Brule Lake parking lot.

Motors are allowed only on the east part of Homer Lake. The rest of the route is strictly for paddlers. The region south of Brule Lake is lightly used most of the season, but Brule is one of the busier lakes in the area, ranking 7th in popularity among all BWCAW entry points.

Anglers will find good populations of walleyes and northern pike in all of the lakes along this route. Brule Lake, in particular, is famous for its good walleye crop. It also harbors smallmouth bass and northern pike.

Most canoeists could easily complete this loop in just 1 day. With some interesting scenery and bountiful wildlife along the route, however, it will be more thoroughly appreciated if you allow 2 full days for exploration along the way.

Day 1 (6 miles): Homer Lake, p. 7 rods, **Vern River,** p. 6 rods, **river, rapids, river, Vern Lake,** p. 65 rods, **Juno Lake.** After 2 short portages along the scenic Vern River, you may have to run, walk or line your canoe through some small, shallow rapids where there is no portage necessary (or available). You could also access Vern Lake by way of a more direct route through Whack Lake, but you would be missing the lovely, short stretch of river connecting Homer and Vern lakes.

With a few rocky outcroppings along its shoreline, Vern Lake is the most scenic of the three lakes south of Brule. A forest of spruce, fir and birch trees borders it. At the northern end of the lake is the most difficult portage. The 65-rod trail has a couple of steep grades, including a steep descent to the west end of Juno Lake.

The forest bordering the west end of Juno Lake was decimated by the same storm that damaged the Homer Lake shoreline. If the 2 campsites near the west end are occupied, continue paddling to a newer site near the middle of this long lake. Located on the north shore, it is large enough for 2 tents.

Day 2 (5 miles): Juno Lake, p. 70 rods, **Brule Lake.** Unlike the preceding portage, which carried you *to* Juno Lake, the 70-rod trail *from* Juno follows an excellent path to the south shore of Brule Lake. Treacherous waves on big Brule Lake can make paddling quite difficult, if not impossible, at times. Don't take any unnecessary risks. If there is a gale wind blowing from the north this day, you might consider backtracking to the Homer Lake landing. A southwest wind, however, should pose no problem on Brule Lake as you follow the south shoreline to the public access.

If you have not made prior arrangements to have your car waiting at the Brule Lake landing, you will have to walk 1.9 miles south to the Homer Lake parking lot at the end of your excursion.

ROUTE #40-2: The Frost Duck Route

5 Days, 44 Miles, 31 Lakes, 4 Rivers, 1 Creek, 36 Portages

DIFFICULTY: Most Rugged

FISHER MAPS: F-5, F-6, F-12

INTRODUCTION: This high-quality wilderness route will lead you into one of the most isolated and pristine regions of the Boundary Waters Canoe Area. From Homer Lake, you will first loop northwest through Vern and Juno lakes to Brule Lake. After portaging from the northwest corner of Brule Lake to Cam Lake, you'll proceed northwest through a series of small and scenic lakes leading to Frost Lake. From the southwest end of Frost Lake, the Frost River will then carry you west through one of the most isolated parts of the BWCA Wilderness. At Fente Lake you will steer a south course through Hub and Mesaba lakes and onward to Alton Lake. Turning toward the east, then, you'll cross busy Sawbill Lake and the "fire lakes" en route to Kelly Lake. Finally, you will paddle down the Temperance River flowage to end your journey at Baker Lake, about 12 miles by road from your starting point.

Most of this route is lightly traveled. Only in the vicinities of Brule, Cherokee and Sawbill lakes are you likely to experience some heavy canoe traffic during the summer months. Wildlife is abundant and scenery is lovely along much of the route. The quiet observer is bound to see moose, beavers and otters. And in the right season, fresh blueberries will surely be a part of your diet.

Portages are all too frequent—averaging more than 7 per day (as many as 13 on the 3rd day). Fortunately, most are short, but the longest is nearly 1½ miles long, and 8 other trails measure at least 100 rods. Several are quite difficult. During dry periods, the going may be even slower and tougher, as parts of the Frost River may be too low for navigation of a loaded canoe. The entire route most certainly deserves a "most rugged" rating. For that reason, it's a good idea to schedule a layover day. You may need the rest after Day 3. Or, if you're not "psyched up" for 13 portages in 1 day, you could just as well spread the third over 2 days by making a short detour from the route to camp on Bologna Lake.

Anglers with energy to spare will find plenty of good opportunities to wet their lines. Walleyes and northern pike occupy many of the lakes, and smallmouth bass and lake trout are found in some lakes along the route.

Day 1 (10 miles): Homer Lake, p. 7 rods, **Vern River,** p. 6 rods, **river, rapids, river, Vern Lake,** p. 65 rods, **Juno Lake,** p. 70 rods, **Brule Lake.** (See comments for Days 1 and 2, Route 40-1.) Five campsites are located in the north-central part of the Brule Lake, in or near Cone Bay. Head there for a 10-mile day of travel—if the wind isn't too strong across the big lake. Otherwise, if the waves are running, you may have to hold up in Jock Mock Bay, 9 miles from your origin. Three campsites are also located in the far-western end of Brule Lake. If you are lucky enough to be there on a calm day, or when there are gentle winds out of the east, it might be wise to forge onward. Those western campsites are about 12 miles from the Homer Lake landing—a big first day. But you may be glad you crossed the open water before the winds changed to westerly.

Day 2 (10 miles): Brule Lake, p. 100 rods, **Cam Lake,** p. 45 rods, **Gasket Lake,** p. 75 rods, **Vesper Lake,** p. 110 rods, **Town Lake,** p. 10 rods, **Cherokee Lake,** p. 13 rods, **Gordon Lake,** p. 140 rods, **Unload Lake, creek, Frost Lake.** Though not too long, the portages in store for you this day are *not* easy. All 4 trails between Brule and Town lakes are very rocky, being strewn with boulders that make walking treacherous. The first carry (100 rods) gradually ascends a hill for 80 rods, then descends to Cam Lake. The 75-rod portage from Gasket to Vesper Lake climbs steeply to pass over the Laurentian Divide. South of that point, water flows eventually to the Atlantic Ocean. From that point onward to Fente Lake (Day 3), the portages are generally downhill as the water ultimately drains north into Hudson Bay of the Arctic Ocean.

The scenery in this lightly traveled area is stunning, enhanced by slopes of large boulders on the west shores of Gasket and Brule lakes. Cherokee is also a beautiful, island-studded lake that attracts many visitors from both the Sawbill Lake and Brule Lake entry points. You'll miss most of the lake—and the people—as you cross only the northern end.

The 140-rod trail leading west from Gordon Lake climbs over a fairly steep hill, but then levels off on a good, smooth path to Unload Lake. The shallow creek joining Unload and Frost lakes may be blocked by a beaver dam that requires a lift-over. Or you can bypass the creek on a 40-rod portage to Frost Lake. It is a rough path that is not often used. But it may be necessary during late summer or an unusually dry year, when the connecting creek is too shallow for a loaded canoe.

There are a couple of excellent campsites on the north shore of Frost Lake, and three other sites. There are some fine sand beaches along the north shore of the lake, while some small cliffs adorn the south shore of this interesting lake. Watch for moose along the sandy shoreline at dawn and dusk.

Day 3 (9 miles): Frost Lake, p. 130 rods, **Frost River, Octopus Lake,** p. 18 rods, **Frost River,** p. 25 rods, **river,** p. 5 rods, **river,** p. 30 rods, **Chase Lake,** p. 20 rods, **Pencil Lake,** p. 60 rods, **Frost River,** p. 10 rods, **river,** p. 5 rods, **river,** p. 12 rods, **river,** p. 20 rods, **river, Afton Lake,** p. 20 rods, **Frost River, rapids, Fente Lake,** p. 300 rods, **Hub Lake.** (See comments for Day 3, Route #39-2.) With 13 portages, you're in for a long, tiring day. If 2 trips are needed to cross each portage, you'll be walking a total of over 6 miles. Furthermore, the 2 biggest challenges of the day are near the end when you're already tired. The 20-rod trail leading northwest from Afton Lake is *very steep and treacherous,* both up and down. Use extreme caution! After that thriller, the rapids flowing into Fente Lake may require a lift-over, unless the water level is quite high. Then you're in for the longest and most exhausting carry of the day. The 300-rod trail gains nearly 130 feet in elevation during the first 80 rods. Fortunately, the rest of the trail is fairly level and has a decent path.

Day 4 (8 miles): Hub Lake, p. 105 rods, **Mesaba Lake,** p. 80 rods, **Hug Lake,** p. 3 rods, **Duck Lake,** p. 80 rods, **Zenith Lake,** p. 460 rods, **Lujenida Lake, Kelso River, Kelso Lake,** p. 10 rods, **Alton Lake.** This is another day of rough portages. Though less than half the *number* of carries you had to endure during the previous day, the total length of those trails is even greater—nearly 7 miles of walking if 2 trips are needed to get your gear across.

After a fairly level trek from Hub to Mesaba Lake, the next 2 ¼-mile carries are uphill, and so is the first 70 rods of the long portage to Lujenida Lake. After gaining nearly 100 feet in elevation to pass over the Laurentian Divide, it descends more than 170 feet en route to the north end of Lujenida Lake. Much of the latter half is fairly level or gently down-sloping as the path closely parallels a creek flowage. You can break up the trek into three shorter segments with brief paddling interludes on 2 ponds. It may be quicker, however, to simply walk non-stop from Zenith to Lujenida. Fortunately, the trail has a good, well-traveled path.

A beaver dam between Duck and Hug lakes makes the short portage there (3 rods) necessary. That dam maintains the water level on

Duck Lake. Without it, the shallow lake is barely deep enough to cross in a heavily loaded canoe.

Plan to camp near the middle of Alton Lake for an 8-mile day of travel. You could also portage directly from Kelso Lake to Sawbill, but Sawbill has fewer campsites and more traffic, including motorboats at the south end of the lake. Alton should be a quieter destination, and anglers may find smallmouth bass, walleyes, northern pike and even some large lake trout in its crystal-clear depths.

Day 5 (7 miles): Alton Lake, p. 30 rods, **Sawbill Lake,** p. 100 rods, **Smoke Lake,** p. 90 rods, **Burnt Lake,** p. 230 rods, **Kelly Lake,** p. 3 rods, **Peterson Lake, Temperance River,** p. 15 rods, **Baker Lake.** (See comments for Day 8, Route #39-2.) Under normal or high water conditions you may be able to avoid the last 2 portages by pulling or paddling your canoe up the shallow rapids connecting Kelly, Peterson and Baker lakes. In fact, when the water is high enough, you can easily paddle right through the channel connecting Kelly and Peterson lakes. On the other hand, when the water is quite low (as it was during the dry summers of 1997 and 1998), the last portage to Baker Lake may stretch to nearly 40 rods on a rocky, brushy path along the river's edge.

Entry Point 41—Brule Lake

SEASONAL PERMITS: 1,032

POPULARITY RANK: 7th

DAILY QUOTA: 10

LOCATION: Brule Lake is 25 airline miles northeast of Tofte and 19 miles northeast of the Sawbill Trail via Forest Routes 170 and 326. These are good gravel roads, but there is another route that involves less driving on gravel. The Caribou Trail is a more winding and hilly road than the Sawbill Trail, but it offers a more direct route to Brule Lake from US Highway 61 at Lake Superior. Designated as County Road 4, the Caribou Trail begins 1 mile northeast of "downtown" Lutsen (10 miles northeast of Tofte). Drive north on the good gravel road (blacktop at first) for 18 miles from Highway 61 to Forest Route 170. Turn left at the T intersection where the Caribou Trail ends and follow F.R. 170 for 1½ miles west to its junction with F.R. 326. Turn right and follow the Brule Lake Road (F.R. 326) 6 miles north to the road's end. The boat landing is on the left side of the road at the west end of a large parking lot.

DESCRIPTION: Camping is not allowed at the Brule Lake boat landing. A good place to spend the night before your trip, however, is not far away. The Crescent Lake Campground is 12 miles by road southwest of Brule Lake (¼ mile south of F.R. 170 from a point 6 miles southwest of the Brule Lake Road turnoff). A fee is charged for camping at any of 33 designated campsites, all of which are available on a first-come-first-served basis. There is also a campsite available for large groups.

Brule is one of the largest lakes in the eastern region of the Boundary Waters. It rests in the shadow of Eagle Mountain, the highest point in Minnesota. A trail to its summit heads north from Forest Route 170 at its junction with Forest Route 158. The panoramic view at 2,301 feet above sea level—all the way to Lake Superior on a clear day—is breathtaking. Dotted with 67 picturesque islands, Brule Lake is one of the more beautiful sights around (though not visible from Eagle Mountain).

Once a popular destination for motorboat anglers, Brule still has a notable walleye population, as well as smallmouth bass and northern pike. The use of this entry point by canoeists increased considerably after the motorboats were banned in 1986. About the same number of permits were issued 20 years ago as now, but more than half of the permits back then were issued to groups using motors. Brule has always been a beautiful lake. Now it is even more desirable for paddlers who seek a quick escape into wilderness solitude.

About ⅔ of the available permits for a Brule Lake entry to the BWCAW are issued each summer. While a reservation may not be necessary for a trip starting on weekdays, you will surely need a reservation if your trip starts on Friday, Saturday, Sunday or Monday.

Brule Lake is large enough to accommodate an influx of canoes. Its vastness is also something to beware of. Strong winds can whip up large waves on the open expanse. The islands and peninsulas at the east end of the lake afford some protection from gales, but there is no protection in the west and central parts of the lake. Be alert to wind direction and use caution.

ROUTE #41-1: **The Mulligan Cliff Loop**
2 Days, 15 Miles, 9 Lakes, 2 Creeks, 11 Portages

DIFFICULTY: Challenging

FISHER MAPS: F-6, F-13

INTRODUCTION: This lovely, short loop will take you north from Brule Lake through a chain of small, slender lakes to beautiful Winchell Lake. The next day, then, you'll return to Brule Lake via a chain of somewhat larger lakes (the Cone lakes) and their interconnecting creeks. It is an ideal weekend loop. Or, for avid anglers, it might be stretched over 3 or 4 days.

Once part of a motor route between Brule and Poplar lakes, the entire route is now reserved strictly for paddlers. You can still see the underwater remnants of old docks that once protruded from the ends of most portages. For strong and experienced paddlers, this loop would surely deserve an "easier" rating. Nine of the 11 portages measure 40 rods or less. Because of 2 longer portages (1 each day), however, the route could be a challenge for groups with weak or inexperienced trippers. Furthermore, paddling may also be a challenge if the waves are running on big Brule Lake.

The forest north of Brule Lake creates a boreal scene, consisting almost entirely of conifers—spruce, fir, pine and cedar trees. Unlike in much of the BWCA Wilderness, where aspens and birch are common, deciduous trees are few and far between in this region.

Anglers will have plenty of opportunities to wet their lines. Walleyes, northern pike and smallmouth bass occupy Brule and the Cone lakes. Winchell also harbors some large lake trout. With any luck at all, your fry pan should be sizzling.

Day 1 (6 miles): Brule Lake, p. 37 rods, **Lily Lake,** p. 32 rods, **Mulligan Lake,** p. 40 rods, **Grassy Creek,** p. 200 rods, **Wanihigan Lake,** p. 14 rods, **Winchell Lake.** All of the portages between Brule and Winchell lakes have generally good paths, and you will see the remains of old boat docks at the ends of most trails. The first three carries are short, but you'll climb a total of nearly 100 feet in elevation. Most of that climb (60 feet) is on the 32-rod trail from Lily to Mulligan Lake, where there is a lovely path through a stand of large, old white pines. Mulligan is a state-designated trout lake, named after the Tofte District's first ranger, John E. Mulligan. Brook trout have been stocked there.

Resting at a Winchell Lake campsite

Grassy Creek is very shallow—barely deep enough for passage of a loaded canoe. Watch carefully for the beginning of the 200-rod portage along the grassy east shore. When the water level is quite low (as it was in 1998), the creek is too shallow to afford direct access to the trail. One must first walk on the floating bog or along the edge of the grassy marsh for 20-40 rods. The actual portage then starts out on a path that's a bit rocky and muddy, as the trail skirts the edge of the creek. After it veers away from the creek, however, it has an excellent path that gradually descends to Wanihigan Lake.

Winchell is a beautiful lake, with rocky cliffs bordering its south shoreline and the nearby Misquah Hills towering nearly 350 feet above the water. There are several nice campsites on the north shore of Winchell Lake, including 5 within a mile of the Wanihigan Lake portage. Winchell is a popular destination for trippers starting at several entry points, so try to claim a campsite as early as possible. From any of those sites you will be able to enjoy a lovely view across the water toward the steep and rocky ridge bordering the south shore of the lake. Toward the west end, you will see the charred evidence of a forest fire that raced through the area in 1995—one of many wildfires that ravaged the BWCAW that year.

Day 2 (9 miles): Winchell Lake, p. 14 rods, **Wanihigan Lake,** p. 14 rods, **Cliff Lake,** p. 160 rods, **North Cone Lake,** p. 2 rods, **Cone Creek, Middle Cone Lake,** p. 25 rods, **Cone Creek, South Cone Lake, Cone Creek,** p. 15 rods, **creek, Brule Lake.** All of the portages between Winchell and Brule lakes have rocky paths that necessitate careful steps. The half-mile trail climbs for about 25 rods from Cliff Lake, but then descends nearly 100 feet to the shore of North Cone Lake. The 2-rod path between North Cone and Middle Cone lakes is little more than a lift-over around small rapids. You can normally avoid a carry by walking, lining or running your canoe through the narrow channel. When the water level is high enough, the final 15-rod portage between South Cone and Brule lakes may not be necessary. Cone Creek is usually deep enough to accommodate canoe traffic. On the other hand, when water levels are quite low, the portage could extend to as long as 30 rods.

Cliff is an especially scenic lake, bordered by a steep, pine-covered ridge along the north shore and rocky cliffs near the east end of the lake. The hills on both sides of this slender lake tower 250 feet above the water.

On a windy day, use caution crossing Brule Lake's open expanse. If necessary, rest during the windiest part of the afternoon at one of the campsites in Cone Bay and wait for the evening calm. There is no need to fight the lake. Lean back and enjoy its beauty.

ROUTE #41-2: The Long Island Flame Loop

6 Days, 52 Miles, 32 Lakes, 4 Rivers, 4 Creeks, 41 Portages

DIFFICULTY: Most Rugged

FISHER MAPS: F-5, F-6, F-12, F-13

INTRODUCTION: This high-quality wilderness route will lead you into one of the most isolated and pristine regions of the Boundary Waters Canoe Area, as well as some popular and well-visited areas. From Brule Lake, you will first head north through a chain of small, slender lakes to beautiful Winchell and Omega lakes. Then you'll follow a westerly course through a series of long and slender lakes leading to Frost Lake. Draining the southwest end of Frost Lake, the Frost River will carry you farther west through one of the most isolated parts of the BWCA Wilderness. From Fente Lake you will steer a southward course through Hub and Mesaba lakes and onward to Alton Lake. Turning toward the east, then, you'll cross busy Sawbill Lake and the "fire lakes" en route to Kelly Lake. From that point, you'll veer northward up the Temperance River flowage to South Temperance Lake, passing through several long and slender lakes along the way. Finally, you will paddle eastward across Brule Lake, back to the public landing where your journey started.

Part of this route is very lightly traveled. In the vicinities of Brule, Long Island and Sawbill lakes, on the other hand, you are likely to experience some heavy canoe traffic during the summer months. Wildlife is abundant throughout the route and the scenery is lovely along much of the loop. The quiet observer is bound to see moose, beavers and otters.

Portages are all too frequent—averaging nearly 7 per day (as many as 13 on the 3rd day). Fortunately, most are short, but the longest is nearly 1½ miles long, and 9 other trails measure at least 100 rods. Several are quite difficult. During dry periods, the going may be even slower and tougher, as parts of the Frost River may be too low for navigation of a loaded canoe. For most folks the route surely deserves a "most rugged" rating. And it's probably a good idea to schedule a lay-over day. You may need the rest after Day 3. Or, if you're not "psyched up" for 13 portages in 1 day, the third day could just as well be spread over 2 days by making a short detour along the route and camping on Bologna Lake.

Anglers with energy to spare will find plenty of good opportunities to test their skills. Walleyes and northern pike are found in most of the lakes. Smallmouth bass and lake trout are found in some lakes along the route.

Day 1 (7 miles): Brule Lake, p. 37 rods, **Lily Lake,** p. 32 rods, **Mulligan Lake,** p. 40 rods, **Grassy Creek,** p. 200 rods, **Wanihigan Lake,** p. 14 rods, **Winchell Lake,** p. 44 rods, **Omega Lake.** (See comments for Day 1, Route #41-1.) The final portage has a level but rocky path between Winchell and Omega lakes. Omega is a rather pretty lake with some small rock cliffs along the shoreline and a few nice campsites. The best site for a larger group is on the south shore near the middle of the lake.

Day 2 (10 miles): Omega Lake, p. 35 rods, **Kiskadinna Lake,** p. 185 rods, **Muskeg Lake,** p. 13 rods, **Muskeg Creek,** p. 20 rods, **Long Island Lake, Long Island River,** p. 5 rods, **river,** p. 28 rods, **Gordon Lake,** p. 140 rods, **Unload Lake, creek, Frost Lake.** The first 2 portages this day are both steep and rocky. Use caution on both, especially when the ground is wet. The first requires a short, steep climb over a small hill, with an even steeper descent. Kiskadinna Lake is plagued with a plethora of dead spruce trees and many windfalls along its entire shoreline, which has very little elevation behind it.

The 185-rod trail to Muskeg Lake starts innocently enough, first climbing slightly to a relatively level, dry ridge that affords a north view through the forest. Then, about midway across the portage, the trail drops steeply to cross a small stream on a log bridge. Beyond the stream the well-traveled path descends more gradually to the shore of Muskeg Lake—a total drop of more than 150 feet. Though not as exhausting as hiking uphill, steep descents are often more difficult and more treacherous, especially when the path is wet.

The short portage at the west end of Muskeg Lake may vary in length from 4 to 13 rods, depending on the water's depth. Or it may not be necessary at all when the water level is high enough to afford paddling through the shallow creek. The tiny creek that follows is quite scenic, with some low rock cliffs near the 20-rod path.

The 140-rod trail leading west from Gordon Lake climbs over a fairly steep hill, but then levels off on a good, smooth path to Unload Lake. The shallow creek joining Unload and Frost lakes may be blocked by a beaver dam that requires a lift-over. Or you can bypass the creek on a 40-rod portage to Frost Lake. It is a rough path that is not often used. But it may be necessary during late summer or an unusually dry year, when the connecting creek is too shallow for a loaded canoe.

There are a couple of excellent campsites on the north shore of Frost Lake, and three other sites. There are some fine sand beaches along the north shore of the lake, while some small cliffs adorn the south shore of this interesting lake. Watch for moose along the sandy shoreline at dawn and dusk.

Day 3 (9 miles): Frost Lake, p. 130 rods, **Frost River, Octopus Lake,** p. 18 rods, **Frost River,** p. 25 rods, **river,** p. 5 rods, **river,** p. 30 rods, **Chase Lake,** p. 20 rods, **Pencil Lake,** p. 60 rods, **Frost River,** p. 10 rods, **river,** p. 5 rods, **river,** p. 12 rods, **river,** p. 20 rods, **river, Afton Lake,** p. 20 rods, **Frost River, rapids, Fente Lake,** p. 300 rods, **Hub Lake.** (See comments for Day 3, Route #40-2.)

Day 4 (8 miles): Hub Lake, p. 105 rods, **Mesaba Lake,** p. 80 rods, **Hug Lake,** p. 3 rods, **Duck Lake,** p. 80 rods, **Zenith Lake,** p. 460 rods, **Lujenida Lake, Kelso River, Kelso Lake,** p. 10 rods, **Alton Lake.** (See comments for Day 4, Route #40-2.)

Day 5 (8 miles): Alton Lake, p. 30 rods, **Sawbill Lake,** p. 100 rods, **Smoke Lake,** p. 90 rods, **Burnt Lake,** p. 230 rods, **Kelly Lake,** p. 65 rods, **Jack Lake.** (See comments for Day 8, Route #39-2.) Kelly and Jack lakes are part of the Temperance River flowage that drains south from North Temperance Lake, eventually all the way to Lake Superior. Hills rise high above the river valley—as much as 250 feet above Kelly and Jack lakes. This area shouldn't be crowded. With only a few campsites available, however, don't delay in claiming yours. Anglers normally find the fishing to be quite good in Jack Lake for walleyes and northern pike.

Day 6 (10 miles): Jack Lake, p. 12 rods, **Weird Lake,** p. 80 rods, **Temperance River,** p. 240 rods, **South Temperance Lake,** p. 10 rods, **creek, Brule Lake.** As you would expect, the only real challenge of the day is the long carry to South Temperance Lake. It gains about 60 feet elevation across the ¾-mile course on a good path that is well maintained and well used.

The region lying east of South Temperance Lake was scarred by a large wildfire that burned 4,450 acres of timber in June of 1996. It was started by lightning and cost $1.5 million to fight. Unlike other "prescribed" natural fires that were allowed to burn in the Wilderness, the South Temperance Fire threatened areas lying outside the BWCAW and was, therefore, not allowed to burn freely. (Also see comments for Day 2, Route #39-1.)

|4

Entry from the **Gunflint Trail** —West

The Northeastern Area

THE NORTHEASTERN PART OF THE BOUNDARY WATERS CANOE IS SERVED by eleven entry points that are accessible from, and to the west of, Cook County Road 12—the Gunflint Trail. These include a few of the busiest and some of the least used entry points in the BWCA Wilderness. Most receive moderate use throughout the summer months.

The Gunflint Trail begins in the center of Grand Marais, on the North Shore of Lake Superior. It leads north for 25 miles, then veers west for another 25 miles, and finally heads north again to its end at Gull Lake, 57 miles northwest of Grand Marais. All of the road is black-top and it's normally in good condition. Resorts, outfitters and public campgrounds are located intermittently along the road's entire course. Traffic is fairly heavy during the summer months (of course, "heavy traffic" to those of us living Up North may not mean what it does to folks from The City).

Grand Marais is the commercial center for all of Cook County. It is a small but bustling community that is supported mostly by the tourism and logging industries. For canoe trippers in need of refuge

Grand Marais is the commercial center for Cook County

before or after their trips, a municipal campground is located near the center of the village. Adjacent to the campground is a municipal indoor swimming pool where a grimy tourist may purchase an inexpensive shower and sauna—as well as soak in the whirlpool bath and the swimming pool.

BWCAW overnight permits are issued at the USFS Visitors' Center at the southwest edge of town, 1 mile from the municipal campground on Highway 61. It is a newer facility that was opened in May of 1996. If you know that you'll be passing through town late at night, after office hours, you can make prior arrangements to pick up your permit at one of several cooperating outfitters located along the Gunflint Trail. For trips starting far up the trail, that may be a practical alternative.

Entrance to Gunflint Trail in downtown Grand Marais

Entry Point 43—Bower Trout Lake

SEASONAL PERMITS: 98

POPULARITY RANK: 45th (tie)

DAILY QUOTA: 1

LOCATION: Bower Trout Lake is 14 airline miles northwest of Grand Marais. From Highway 61, drive north on the Gunflint Trail for nearly 17 miles to its junction with Forest Route 325 (South Brule Road). It's on the west (left) side of the Gunflint Trail, 1 mile past the Greenwood Road turnoff. Turn left and follow this good but narrow, winding and hilly gravel road west for 6 miles to a **T**-intersection with Forest Route 152 (Lima Grade Road). Turn left there and proceed southeast on F.R. 152 for 0.3 mile to Forest Route 152H on the right. Turn right and drive 0.3 mile west, past a large gravel pit on the right, to a small parking lot on the left side of this narrow 1-lane road. Although the road appears to continue past this point, don't drive any farther. A short distance beyond the parking spot, the old road enters a swampy area and becomes impassable.

DESCRIPTION: The unimproved parking lot is barely large enough for 3-4 vehicles, but that many more cars may also park along the edge of the narrow road. A 67-rod portage trail continues on down the same old, overgrown road. After the muddy section, the level path has a good, dry surface on the final 40-rod stretch to the north shore of Bower Trout Lake.

There are no designated campgrounds in the immediate vicinity of this entry point. The Kimball Lake Campground is the most convenient USFS facility. It is located just 2 miles east of the Gunflint Trail via Forest Route 140 from their intersection 10.7 miles north of Highway 61. Ten campsites are available on a first-come-first-served basis. A camping fee is charged. If that campground is full, you could stay at the much larger East Bearskin Lake Campground, located farther up the Gunflint Trail (see Entry Point 64).

Along with Ram Lake and Morgan Lake, its neighbors to the north, Bower Trout Lake is one of the least accessible entry points served by the Gunflint Trail. Nevertheless, its popularity has grown considerably during the past 20 years—up about 75% since 1977. With a quota of only 1 group per day, Bower Trout ranks high among all entry points with quotas filled the greatest number of days each summer. A reservation is advised. Canoeists who prefer scenic solitude have discovered that Bower Trout Lake is a delightful point of Wilderness entry. And, with but a few notable exceptions, travel here is fairly easy.

The BWCA Wilderness Act of 1978 prohibited motorboats in this part of the Boundary Waters. The only motors you may hear are in vehicles using the nearby roads.

ROUTE #43-1: The Lily Horseshoe Route

3 Days, 27 Miles, 15 Lakes, 1 River, 1 Creek, 18 Portages

DIFFICULTY: Challenging

FISHER MAP: F-13

INTRODUCTION: This scenic little route will lead you first through the quiet lakes, ponds and creeks that compose the upper reaches of the South Brule River and then north to the headwaters of the North Brule River. From Bower Trout Lake you'll paddle west through Marshall, Swan and Vernon lakes to Brule Lake. From the north shore of that awesome lake, you will proceed north through a series of small lakes to lovely Winchell Lake. Then you'll steer east and cross Winchell, Gaskin and Horseshoe lakes. Finally, the route veers north to cross Caribou and Lizz lakes en route to Poplar Lake. You'll end this journey at a public landing at the northwest end of Poplar Lake, at least 15 miles by road from your origin (via the back roads).

While most of the portages are relatively short and easy to negotiate, there are just enough long trails for this route to warrant a "challenging" rating. Most groups should have no problem completing the route in 3 days. Weak or inexperienced trippers and serious anglers, however, might consider adding an extra day to their itinerary. There is usually very good fishing along the route for walleyes, smallmouth bass and northern pike.

The least traveled part of the route is encountered on the first day, from Bower Trout to Vernon Lake. You'll probably see numerous other parties during the last 2 days in the region between Brule Lake (the 7th most popular entry point in the BWCAW) and Lizz Lake (ranked 13th). In mid-summer, get an early start each day and try to find your campsite early in the afternoon.

Day 1 (8 miles): P. 67 rods, **Bower Trout Lake,** p. 90 rods, **Marshall Lake,** p. 28 rods, **South Brule River, Dugout Lake, South Brule River, Skidway Lake,** p. 35 rods, **South Brule River,** p. 40 rods, **river,** p. 40 rods, **Swan Lake, South Brule River,** p. 292 rods, **Vernon Lake.** This is an interesting day on small lakes and river segments bordered by hills on both sides. The portage landings at both ends of Bower Trout Lake may be muddy and shallow when the water level is low. After launching onto Bower Trout Lake, all the ensuing portages are generally uphill as you navigate through the South Brule River flowage, but you will gain a total of only 108 feet from Bower Trout to Vernon Lake. The paths are well beaten and, for the most part, in pretty good condition. The beginnings of the 90-rod and 35-rod trails, however, are quite rocky. The first 40-rod path may also be muddy near the beginning.

Along the shores of Dugout and Skidway lakes, as well as on the 35-rod portage, you will see the charred stumps from a forest fire that scoured the area in 1995. It affords a unique perspective—one of the few places in the BWCA Wilderness where you can actually see a landscape that is not concealed by dense forests. It allowed my wife and me to observe a cow moose and her calf meander along the hillside overlooking Dugout Lake, after they had retreated from the water's edge during our approach. Moose populations thrive in areas that have been recently burned. So do blueberries, so keep a watchful eye for both.

When the water level is low, watch out for submerged rocks in the narrow river channels at both ends of Dugout Lake. You may have to step out of your canoe and guide it through the shallow "rapids." While always vigilant for submerged rocks, also don't forget to look up occasionally. The hills to the south of Marshall Lake rise to over 500 feet above the water.

Swan is a lovely lake with some nice campsites—a good place to rest before your last and longest portage. A logging camp served by a railroad once operated at the north end of the lake. The old railroad grade parallels the South Brule River flowage, just north of the route that brought you here.

From the west end of Swan Lake, the narrow South Brule River meanders for about half a mile en route to the 292-rod portage. Watch for the take-out on the south (left) side of the crystal-clear stream. About 50 rods from the start, the trail crosses a creek and then climbs gradually for the next half-mile, gaining 100 feet in elevation along the way. Over the final 80 rods, however, the trail descends more steeply down to the east end of Vernon Lake. In spite of its length, the portage is not too difficult and has a good path most of the way. You'll see the dilapidated remains of the Alger Smith logging camp near the beginning of the portage. It operated from 1920 to 1923.

Watch out for rocks and boulders in the shallow east end of Vernon Lake right after the put-in. There is a nice campsite on the north shore of the lake, situated in a grove of birch trees, with space for 2 or 3 tents. Anglers should find walleyes, northern pike and smallmouth bass nearby. You might even pull a lake trout from the cool, clear water. They were stocked there in 1997.

Day 2 (9 miles): Vernon Lake, p. 49 rods, **Brule Lake,** p. 37 rods, **Lily Lake,** p. 32 rods, **Mulligan Lake,** p. 40 rods, **Grassy Creek,** p. 200 rods, **Wanihigan Lake,** p. 14 rods, **Winchell Lake.** The first portage this day will get your heart pumping. There you will climb steeply for 40 of the 49 rods, gaining over 110 feet in elevation, before dropping down to the far-eastern shore of Brule Lake, 83 feet above Vernon Lake.

If there is a strong west wind blowing across big Brule Lake, the next 3½ miles of paddling may be the most exhausting (and potentially treacherous) part of your journey. If you get an early start, however, you may get across the lake before the mid-day winds pick up. (Also see comments for Day 1, Route #41-1.)

Plan to camp near the center of Winchell Lake for a 9-mile day of travel. If the campsites appear to be filling up, however, you might be well advised to take the first good site you come to.

Day 3 (10 miles): Winchell Lake, p. 60 rods, **Gaskin Lake,** p. 102 rods, **Horseshoe Lake,** p. 20 rods, **Caribou Lake,** p. 73 rods, **Lizz Lake,** p. 51 rods, **Poplar Lake.** Although it's the longest, in terms of miles traveled, this day is also your easiest. A boreal forest of white pines, cedars and spruce trees borders Winchell, Gaskin and Horseshoe lakes. There are very few deciduous trees in this region and rather low terrain compared to the Misquah Hills region south of Winchell Lake.

The 2 longest portages pass over big hills, but the paths are well built, well maintained and well used. Most of the 60-rod trail is downhill. Watch for some large white pines and cedar trees near the middle of the 102-rod trail. The final 3 portages have good paths that are well traveled by the many visitors who enter the BWCAW at Lizz Lake.

Poplar Lake lies entirely outside the Wilderness. You'll see several resorts and private cabins along its north shoreline en route to the public boat landing at the far-west end of the lake.

ROUTE #43-2: The Cherokee Vista Loop

5 Days, 45 Miles, 25 Lakes, 2 Rivers, 2 Creeks, 29 Portages

DIFFICULTY: Challenging

FISHER MAPS: F-6, F-12, F-13

INTRODUCTION: This interesting loop should appeal to anyone who lives by the old adage, "variety is the spice of life." During a span of 5 days, you'll encounter lakes ranging from tiny to huge, terrain that varies from quite hilly to nearly flat, some lovely streams and portages that range from easy to rugged. The route will lead you first through the quiet lakes, ponds and creeks that compose the upper reaches of the South Brule River and then west to Brule Lake. After crossing a vast expanse of open water, you'll reenter a world of smaller lakes and interconnected streams as you cross over the Laurentian Divide and then steer north through island-studded Cherokee Lake to Long Island Lake. From there you'll plot an eastward course through a chain of several long and slender lakes to Horseshoe Lake. At that point, you'll veer south through the Misquah Hills and across a chain of small lakes leading to Ram Lake. After portaging out of the BWCA Wilderness, you'll end your journey at the Ram Lake parking lot, 1 mile by road north of your origin.

You'll probably see the fewest other people during the first and last days of your journey, in the hilly region closest to Forest Route 152. The rest of the route entertains many more visitors who access the Wilderness from several popular entry points. Nevertheless, it's an interesting loop that is worth sharing with others. Just don't wait too late in the afternoon to claim your campsites.

While there are a couple of days that might deserve a "most rugged" rating, there are also 2 days that many trippers would consider "easier." Overall, "challenging" seems appropriate, with an average of about 6 portages per day. Each day does present at least one significant challenge, with at least 1 steep hill to surmount. So, if your group is weak on portages, beware. You could find a more appropriate route. Or, at the very least, allow an extra day.

Anglers should find some excellent fishing along this route for walleyes, northern pike and smallmouth bass. Lake trout are also found in several of the lakes. Serious anglers may also want to stretch this route over 6 or 7 days to better avail themselves of the fishing opportunities along the way.

Day 1 (8 miles): P. 67 rods, **Bower Trout Lake,** p. 90 rods, **Marshall Lake,** p. 28 rods, **South Brule River, Dugout Lake, South Brule River, Skidway Lake,** p. 35 rods, **South Brule River,** p. 40 rods, **river,** p. 40 rods, **Swan Lake, South Brule River,** p. 292 rods, **Vernon Lake.** (See comments for Day 1, Route #43-1.)

Day 2 (10 miles): Vernon Lake, p. 49 rods, **Brule Lake,** p. 10 rods, **creek, South Temperance Lake,** p. 55 rods, **North Temperance Lake.** The first portage this day will get your heart pumping. There you will climb steeply for 40 of the 49 rods, gaining over 110 feet in elevation, before dropping down to the far-eastern shore of Brule Lake, 83 feet above Vernon Lake.

If there is a light breeze from the east or no wind at all, this day should be quite easy as you cross big Brule Lake. If the wind is strong from any direction, however, brace yourself. A strong head wind is always a retarding menace, but also beware the strong *tail* wind. When starting across a wide-open expanse of water with a strong wind at your back, the lake ahead of you may appear relatively calm and quite safe. As you proceed farther and farther out from the lee side of a sheltering shoreline, however, the waves grow higher and higher. Suddenly you may find your canoe in rougher water than you can handle, resulting in either a swamped or a capsized canoe. Wind can be either a friend or a foe, depending on how much respect you have for it and how much good judgment you demonstrate in its presence. It is always best to paddle close to the shoreline of a large lake. Not only is it safer, it is also far more interesting. That's where the wildlife resides.

The region lying east of South Temperance Lake was scarred by a large wildfire that burned 4,450 acres of timber in June of 1996. It was started by lightning and cost $1.5 million to fight. Unlike other "prescribed" natural fires that were allowed to burn in the Wilderness, the South Temperance Fire threatened areas lying outside the BWCAW and was, therefore, not allowed to burn freely.

North Temperance Lake is a scenic place to spend your night. Steep hills rising more than 200 feet above the water border the north

The portage trail from Ram Lake

end of the lake. Don't delay in claiming your campsite, as this part of the Wilderness entertains visitors from several popular entry points.

Day 3 (9 miles): North Temperance Lake, p. 105 rods, **Sitka Lake,** p. 140 rods, **Cherokee Lake,** p. 13 rods, **Gordon Lake,** p. 28 rods, **Long Island River,** p. 5 rods, **river, Long Island Lake.** Portaging will have its ups and downs this day as you pass through the Laurentian Highlands. South of Sitka Lake, water flows eventually to the Atlantic Ocean. On the north side of the Laurentian Divide, the water ultimately drains into the Arctic Ocean. The most exhausting carry of the day is on the hilly 140-rod portage connecting Sitka and Cherokee lakes.

Beautiful Cherokee Lake attracts many visitors from both the Sawbill Lake and Brule Lake entry points. Expect to share this lovely setting with other people. Long Island is also a very popular lake that attracts visitors from several directions. Try to claim your campsite early in the afternoon. There are numerous good sites from which to choose. Nine miles of travel will put you in the east end of the lake, which harbors lake trout and northern pike.

Day 4 (9 miles): Long Island Lake, p. 20 rods, **Muskeg Creek,** p. 13 rods, **Muskeg Lake,** p. 185 rods, **Kiskadinna Lake,** p. 35 rods, **Omega Lake,** p. 32 rods, **Hensen Lake,** p. 80 rods, **Gaskin Lake.** The tiny creek connecting Long Island and Muskeg lakes is quite scenic, with some low rock cliffs near the 20-rod path. The short portage at the east end of the creek may vary in length from 4 to 13 rods, depending on the water's depth. Or it may not be necessary at all when the water is high enough to afford paddling through the shallow stream.

That was the easy part of the day. Now get ready for a challenge. The 185-rod portage gains more than 150 feet in elevation from Muskeg Lake to Kiskadinna Lake. After the first leg of the ascent, the trail levels off briefly to cross a stream on a log bridge. Beyond the stream the well-beaten path climbs more steeply to a high, dry ridge that affords a north view through the forest. The last half of the trek is relatively level until it descends to the west end of Kiskadinna Lake.

Kiskadinna is one of the least attractive lakes in the area, plagued with a plethora of dead spruce tees and many windfalls along its entire shoreline, which has very little elevation behind it. This is moose country, though, so you can focus all of your attention on searching for wildlife, if not admiring the scenery.

At the east end of that long, slender lake is another steep—but much shorter—climb over a small hill that separates Kiskadinna and Omega lakes. That short trek will put you back on the southeast side of the Laurentian Divide. Omega is a pretty little lake with some small rock cliffs along the shoreline and a few nice campsites. The short portage (32 rods) leading to Hensen Lake is flat but rocky, and it could be wet.

The first half of the final portage (80 rods) climbs a low hill, then descends more steeply to the west end of Gaskin Lake. There are several nice campsites on the lake, but also a good deal of competition for them. It's a popular destination for visitors entering the Wilderness from Poplar Lake. Anglers find lake trout, walleyes and northern pike there.

Day 5 (9 miles): Gaskin Lake, p. 102 rods, **Horseshoe Lake,** p. 21 rods, **Vista Lake,** p. 50 rods, **Misquah Lake,** p. 190 rods, **Little Trout Lake,** p. 60 rods, **Rum Lake,** p. 55 rods, **Kroft Lake,** p. 80 rods, **Ram Lake,** p. 90 rods. Get ready for your toughest day of portages. Most of the trails are plagued with rocks, roots and boulders, and you will pass over some BIG hills. Be glad you're heading this way, though; it's even tougher for those heading in the opposite direction. Fortunately, the day also affords some of the most striking scenery of the trip, as you pass through the rugged Misquah Hills. Furthermore, you'll be leaving most people behind and entering perhaps the least visited part of the entire loop.

You'll start right off with a long walk over a big hill, but the path is well built, well maintained and well used. Watch for some large white pines and cedar trees near the middle of the 102-rod trail.

After the next 2 short, rocky portages, take time to rest on scenic Misquah Lake before tackling the roughest portage of all. A steep ridge looms nearly 300 feet above the east shore of the lake—a hint of what's to come.

The portage from Misquah Lake to Little Trout Lake is one of the toughest in this part of the BWCA Wilderness. From the rocky landing at Misquah Lake, the trail first gradually climbs up along the side of a hill, and then descends to a wet, boggy spot. Then the real "fun" begins—a steep climb up and over a large hill where you will gain more than 80 feet in less than 25 rods. After dropping steeply into another wet bog, you will have yet another steep hill over which to climb, before descending steeply to the rocky shore of Little Trout Lake.

As if that weren't enough, the next portage climbs over another big, steep hill. It gains nearly 100 feet in elevation during the first 30 rods and then descends about 80 feet to the shore of Rum Lake. The last 3 portages will seem easy compared to the previous 2, although there will still be a couple of short climbs before the final long descent from Ram Lake. Get your drinking water from Little Trout Lake. Rum and Kroft lakes are very murky by comparison.

The final trail is rather unusual, with a wide right-of-way that affords a panoramic view from the portage. The trail descends more than 125 feet in elevation from Ram Lake to the parking area $\frac{1}{10}$ mile from the road.

If you didn't leave a car at the Ram Lake entry point, of course, you must walk yet another mile back to your origin at the Bower Trout Lake parking lot. It's not a bad hike, however, on the down-sloping gravel road.

Entry Point 44—Ram Lake

SEASONAL PERMITS: 102

POPULARITY RANK: 43rd

DAILY QUOTA: 1

LOCATION: Ram Lake is 15 airline miles northwest of Grand Marais. From Highway 61, drive north on the Gunflint Trail for nearly 17 miles to its junction with Forest Route 325 (South Brule Road). It's on the west (left) side of the Gunflint Trail, 1 mile past the Greenwood Road turnoff. Turn left and follow this good but narrow, winding and hilly gravel road west for 6 miles to a **T**-intersection with Forest Route 152 (Lima Grade Road). Turn right onto F.R. 152 and proceed 0.3 mile to the Ram Lake turnoff on the left side of the road. Turn left there and drive 0.1 mile to the end of the access road (or stop anywhere along the way if you don't feel comfortable continuing on this unimproved road). A 90-rod portage leads from the parking area uphill to Ram Lake.

DESCRIPTION: There really isn't any "designated" parking lot at this entry point. People leave their vehicles wherever it is convenient. Since there isn't much demand for the available space, however, you should have no problem finding a place to park.

There are no designated campgrounds in the immediate vicinity of this entry point. The Kimball Lake Campground is the most convenient USFS facility. It is located just 2 miles east of the Gunflint Trail via Forest Route 140 from their intersection 10.7 miles north of Highway 61. Ten campsites are available on a first-come-first-served basis. A camping fee is charged. If that campground is full, you could also stay at the much larger East Bearskin Lake Campground, located farther up the Gunflint Trail (see Entry Point 64).

Ram is a crystal-clear, state-designated trout lake that is stocked with rainbow and lake trout. It's a good entry point for strong canoeists who want a quick escape to solitude—the essence of true wilderness.

This is no place, however, for the weak or timid. Since 3 of the first 5 portages require steep climbs, there are no easy routes from Ram Lake. In fact, this is one of the most physically challenging entry points in all of the Boundary Waters. The BWCA Wilderness Act of 1978 prohibited motorboats in this part of the Boundary Waters. The only motors you may hear are in vehicles using the nearby roads until you penetrate deeper into the Wilderness.

Along with its neighboring entry points to the north and south, Ram Lake is one of the least accessible entry points served by the Gunflint Trail. But more and more people have learned that, in spite of its remoteness and the exhausting access trail, it is worth visiting. With a quota of only 1 group per day, Ram Lake ranks high among all entry points with quotas filled the greatest number of days each summer. A reservation is usually necessary.

Besides the 2 routes suggested below, you could also enjoy a 5-day expedition west to lovely Cherokee Lake by reversing Route #43-2.

ROUTE #44-1: **The Misquah Hills Route**

2 Days, 10 Miles, 8 Lakes, 9 Portages

DIFFICULTY: Most Rugged

FISHER MAP: F-13

INTRODUCTION: This short but exhausting route is a good choice for those who seek nice scenery, immediate solitude and some good fishing. From Ram Lake you will paddle and portage northwest through a chain of small lakes leading to Vista Lake. The next morning you will plot an eastbound course through Jake and Morgan lakes to exit the BWCA Wilderness on the Morgan Lake Trail. The route ends at Forest Route 315, 5 miles by road from its origin.

This entire route is contained in a pretty part of the Wilderness that entertains relatively few visitors. Nevertheless, campsites are limited and, during the busiest part of the summer, they do fill up. So it's a good idea to get an early start and claim your campsite while the sun is still high in the sky.

Covering only 10 miles, this route could "easily" be completed in just 1 day by strong and experienced canoeists traveling with little gear. For most groups, however, traveling just 5 miles each day in this hilly country will be challenge enough. It should also allow time for fishing while you're resting between portages. Anglers will find trout in the cool, clear waters of Ram, Little Trout and Misquah lakes and a good population of walleyes in Vista Lake.

If the quota for Ram Lake is filled on the day you want to enter the BWCAW, you could just as well take this route in reverse by entering the Wilderness at Morgan Lake (see Entry Point 45)—IF you don't mind starting your trip with a 1-mile portage.

Day 1 (5 miles): P. 90 rods, **Ram Lake,** p. 80 rods, **Kroft Lake,** p. 55 rods, **Rum Lake,** p. 60 rods, **Little Trout Lake,** p. 190 rods, **Misquah Lake,** p. 50 rods, **Vista Lake.** The portage leading from the parking area to Ram Lake is all uphill and rather steep in places. The trail skirts the south edge of a wide-open swath of hillside that affords a rather impressive view from the top, as well as at points along the way—more like vistas from a mountain hiking trail than from a typical BWCAW portage. The well-beaten path is narrow and cluttered with rocks, boulders and roots that make walking hazardous, especially when the trail is wet. Be very careful at the end, in particular, where the trail drops steeply over the final 3 rods to the shore of Ram Lake.

The next 2 portages aren't difficult. But the 60-rod trail from Rum Lake surmounts a steep hill, gaining more than 80 feet in elevation before descending nearly 100 feet to Little Trout Lake. And that's just a "warm-up" for the next long trek. The 190-rod trail to Misquah Lake ranks among the most exhausting portages in the BWCAW. You'll climb over 2 steep hills during the first 100 rods on a rough and rocky path that dips twice through low wet, boggy spots. Then you'll climb over another large hill en route to the rocky landing at the south end of Misquah Lake.

Misquah Lake provides a beautiful setting in which to rest and catch your breath. A steep ridge looms nearly 300 feet above the east shore of the lake.

Most visitors to Vista Lake access it from the north. There are a couple of nice campsites in the south and central parts of the lake. Anglers are attracted to the lake because it boasts a good population of fairly large walleyes and northern pike. If you arrive early in the afternoon, resist the temptation to continue onward. There are no designated USFS campsites on Jake and Morgan lakes. If necessary, however, you may veer to the south of the main route to Lux and Carl lakes. Each of them has 1 campsite.

Day 2 (5 miles): **Vista Lake,** p. 35 rods, **Jake Lake,** p. 55 rods, **Morgan Lake,** p. 320 rods. All 3 of these portages may be used more by moose than by human beings. In spite of light use, however, they do have good paths. The final portage is long, but mostly downhill after the first 80 rods, with a fairly smooth, good path most of the way. A picturesque beaver pond marks the halfway point. The worst part of the entire trail is the last 7 rods, where it passes through a swampy area next to the road.

If you didn't shuttle a car here before you started this route, you'll have to end this trip with a 5-mile hike south on Forest Routes 315 and 152 to the Ram Lake parking lot.

ROUTE #44-2: The Winchell Swan Loop

5 Days, 32 Miles, 21 Lakes, 1 River, 1 Creek, 23 Portages

DIFFICULTY: Challenging

FISHER MAP: F-13

INTRODUCTION: This interesting route will lead you through the scenic Misquah Hills region of the BWCAW's southeast corner. From Ram Lake you will first paddle and portage through a chain of small lakes leading northwest to Vista Lake. At Horseshoe Lake, the route veers southwest across Gaskin, Winchell and Cliff lakes. The "Cone Chain" then carries you south to big Brule Lake where the route turns east. From Brule Bay you'll portage to Vernon Lake and then on to Swan Lake. From there, you'll paddle through the lakes, ponds and creeks that compose the upper stretch of the South Brule River en route to Bower Trout Lake. The route ends at a small parking lot 67 rods from the north shore of Bower Trout Lake, 1 mile by road from your origin.

The trip begins and ends on the highest notes, perhaps, as this corner of the Wilderness offers some lovely scenery, and there are fewer people than in the region north of Brule Lake. You may not completely escape from other people anywhere along this route, but the lakes from Horseshoe to Brule entertain far more visitors than do those crossed during your first and last days.

Covering only 32 miles, this route could surely be completed in just 4 days by most experienced parties. Spread over 5 days, however, you will have more time to appreciate the scenic, hilly terrain that surrounds the waterways. Also, the anglers in your group will have plenty of time to seek out the walleyes, northern pike, smallmouth bass and lake trout that inhabit these lakes. Portages are generally short and easy, but there are enough long ones to warrant a "challenging" rating. Indeed, your first day might well deserve a "most rugged" rating—especially if you're not in the very best physical condition. Only 4 portages exceed 100 rods in length, but several shorter carries seem much longer.

Day 1 (5 miles): P. 90 rods, **Ram Lake,** p. 80 rods, **Kroft Lake,** p. 55 rods, **Rum Lake,** p. 60 rods, **Little Trout Lake,** p. 190 rods, **Misquah Lake,** p. 50 rods, **Vista Lake.** (See comments for Day 1, Route #44-1.) If you arrive early in the afternoon, resist the temptation to forge onward. Visitors entering the Wilderness from Poplar Lake to the north often occupy the campsites on Horseshoe and Gaskin lakes.

Day 2 (7 miles): **Vista Lake,** p. 21 rods, **Horseshoe Lake,** p. 102 rods, **Gaskin Lake,** p. 60 rods, **Winchell Lake.** Although it's one of the longest, in terms of miles traveled, this will surely be your easiest day of the trip—and a welcome relief after the previous day. The first portage is nearly level but has a rocky path. The next 2 trails pass over big hills, but the well-traveled paths are in good condition. Watch for some large white pines and cedar trees near the middle of the 102-rod trail.

A boreal forest of white pines, cedars and spruce trees borders Horseshoe, Gaskin and Winchell lakes. There are very few deciduous trees in this region and rather low terrain between Vista and Winchell lakes compared to the Misquah Hills region lying south of those lakes.

Plan to camp near the center of Winchell Lake for a 7-mile day of travel. Winchell is a beautiful lake with the nearby Misquah Hills towering nearly 350 feet above the water. There are several nice campsites on the north shore of the lake. This is a popular destination for trippers starting at several entry points, so try to claim a campsite as early as possible. From any of the sites you will be able to enjoy a view across the water toward the steep and rocky ridge bordering the south shore of the lake. The deep and very clear water harbors some large lake trout and northern pike. Toward the west end, you will see the charred evidence of a forest fire that raced through the area in 1995—one of many wildfires that ravaged the BWCAW that year.

Day 3 (7 miles): **Winchell Lake,** p. 14 rods, **Wanihigan Lake,** p. 14 rods, **Cliff Lake,** p. 160 rods, **North Cone Lake,** p. 2 rods, **Cone Creek, Middle Cone Lake,** p. 25 rods, **Cone Creek, South Cone Lake, Cone Creek,** p. 15 rods, **creek, Brule Lake.** (See comments for Day 2, Route #41-1.) Claim a campsite as early in the afternoon as possible. Brule is one of the most popular entry points in the BWCAW, and campsites there are often at a premium. By camping in or near Cone Bay, you won't have to cross the widest expanse of the big lake during the afternoon, when wind and waves are normally the worst for paddlers.

Crystal-clear Brule Lake is known for its good fishing. Some large walleyes and northern pike lurk beneath its surface. It also harbors smallmouth bass.

Day 4 (8 miles): Brule Lake, p. 49 rods, **Vernon Lake,** p. 292 rods, **South Brule River, Swan Lake.** On a windy day, use caution crossing Brule Lake's open expanse. Stay close to the shore and use the lee sides of islands and peninsulas for protection, if necessary.

The first and shorter of the 2 portages descends steeply to Vernon Lake. After rising about 30 feet during the first 5 rods from the shore of Brule Bay, the trail then plunges over 110 feet during the final 40 rods. Use caution, especially when the path is wet and slippery.

Watch out for rocks and boulders in the shallow east end of Vernon Lake, just before the portage landing. The longest carry of this route (292 rods) is not as challenging as some of the shorter trails crossed earlier. After climbing for 80 rods, you'll then descend for about half a mile on a good path that loses 100 feet of elevation. About 50 rods from the end of the trail, you will cross a small creek and then continue on a fairly level path to the South Brule River. Near the end of the portage, you may see the dilapidated remains of the Alger Smith logging camp. It operated in this area from 1920 to 1923.

The narrow, crystal-clear river meanders for about half a mile en route to Swan Lake. Swan is a lovely lake with 3 nice campsites. One of them is at the former site of a logging camp that once operated at the north end of the lake. It was served by a railroad. The old railroad grade parallels the north side of the South Brule River flowage.

Day 5 (5 miles): Swan Lake, p. 40 rods, **South Brule River,** p. 40 rods, **river,** p. 35 rods, **Skidway Lake, South Brule River, Dugout Lake, South Brule River,** p. 28 rods, **Marshall Lake,** p. 90 rods, **Bower Trout Lake,** p. 67 rods. You'll be traveling downstream again this day as you ply the waters of the South Brule River flowage—descending 46 feet from Swan to Bower Trout Lake. All of the portages, therefore, are generally downhill. The paths are well beaten and, for the most part, in pretty good condition.

Along the shores of Skidway and Dugout lakes, as well as on the 35-rod portage, you will see the charred stumps from a forest fire that scoured the area in 1995. It affords a unique perspective—one of the few places in the BWCA Wilderness where you can actually see a landscape that is not concealed by dense forests. It allowed my wife and me to observe a cow moose and her calf meander along the hillside overlooking Dugout Lake, after they had retreated from the water's edge during our approach. Moose populations thrive in areas that have been recently burned. So do blueberries, so keep a watchful eye for both.

When the water level is low, watch out for submerged rocks in the narrow river channels at both ends of Dugout Lake. You may have to step out of your canoe and guide it through the shallow "rapids." While always vigilant for submerged rocks, also don't forget to look up occasionally. The hills to the south of Marshall Lake rise to over 500 feet above the water.

The portage landings at both ends of Bower Trout Lake may be muddy when the water level is low in that shallow lake. From the landing on the lake's north shore, your final portage follows the good, level path of an old railroad grade. As you approach the unimproved parking lot, you'll pass through a wet and muddy spot, but most of the trail is dry. If you didn't leave a car at the Bower Trout Lake entry point, you must walk another mile back to your origin—a gradual uphill trek along Forest Route 152.

Entry Point 45—Morgan Lake

SEASONAL PERMITS: 74

POPULARITY RANK: 52nd

DAILY QUOTA: 1

LOCATION: Morgan Lake is 17 airline miles northwest of Grand Marais. From Highway 61 in Grand Marais, drive 21 miles north via the Gunflint Trail to the Lima Mountain Road (Forest Route 152). Turn left there and proceed 2.3 miles west on this fair gravel road to an unmarked **Y**-intersection. Bear right for another $1/10$ mile to the junction of Forest Route 315. Turn right and proceed 1.9 miles north to the Morgan Lake portage on the left side of the road.

DESCRIPTION: There is a small parking space, large enough for only 2 or 3 vehicles, off the road. Fortunately, there isn't much demand for the space.

There are no designated campgrounds in the immediate vicinity of this entry point. The Kimball Lake Campground is the most convenient USFS facility. It is located just 2 miles east of the Gunflint Trail via Forest Route 140 from their intersection 10.7 miles north of Highway 61. Ten campsites are available on a first-come-first-served basis. A camping fee is charged. If that campground is full, you could stay at the much larger East Bearskin Lake Campground, located farther up the Gunflint Trail (see Entry Point 64).

Access to Morgan Lake is by way of a 1-mile trail that begins at the parking spot. A portage of this length is a rugged way to begin any canoe trip, but don't let that discourage you. The trail has a good path that is fairly easy to negotiate. A 6-rod boardwalk crosses a swamp at the beginning of the portage. Most of the trail is on dry, level-to-gently-rolling terrain. It passes through a lovely upland forest of aspen and birch, mixed with pine, fir and spruce. The only steep part is where the trail abruptly drops to cross a small creek draining a large bog. Just before reaching the creek, you will pass an opening that affords a nice view of the bog—a good place to watch for moose. Beyond the creek, then, is the only significant climb, back up to high ground, before you gradually descend to the east shore of Morgan Lake.

Along with its neighboring entry points to the south, Morgan Lake is one of the least accessible BWCAW entries along the Gunflint Trail. It is also one of the most overlooked. Less than half the available overnight permits were issued in 1997. No daytime use permits were written. Few people avail themselves of this good, quick way to escape into wilderness. So this is a good choice for anyone looking for solitude who doesn't mind shedding some sweat to find it.

An attempt to reclaim Morgan and its 3 neighboring lakes for brook trout failed. Morgan and Jake lakes were stocked with trout in 1989, and Lux Lake was stocked in 1988. Don't bother fishing for the trout. About all the stocking did was provide good meals for the northern pike that somehow survived the reclamation effort.

In addition to the 2 routes described below, you could also "enjoy" a rugged 2-day challenge by reversing Route #44-1. You'll travel right through the heart of the Misquah Hills and take out at Ram Lake. It's recommended only for those in very good physical condition.

ROUTE #45-1: The Vista Swallow Route

2 Days, 16 Miles, 10 Lakes, 10 Portages

DIFFICULTY: Challenging

FISHER MAP: F-13

INTRODUCTION: This short route takes you through some of the least visited lakes and some of the most visited lakes in this part of the BWCA Wilderness. From the end of the long portage, you'll paddle west to Vista Lake and then veer north to Horseshoe Lake. From the west end of that long, slender lake, you will portage to Gaskin Lake. After a night on that popular lake, you will portage northward and cross 3 small, slender lakes en route to Meeds Lake. After paddling across the largest lake on this route, you'll endure another mile-long carry as you exit the Boundary Waters via the trail to Poplar Lake. This route ends at the public landing at the northwest end of Poplar Lake, about 10 miles by road from your origin (via the back roads).

Some might argue that this route deserves a "most rugged" rating because of the 2 mile-long portages. Indeed, it's not a route for everyone. Most of the portages, however, are relatively short and not difficult. And even the 2 long carries are not as bad as they might seem. Nevertheless, if you need 2 trips to get all your gear across the portages, you'll start and end the trip with 3 miles of hiking. Pack accordingly.

The anglers in your group will have good opportunities to supplement your diet with fresh fish. You'll be paddling across some good walleye lakes. And there are plenty of northern pike as well.

Day 1 (8 miles): P. 320 rods, **Morgan Lake,** p. 55 rods, **Jake Lake,** p. 35 rods, **Vista Lake,** p. 21 rods, **Horseshoe Lake,** p. 102 rods, **Gaskin Lake.** After the first portage, unless there is a strong west wind, this should be a fairly easy day of travel. The 3 short portages are fairly level, but the 21-rod path to Horseshoe Lake is quite rocky. The only big hill comes at the other end of Horseshoe Lake. Watch for some big, old pine and cedar trees on the top of the hill near the mid-point of the trail.

Horseshoe and Gaskin lakes are part of a popular route that originates at Poplar Lake and enters the BWCAW at Lizz Lake. There are numerous campsites on Gaskin Lake, but also plenty of competition for them. So try to claim your site as early in the day as possible, especially during peak season.

Day 2 (8 miles): Gaskin Lake, p. 80 rods, **Hensen Lake,** p. 58 rods, **Pillsbery Lake,** p. 93 rods, **Swallow Lake,** p. 110 rods, **Meeds Lake,** p. 320 rods, **Poplar Lake.** This is a tougher day than the first. Not only are the first 4 portages more frequent than those crossed the previous day, they are also longer and not as well used. If you need 2 trips to get your gear across, you'll be walking more than 6 miles this day (4 miles with gear). The first trail gains about 60 feet elevation as you cross over a ridge separating Gaskin and Hensen lakes. Elevation is not factor on the next 3 trails, and they are not difficult.

Until recently, the 1-mile trail from Meeds to Poplar Lake was downright nasty. Fortunately, most of the wet and muddy spots were bridged by boardwalks during the summer of 1998 when portage crews upgraded the trail. The portage starts with a gradual ascent, soon exits the BWCA Wilderness, and then crosses an old logging road that is now part of the Banadad Ski Trail. The final 200 rods of trail are mostly downhill, including a steep descent at the end.

On Poplar Lake, which lies entirely outside the BWCAW, you'll see several private cabins and resorts along the northeast shore of the lake. The public landing is at the end of a quiet bay in the lake's northwest corner.

ROUTE #45-2: The Cherokee Swan Route

5 Days, 44 Miles, 22 Lakes, 2 Rivers, 2 Creeks, 26 Portages

DIFFICULTY: Challenging

FISHER MAPS: F-12, F-13

INTRODUCTION: This is an excellent route for anyone who likes the variety of large and small lakes, rivers and slender lakes that look like rivers, portages of all lengths and challenges, and scenery that changes every day. From the end of the Morgan Lake portage, you'll paddle west to Vista Lake and then veer north to Horseshoe Lake. From the west end of that long, slender lake, you will portage to Gaskin Lake. After a night on that popular lake, you will portage north to a chain of long, slender lakes that lead west to Long Island Lake. The Long Island River will then carry you south to lovely Gordon and Cherokee lakes. After crossing the Laurentian Divide for the second time, the

Moose in the South Brule River

route turns east and crosses the full length of big Brule Lake en route to Vernon Lake. Finally, the South Brule River system of lakes, pools and rapids will lead you farther east to Bower Trout Lake. From there you will portage out of the BWCA Wilderness and end your journey at a small parking lot, about 6 miles by road from your origin.

Most of the 26 portages are neither long nor difficult. There are enough long and difficult trails, however, to challenge even a seasoned tripper. Only 6 exceed 100 rods in length and the steepest, fortunately, are downhill. Nevertheless, groups with less experience or weaker members might be wise to add an extra day to the itinerary. The same holds true for avid anglers who want to avail themselves of the opportunities to fish along the route. They will find northern pike in many of the lakes and walleyes, smallmouth bass and lake trout in some.

While parts of this route receive very light use—especially at the beginning and end—you're likely to see quite a few people in the vicinities of Gaskin, Long Island, Cherokee and Brule lakes. The west end of the loop entertains visitors from several popular entry points. But don't let that discourage you; the scenery is well worth sharing.

Day 1 (8 miles): P. 320 rods, **Morgan Lake,** p. 55 rods, **Jake Lake,** p. 35 rods, **Vista Lake,** p. 21 rods, **Horseshoe Lake,** p. 102 rods, **Gaskin Lake.** (See comments for Day 1, Route #45-1.)

Day 2 (10 miles): Gaskin Lake, p. 80 rods, **Hensen Lake,** p. 32 rods, **Omega Lake,** p. 35 rods, **Kiskadinna Lake,** p. 185 rods, **Muskeg Lake,** p. 13 rods, **Muskeg Creek,** p. 20 rods, **Long Island Lake.** The first trail gains about 60 feet elevation as you cross over a ridge separating Gaskin and Hensen lakes. The second short trail, from Hensen to Omega Lake, is flat but rocky and it may be wet. Omega is a more scenic lake than most in this chain of long and narrow lakes, with some small rock cliffs along the shoreline.

The next 2 portages are both steep and rocky. Use caution, especially when the ground is wet. The first passes over the Laurentian Divide and requires a short, steep climb over a small hill, with an even steeper descent. The northwest part of this loop lies north of the Divide, where the water flows ultimately north to the Arctic Ocean. The beginning and end of this route, however, lie on the side of the Divide where the water flows east to the Atlantic Ocean via the Great Lakes.

Kiskadinna Lake is plagued with a plethora of dead spruce trees and many windfalls along its entire shoreline, which has very little elevation behind it—not one of the prettier lakes in the BWCAW.

The 185-rod trail to Muskeg Lake starts innocently enough, first climbing slightly to a relatively level, dry ridge that affords a north view through the forest. Then, about midway across the portage, the trail drops steeply to cross a small stream on a log bridge. Beyond the stream the well-beaten path descends more gradually to the shore of Muskeg Lake—a total drop of more than 150 feet. Though not as exhausting as hiking uphill, steep descents are often more difficult and more treacherous, especially when the path is wet. Step carefully.

The short portage at the west end of Muskeg Lake may vary in length from 4 to 13 rods, depending on the water's depth. Or it may not be necessary at all when the water level is high enough to afford paddling through the shallow creek. The tiny creek that follows is quite scenic, with some low rock cliffs near the 20-rod path.

Long Island Lake has several fine campsites large enough to accommodate groups with 3-4 tents. Several sites also have sandy beaches when high water is not covering them. The lake attracts visitors from the Cross River entry point to the north, as well as from Brule and Sawbill lakes to the south. Don't delay in claiming your site for the night. Then relax while you search for one of the large lake trout that inhabit the lake.

Day 3 (9 miles): Long Island Lake, Long Island River, p. 5 rods, **river,** p. 28 rods, **Gordon Lake,** p. 13 rods, **Cherokee Lake,** p. 140 rods, **Sitka Lake,** p. 105 rods, **North Temperance Lake.** This is a delightful day of paddling through one of the more scenic parts of the Boundary Waters, with easy portages connecting Long Island, Gordon and Cherokee lakes. Beautiful island-studded Cherokee Lake is a very popular destination for paddlers entering the Wilderness at Sawbill and Brule lakes. And the narrow route leading to it from Long Island Lake is also lovely.

Your first long carry of the day (140 rods) will get your heart pumping fast. It is a hilly trail that rises over 90 feet in elevation before dropping to the north shore of Sitka Lake. The next trail also has its ups and downs, as it crosses the Laurentian Divide.

North Temperance Lake is a scenic place to spend your night. Steep hills rising more than 200 feet above the water border the north end of the lake. Don't delay in claiming your campsite, as this part of the Wilderness entertains visitors from several popular entry points.

Day 4 (9 miles): North Temperance Lake, p. 55 rods, **South Temperance Lake, creek,** p. 10 rods, **Brule Lake,** p. 49 rods, **Vernon Lake.** If the wind is not a problem, this should be your easiest day of the entire trip. If the wind is strong from any direction, however, brace yourself. A strong head wind is always a retarding menace, but also beware the strong *tail* wind. When starting across a wide-open expanse of water with a strong wind at your back, the lake ahead of you may appear relatively calm and quite safe. As you proceed farther and farther out from the lee side of a sheltering shoreline, however, the waves grow higher and higher. Suddenly you may find your canoe in rougher water than you can handle, resulting in either a swamped or a capsized canoe. Wind can be either a friend or a foe, depending on how much respect you have for it and how much good judgment you demonstrate in its presence. It is always best to paddle close to the shoreline of a large lake. Not only is it safer, it is also far more interesting. That's where the wildlife resides.

The region lying east of South Temperance Lake was scarred by a large wildfire that burned 4,450 acres of timber in June of 1996. It was started by lightning and cost $1.5 million to fight. Unlike other "prescribed" natural fires that were allowed to burn in the Wilderness, the South Temperance Fire threatened areas lying outside the BWCAW and was, therefore, not allowed to burn freely.

The 49-rod portage at the east end of Brule Lake descends steeply to Vernon Lake. After rising about 30 feet during the first 5 rods from the shore of Brule Bay, the trail then plunges over 110 feet during the final 40 rods. Use caution, especially when the path is wet and slippery.

There is a nice campsite on the north shore of Vernon Lake, situated in a grove of birch trees, with space for 2 or 3 tents. Anglers should find walleyes, northern pike and smallmouth bass nearby. You might even pull a lake trout from the cool, clear water. They were stocked there in 1997.

Day 5 (8 miles): Vernon Lake, p. 292 rods, **South Brule River, Swan Lake,** p. 40 rods, **South Brule River,** p. 40 rods, **river,** p. 35 rods, **Skidway Lake, South Brule River, Dugout Lake, South Brule River,** p. 28 rods, **Marshall Lake,** p. 90 rods, **Bower Trout Lake,** p. 67 rods. (See comments for Day 4, paragraphs 3 and 4, and Day 5, Route #44-2.)

Entry Point 47 — Lizz Lake & Swamp Lake

Seasonal Permits: 685 (with Meeds Lake in 1997)

Popularity Rank: 13th (with Meeds Lake in 1997)

Daily Quota: 4

Location: Lizz Lake is located 21 airline miles northwest of Grand Marais and 1 short portage south of Poplar Lake. From Highway 61 in Grand Marais, follow the Gunflint Trail northwest for 32 miles, past Poplar Lake, to County Road 92 on the south (left) side of the road. Watch carefully for the USFS sign 1.8 miles past Windigo Lodge. Turn left there and follow the county road ½-mile west to its intersection with a 1-lane gravel road (left). Drive 1 mile south on this good, but narrow gravel road to the Poplar Lake boat landing.

Description: Near the end of the road, you'll see a spur road that leads right 0.2 mile to the boat landing. Parking is not permitted at the landing. Instead, proceed 0.1 mile past that corner to a large parking lot that accommodates 50-60 vehicles. A 15-rod path leads from the parking lot down to the west end of Poplar Lake, on wooden stairs part of the way.

There are 2 good campgrounds located close to Poplar Lake. The Iron Lake Campground is the closer, as well as the smaller, located about 4 miles west of the Poplar Lake boat landing via County Road 92. The 7 campsites are available by reservation and operated by a concessionaire, Way of the Wilderness Outfitters. The narrow county road is recommended for high-clearance vehicles but, if you drive slowly and carefully, any car should make it without difficulty. If that campground is filled up, another convenient place to spend the night before your canoe trip is at the Flour Lake Campground. Operated by Golden Eagle Lodge, the 35 campsites there may also be reserved in advance. It is located 2½ miles east of the Gunflint Trail on County Road 66 (see Entry Point 62). Reservations for either of the campgrounds may be

made by calling the National Recreation Reservation Service (see Chapter 2). A camping fee is charged at both campgrounds.

In addition to Lizz and Swamp lakes, the Meeds Lake and Skipper Lake entry points are also accessible from Poplar Lake. Lizz Lake is the most popular of the 4, as it offers the easiest entry into the Boundary Waters. Prior to 1999, the USFS grouped Lizz, Swamp and Meeds lakes together with the same quota, since they serve essentially the same geographic region. Because so many visitors opted to enter at Lizz Lake, however, the Forest Service decided to separate Meeds Lake from the other 2 and gave each a separate quota.

Poplar Lake lies entirely outside the BWCA Wilderness. You'll see numerous private cabins and several resorts along the northeast shore of the lake. The public landing is at the end of a quiet bay in the lake's northwest corner. Motorboats are permitted on Poplar Lake, of course, but they are not allowed to enter the Wilderness via any of the 4 entry points accessible from Poplar. The northwest half of Lizz Lake, however, does lie outside the BWCAW, so you could see a motorboat past the first portage.

If your heart is set on an easy BWCAW entry through Lizz Lake, make your reservation early. In 1997, only ⅔ of the available permits were issued to visitors. But then there was a quota of 7 permits per day. With the quota now at 4 daily permits, most of the pressure from visitors entering the Wilderness from Poplar Lake will be at the Lizz Lake entry point. Lizz is likely to be one of the most difficult entry points for which to get a permit, as it was a few years ago.

Travel in this area is generally easy. Portage trails are well worn. Campsites are plentiful. Fishing is usually quite good. But the scenery in the immediate vicinity of Lizz Lake is not exceptional. This is a rather special area with a boreal forest of spruce, fir, cedar and pine. You'll see few of the aspen and birch trees that characterize much of the BWCA Wilderness. Nevertheless, for a weekend away from the city, it's lovely. And, for those with more time to paddle, Lizz Lake does provide easy access to the scenic Misquah Hills region and to some of the prettiest lakes in the Boundary Waters.

In addition to the 2 routes described below, you may also reverse route #48-1 for a challenging 2-day loop.

ROUTE #47-1: The Horseshoe Hensen Loop

3 Days, 22 Miles, 11 Lakes, 11 Portages

DIFFICULTY: Challenging

FISHER MAP: F-13

INTRODUCTION: This short loop will take you south from Poplar Lake, through Lizz and Caribou lakes to Horseshoe Lake. After portaging from the west end of Horseshoe to Gaskin Lake, you will continue paddling west through the prettiest part of the loop—Winchell Lake. From the northwest end of Winchell Lake, then, you will portage north to Omega Lake. From there, you will begin your northeast journey back to Poplar Lake by following a chain of small, narrow lakes leading to Meeds Lake. You will exit the Boundary Waters on a one-mile trail from Meeds to Poplar Lake and then return to the public landing at the northwest corner of the lake.

With only 3 or 4 portages each day, this is an easier loop than most. But don't think it's a stroll in the park. You'll have one challenging portage over a big hill each day. And the final carry is a mile long. For inexperienced or weaker groups, this route definitely deserves a "challenging" rating. When that's the case, an extra day on the itinerary might even be in order (with campsites on Horseshoe, Winchell and Pillsbery lakes).

There may be no place on this route where you will feel completely isolated. But you will probably encounter fewer people on the north part of the loop, from Omega Lake to Meeds Lake, than during the first half of the route. Winchell Lake, in particular, attracts many visitors from the Brule Lake entry point to the south, as well as from the Poplar Lake entry points. During the peak summer season, try to get an early start each morning and make camp early each afternoon.

Anglers will have some good opportunities to test their skills. Walleyes and northern pike occupy much of the water along the route. Lake trout may also be found in the deeper water of Winchell Lake, and perhaps in Gaskin Lake, too.

Day 1 (7 miles): Poplar Lake, p. 51 rods, **Lizz Lake**, p. 73 rods, **Caribou Lake,** p. 20 rods, **Horseshoe Lake,** p. 102 rods, **Gaskin Lake.** You will be on a well-traveled route all day. Portage trails are wide and relatively smooth. Only the final trail presents any challenge, as it climbs rather steeply over a large hill. Watch for some big, old pine and cedar trees on top of the hill near the mid-point of the portage.

There are numerous campsites on Gaskin Lake, but also plenty of competition for them. So try to claim your site as early in the day as possible, especially during peak season. Gaskin is known to harbor a few large walleyes, as well as smallmouth bass, northern pike and some lake trout.

Day 2 (7 miles): Gaskin Lake, p. 60 rods, **Winchell Lake,** p. 45 rods, **Omega Lake,** p. 20 rods, **Hensen Lake.** Winchell is a beautiful lake, with rocky cliffs bordering its southern shoreline and the nearby Misquah Hills towering nearly 350 feet above the water. But it may also be the windiest. When a strong west wind prevails, travel is quite slow across this long lake. Toward the west end, you will see the charred evidence of a forest fire that raced through the area in 1995—one of many wildfires that ravaged the BWCAW that year.

The only challenging portage of the day is the first—60 rods over a big hill that separates Gaskin and Winchell lakes. The next 2, shorter trails are nearly flat, but quite rocky. So watch your step.

You'll probably see fewer people north of Winchell Lake than on the route from Poplar Lake to Winchell. The campsites on Hensen Lake are small, with few good tent sites. If you're traveling with a larger group, you might be happier camped on Omega Lake, which has a couple of nice, larger sites.

Day 3 (8 miles): Hensen Lake, p. 58 rods, **Pillsbery Lake,** p. 93 rods, **Swallow Lake,** p. 110 rods, **Meeds Lake,** p. 320 rods, **Poplar Lake.** Traveling across fairly level terrain, none of the 3 portages between Hensen and Meeds lakes is difficult. So you can save your energy for the final carry—the longest of the route. Prior to 1999, the 1-mile trail from Meeds to Poplar Lake was downright nasty. Fortunately, most of the wet and muddy spots were bridged by boardwalks during the summer of 1998 when portage crews upgraded the trail. The portage starts with a gradual ascent, soon exits the BWCA Wilderness, and then crosses an old logging road that is now part of the Banadad Ski Trail. The final 200 rods of trail are mostly downhill, including a steep descent at the end.

ROUTE #47-2: **The Cliff and Muskeg Loop**
6 Days, 45 Miles, 25 Lakes, 1 River, 3 Creeks, 27 Portages

DIFFICULTY: Challenging

FISHER MAPS: F-12, F-13

INTRODUCTION: This well-traveled route will lead you through some of the most popular and prettiest lakes lying southwest of the Gunflint Trail. From Poplar Lake, you'll first head south to Horseshoe Lake. Then you will veer southwest through Gaskin, Winchell and the Cone chain of lakes to big Brule Lake. From the west end of Brule, you will steer northwest through the Temperance lakes to Cherokee Lake and then straight north to Long Island Lake. Following your easiest day, you will then confront your most challenging portage en route to a series of long, slender lakes that lead east to Meeds Lake. You will exit the Boundary Waters on a one-mile trail from Meeds to Poplar Lake and then return to the public landing at the northwest corner of the lake.

Overall, this is a fairly easy loop, with just enough longer portages to warrant a "challenging" rating. Of the 27 carries along the route, only 8 exceed 80 rods in length, and they are spread fairly evenly along the course. More than half are less than 50 rods. Most groups should have no problem completing the route in 6 days. Many could do it in just 5. But avid anglers and weak or inexperienced parties might consider spreading the route over 7 days, perhaps with a layover day on beautiful Cherokee Lake.

Most of this route is fairly well traveled during the busier summer months. The parts from Poplar to Winchell, on Brule Lake, and from Cherokee to Long Island Lake entertain the most visitors. You will probably enjoy the most isolation during the eastbound journey from Long Island to Poplar Lake. Motorboats are prohibited from the entire route contained in the BWCAW. Only on Poplar Lake and the northwest end of Liz Lake, which lie outside the Boundary Waters, are motors permitted.

Anglers will find most species of game fish in these lakes, including walleyes, northern pike, smallmouth bass and lake trout.

Day 1 (9 miles): Poplar Lake, p. 51 rods, **Lizz Lake,** p. 73 rods, **Caribou Lake,** p. 20 rods, **Horseshoe Lake,** p. 102 rods, **Gaskin Lake,** p. 60 rods, **Winchell Lake.** (See comments for Day 1, Route #47-1.) The final portage requires another heart-pounding climb—60 rods over a big hill that separates Gaskin and Winchell lakes. Plan to camp near the east end of Winchell Lake for a 9-mile day of travel. Winchell is a beautiful lake, with rocky cliffs bordering its southern shoreline and the nearby Misquah Hills towering nearly 350 feet above the water. There are several nice campsites on the north shore of Winchell Lake. Winchell is a popular destination for trippers starting at several entry points, so try to claim a campsite as early as possible. The deep water is very clear and harbors some large lake trout and northern pike.

Day 2 (8 miles): Winchell Lake, p. 14 rods, **Wanihigan Lake,** p. 14 rods, **Cliff Lake,** p. 160 rods, **North Cone Lake,** p. 2 rods, **Cone Creek, Middle Cone Lake,** p. 25 rods, **Cone Creek, South Cone Lake,**

Going up the steep portage from Muskeg Lake to Kiskadinna Lake

Cone Creek, p. 15 rods, **creek, Brule Lake.** When a strong west wind prevails, travel is quite slow across Winchell Lake. Toward the west end, you will see the charred evidence of a forest fire that raced through the area in 1995—one of many wildfires that ravaged the BWCAW that year. (Also see comments for Day 3, Route #44-2.)

Day 3 (8 miles): Brule Lake, p. 10 rods, **creek, South Temperance Lake,** p. 55 rods, **North Temperance Lake,** p. 105 rods, **Sitka Lake,** p. 140 rods, **Cherokee Lake.** With an early start during the morning calm, you are most likely to enjoy a smooth surface across the main part of Brule Lake. You'll be traveling through a very attractive part of the BWCA Wilderness this day. North Temperance is a particularly scenic lake. Steep hills rising more than 200 feet above the water border the north end of the lake. Cherokee is also a beautiful, island-studded lake that attracts many visitors from all directions.

The region lying east of South Temperance Lake was scarred by a large wildfire that burned 4,450 acres of timber in June of 1996. It was started by lightning and cost $1.5 million to fight. Unlike other "prescribed" natural fires that were allowed to burn in the Wilderness, the South Temperance Fire threatened areas lying outside the BWCAW and was, therefore, not allowed to burn freely.

Portaging will have its ups and downs as you hike through the Laurentian Highlands. South and east of Sitka Lake, water flows eventually to the Atlantic Ocean. On the north side of the Laurentian Divide, the water ultimately drains into the Arctic Ocean. The only exhausting carry of the day is on the hilly 140-rod portage connecting Sitka and Cherokee lakes.

There are many campsites on Cherokee Lake. But there is also a great deal of demand for them by visitors from at least 3 entry points. So don't delay in claiming your site for the night. Then take time to explore this lovely lake. Lake trout and northern pike inhabit its depths.

Day 4 (5 miles): Cherokee Lake, p. 13 rods, **Gordon Lake,** p. 28 rods, **Long Island River,** p. 5 rods, **river, Long Island Lake.** Consider this virtually a layover day. With just 5 miles of paddling interrupted by 3 easy portages, you should have no problem settling into a campsite by mid-day. Or take time along the way for a side trip to Frost Lake, where superb sand beaches border the north rim of the lake. There is a good chance you could find some lake trout in the northwest corner of the lake. And you also just might catch a glimpse of a moose browsing along the shore.

Like Cherokee, Long Island is also a very popular lake that attracts visitors from several directions. Try to claim your campsite as early as possible. There are numerous good sites from which to choose. Five miles of travel will put you in the east-central part of the lake, which also harbors lake trout and northern pike. Rest up; you'll need your energy tomorrow.

Day 5 (7 miles): Long Island Lake, p. 20 rods, **Muskeg Creek,** p. 13 rods, **Muskeg Lake,** p. 185 rods, **Kiskadinna Lake,** p. 35 rods, **Omega Lake,** p. 32 rods, **Hensen Lake.** (See comments for Day 4, paragraphs 1-4, Route #43-2.) The campsites on Hensen Lake are small, with few good tent sites. If you're traveling with a larger group, you might be happier camped on Omega Lake, which has a couple of nice, larger sites.

Day 6 (8 miles): Hensen Lake, p. 58 rods, **Pillsbery Lake,** p. 93 rods, **Swallow Lake,** p. 110 rods, **Meeds Lake,** p. 320 rods, **Poplar Lake.** (See comments for Day 3, Route #47-1.)

Entry Point 48—Meeds Lake

SEASONAL PERMITS: 685 (with Lizz Lake in 1997)

POPULARITY RANK: 13th (with Lizz Lake in 1997)

DAILY QUOTA: 3

LOCATION: Meeds Lake is located 21 airline miles northwest of Grand Marais and 1 long portage south of Poplar Lake. From Highway 61 in Grand Marais, follow the Gunflint Trail northwest for 32 miles, past Poplar Lake, to County Road 92 on the south (left) side of the road. Watch carefully for the USFS sign 1.8 miles past Windigo Lodge. Turn left there and follow the county road ½-mile west to its intersection with a 1-lane gravel road (left). Drive 1 mile south on this good but narrow gravel road to the Poplar Lake boat landing.

DESCRIPTION: Near the end of the road, you'll see a spur road that leads right 0.2 mile to the boat landing. Parking is not permitted at the landing. Instead, proceed 0.1 mile past that corner to a large parking lot that accommodates 50-60 vehicles. A 15-rod path leads from the parking lot down to the west end of Poplar Lake, on wooden stairs part of the way.

There are 2 good campgrounds located close to Poplar Lake. The Iron Lake Campground is the closer, as well as the smaller, located about 4 miles west of the Poplar Lake boat landing via County Road 92. The 7 campsites are available by reservation and operated by a concessionaire, Way of the Wilderness Outfitters. The narrow county road is recommended for high-clearance vehicles but, if you drive slowly and carefully, any car should make it without difficulty. If that campground is filled up, another convenient place to spend the night before your canoe trip is at the Flour Lake Campground. Operated by Golden Eagle Lodge, the 35 campsites there may also be reserved in advance. It is located 2½ miles east of the Gunflint Trail on County Road 66 (see Entry Point 62). Reservations for either of the campgrounds may be

made by calling the National Recreation Reservation Service (see Chapter 2). A camping fee is charged at both campgrounds.

In addition to Meeds Lake, the Lizz-Swamp and Skipper Lake entry points are also accessible from Poplar Lake. Lizz Lake is the most popular of the 4 lakes, as it offers the easiest entry into the Boundary Waters. Meeds Lake is the most challenging of these entry points, and Skipper Lake is a close second—both requiring a mile-long portage from Poplar Lake. Prior to 1999, the USFS grouped Lizz, Swamp and Meeds lakes together with the same quota, since they serve essentially the same geographic region. Because so many visitors opted to enter at Lizz Lake, however, the Forest Service decided to separate Meeds Lake from the other 2 and gave each a separate quota.

Poplar Lake lies entirely outside the BWCA Wilderness. You'll see numerous private cabins and several resorts along the northeast shore of the lake. The public landing is at the end of a quiet bay in the lake's northwest corner. Motorboats are permitted on Poplar Lake, of course, but they are not allowed to enter the Wilderness via any of the 4 entry points accessible from Poplar.

Travel in this area is generally easy. Portage trails are well worn. Campsites are plentiful. Fishing is usually quite good. But the scenery in the immediate vicinity of Meeds Lake is not exceptional. This is a rather special area with a boreal forest of spruce, fir, cedar and pine. You'll see few of the aspen and birch trees that characterize much of the BWCA Wilderness. Nevertheless, for a weekend away from the city, it's lovely. And, for those with more time to paddle, Meeds Lake does provide easy access to the scenic Misquah Hills region and to some of the prettiest lakes in the Boundary Waters.

Prior to 1999, the 1-mile trail from Meeds to Poplar Lake was downright nasty. Fortunately, most of the wet and muddy spots were bridged by boardwalks during the summer of 1998 when portage crews upgraded the trail. The trail climbs steeply for the first 30 rods and then surmounts several smaller hills, eventually gaining nearly 100 feet elevation. The worst will be over when you enter the BWCA Wilderness and cross an old logging road that is now part of the Banadad Ski Trail. The final 100 rods of the trail are mostly downhill on a gradual slope to the north shore of Meeds Lake.

Yes, it's work. But the wilderness canoeist may consider it well worth the effort. You'll sense a feeling of isolation—the essence of true wilderness—much quicker here than by entering the BWCAW through Lizz Lake. People are far scarcer, and motorboats are not permitted.

ROUTE #48-1: The Hensen Horseshoe Loop

2 Days, 16 Miles, 9 Lakes, 9 Portages

DIFFICULTY: Challenging

FISHER MAPS: F-13

INTRODUCTION: This weekend route will take you from Poplar Lake southwest to Meeds Lake. Then you'll portage from the west end of Meeds Lake and paddle south across several small, narrow lakes to Gaskin Lake. Turning to the east, you'll follow a more popular route back to Poplar Lake through Horseshoe, Caribou and Lizz lakes.

Except for the very first portage, this is an easy route. An ambitious group of paddlers could surely complete the loop in a day. But, then, an avid angler may want to stretch it over 3 days to take advantage of the walleye, northern pike and smallmouth bass that inhabit some of the waters.

You will probably see fewer people during the first half of the loop. From Gaskin Lake back to Poplar Lake is a more popular stretch. Don't expect complete isolation anywhere along the loop, especially during the peak summer season. Nevertheless, campsites are plentiful and, normally, the supply is greater than the demand.

Day 1 (8 miles): Poplar Lake, p. 320 rods, **Meeds Lake,** p. 110 rods, **Swallow Lake,** p. 93 rods, **Pillsbery Lake,** p. 58 rods, **Hensen Lake,** p. 80 rods, **Gaskin Lake.** All of the lakes this day are remarkably similar. They have low shorelines with little elevation behind them, and the bordering forest consists largely of spruce and cedar trees with occasional scattered white pines—a boreal scene with few rock out-croppings or cliff faces to break up the dark green border of the lakes.

On the other hand, the portages do vary considerably. Your first portage is downright rugged, but the rest will seem easy by comparison (unless you're an "armchair canoeist" who hasn't been on the water since last year's weekend extravaganza). After crossing Meeds Lake you won't have much rest on the water between portages. Most of your day will be on your feet, not on your seat. If you need 2 trips to get your gear across the portages, you'll be walking more than 6 miles. That's a rough way to start any trip.

There are numerous campsites on Gaskin Lake, but also plenty of competition for them. So try to claim your site as early in the day as possible, especially during peak season. Gaskin is known to harbor a few large walleyes, as well as smallmouth bass, northern pike and some lake trout. Eight miles of travel will put you near the center of the lake.

Day 2 (8 miles): Gaskin Lake, p. 102 rods, **Horseshoe Lake,** p. 20 rods, **Caribou Lake,** p. 73 rods, **Lizz Lake,** p. 51 rods, **Poplar Lake.** After your first portage, you'll find the going quite easy all the way back to Poplar Lake. That first trail surmounts a large hill separating Gaskin and Horseshoe lakes. Watch for some big, old pine and cedar trees on top of the hill near the middle of the portage. All the trails this day have good, well-maintained paths that receive a good deal of use.

ROUTE #48-2: The Frost River Route

7 Days, 55 Miles, 36 Lakes, 2 Rivers, 1 Creek, 45 Portages

DIFFICULTY: Challenging

FISHER MAPS: F-12, F-13

INTRODUCTION: This route has a dichotomy. It includes some of the easiest portages and most visited lakes in the east part of the BWCA Wilderness. But it also includes some of the most difficult portages and least visited parts of the Wilderness. After the long portage from Poplar to Meeds Lake, you will head west on a chain of long and slender lakes to Long Island Lake and then on to Frost Lake. From there you will paddle down the remote and wild Frost river system of pools, creeks and elongated lakes to Mora Lake—the western tip of this big loop. From that point, you'll steer a northeast course across Crooked and Tuscarora lakes to Snipe and Cross Bay lakes. A southbound course from there will return you to Long Island Lake. From the northeast corner of that long lake, you will then steer northeastward through a chain of lakes that sees the fewest visitors in this part of the BWCA Wilderness. From Banadad Lake, you'll continue paddling east across Rush and Skipper lakes and then portage out of the Wilderness and back to Poplar Lake.

This is a wonderful route for anyone who doesn't mind working hard to achieve a high-quality wilderness experience. Fine scenery and bountiful wildlife characterize much of this varied loop. On your third day, in particular, you will be in one of the most pristine and seldom-visited parts of the BWCA Wilderness: the Frost River. Likewise, your final 2 days will also be shared by few if any other humans. In these isolated regions moose demonstrate little or no fear of your intrusion.

Motors are not allowed on any part of the route, and much of the loop entertains relatively few visitors during all but the peak summer periods. Even then, only in the region from Crooked Lake to Long Island Lake are you likely to encounter many other people.

With an average of nearly 7 portages per day, including one day with 11 carries, some might argue that this route deserves a "most rugged" rating. Fortunately, most of the carries are short. Only 10 are longer than 100 rods (2 each measure a mile), and 23 are less than 50 rods long. Nevertheless, this route is recommended for only seasoned trippers who are in good physical condition. Others should seriously consider adding at least one extra day to their itineraries.

Day 1 (9 miles): Poplar Lake, p. 320 rods, **Meeds Lake,** p. 110 rods, **Swallow Lake,** p. 93 rods, **Pillsbery Lake,** p. 58 rods, **Hensen Lake,** p. 32 rods, **Omega Lake.** (See comments for Day 1, paragraphs 1 and 2, Route #48-1.) As soon as you leave Poplar Lake, this should be a fairly quiet day of paddling on a chain of lakes that entertains relatively few visitors. Campsites throughout this chain of long and slender lakes are often small, with only 1 good tent site at each. The best are found on Omega Lake, so it's worth making that lake your destination. If your group is large, head for a nice campsite with a western exposure on the south shore near the center of the lake.

Day 2 (10 miles): Omega Lake, p. 35 rods, **Kiskadinna Lake,** p. 185 rods, **Muskeg Lake,** p. 13 rods, **Muskeg Creek,** p. 20 rods, **Long Island Lake, Long Island River,** p. 5 rods, **river,** p. 28 rods, **Gordon Lake,** p. 140 rods, **Unload Lake, creek, Frost Lake.** (See comments for Day 2, Route #41-2.)

Day 3 (7 miles): Frost Lake, p. 130 rods, **Frost River, Octopus Lake,** p. 18 rods, **Frost River,** p. 25 rods, **river,** p. 5 rods, **river,** p. 30 rods, **Chase Lake,** p. 20 rods, **Pencil Lake,** p. 60 rods, **Frost River,** p. 10 rods, **river,** p. 5 rods, **river,** p. 12 rods, **river,** p. 20 rods, **river, Afton Lake.** (See comments for Day 3, Route #39-2.)

Day 4 (7 miles): Afton Lake, p. 20 rods, **Frost River, rapids, Fente Lake,** p. 15 rods, **Whipped Lake,** p. 100 rods, **Mora Lake,** p. 10 rods, **Tarry Lake,** p. 50 rods, **Crooked Lake,** p. 55 rods, **Owl Lake,** p. 63 rods, **Tuscarora Lake.** You are in for a challenge right away this day. The 20-rod trail that leads northwest from Afton Lake is *very steep*, both up and down. Use extreme caution! After that thriller, however, this day will probably seem easy compared to the previous day. Most of the portages have remarkably good paths, constructed back when labor-intensive work was not a problem. At both ends of most portages, you can still see remnants of old rock cribs and/or log frames that once held docks to ease the landings at these portages.

The rapids flowing into Fente Lake may require a lift-over, unless the water level is quite high. The long trail connecting Whipped and Mora lakes (100 rods) has an excellent path on a gentle slope over a low hill. Mora is a pretty lake, bordered by mixed forest with some exposed rock along the shore. At the north end of Tarry Lake, the smoothest place to take out is 3 rods east of a boulder field where many start the 50-rod portage to Crooked Lake.

Crooked is another lovely lake with several very nice campsites, which can accommodate larger groups with more tents than any of the sites on Mora Lake. The 55-rod trail to Owl Lake is uphill most of the way and quite rocky (large boulders) for about 10 rods where the path crosses a creek. The next portage (63 rods) is also uphill for all but the final 25 rods to Tuscarora Lake.

Tuscarora is a pretty lake, with numerous rock outcrops and low cliffs, surrounded by low hills. It has several nice campsites that are large enough to accommodate larger groups. Seven miles of travel should place you near the middle of this big lake.

Day 5 (9 miles): Tuscarora Lake, p. 255 rods, **Hubbub Lake,** p. 69 rods, **Copper Lake,** p. 100 rods, **Snipe Lake,** p. 47 rods, **Cross Bay Lake,** p. 56 rods, **Rib Lake,** p. 37 rods, **Lower George Lake,** p. 28 rods, **Karl Lake, Long Island Lake.** It won't take long to get your blood racing this day. The second longest portage to date (third longest of the whole route) crosses Howl Swamp en route to Hubbub Lake. Fortunately, there is a board walk across the swamp and the entire path is in good condition. After a short climb up from the shore of Tuscarora Lake, the trail soon levels off and continues quite level until the descent to Howl Swamp. The latter half of the trail is more undulating, but has no exhausting climbs. The boardwalk was in need of repairs in 1998. Watch your step!

The 69-rod trail to Copper Lake is uphill except for the final 15 rods. It was quite brushy and overgrown in June of 1998, but a portage crew was working the area. The next portage (100 rods) first skirts the edge of a large swamp, then climbs over a low hill en route to Snipe Lake.

Snipe is a very pretty little lake, with a rocky shoreline populated mostly by spruce trees. The portage from the east end of the lake drops rather steeply down to Cross Bay Lake. It's easy going from there on to Long Island Lake. The next 3 trails are generally uphill, though not steep, and the paths are in excellent condition. This is good moose country, so keep a watchful eye.

Portaging through low water in the Frost River

The center of Long Island Lake is about 9 miles from your campsite on Tuscarora Lake. If you need plenty of space for a larger group, you'll find a very nice campsite on the south shoreline with a western exposure. Two smaller sites share an island just north of the larger site.

Day 6 (6 miles): Long Island Lake, p. 109 rods, **Cave Lake,** p. 195 rods, **Ross Lake,** p. 180 rods, **Sebeka Lake,** p. 95 rods, **Banadad Lake.** The chain of lakes and portages leading from Long Island to Banadad Lake is the most rugged part of the journey. All portages are generally uphill, and they get progressively steeper as you approach Banadad Lake. They are not as well maintained as those to the south. Nor do they receive much traffic (except by moose). Windfalls may block the trails.

The first portage is the most level, but it has some rough footing. The 195-rod trail climbs gently most of the way to Ross Lake. It descends 3 times to cross low, wet and muddy areas, followed by steeper climbs. The 180-rod trail is the best of the lot, with a pretty good path through a more mature and scenic forest. But it crosses several slanted rock slopes that may be very slippery when wet. It also presents some fairly steep climbs, until the final descent to Sebeka Lake. The steepest path is on the last portage. Don't let the shorter length fool you. It is the roughest of the lot. It climbs steeply before descending to a wet and muddy area. Then it climbs even more steeply, followed by a steep descent to another bog. Finally, it climbs more gently to the west end of Banadad Lake.

Ross, Sebeka and Banadad lakes are much more scenic than the lakes to the south. Hills border these lakes, and there are rock outcrops and cliffs and a mixed forest habitat—a lovely contrast from the region to the south and west. There is a very nice, elevated island campsite with tall pines and birch trees near the west end of Banadad Lake. Stop there. You won't do any better farther down the lake.

Day 7 (7 miles): Banadad Lake, p. 10 rods, **Rush Lake,** p. 50 rods, **Little Rush Lake,** p. 21 rods, **Skipper Lake,** p. 320 rods, **Poplar Lake.** Once again, after leaving the west end of Banadad Lake, the terrain is lower and the forest more boreal, dominated by spruce trees. Much of this area was logged extensively from 1954 to 1972.

The 10-rod portage crosses the Banadad Ski Trail, and there is a wooden bridge across the creek for skiers. This and the next 2 portages are flat, but quite rocky with some wet spots. When the water level is high enough, the 21-rod portage can be avoided by paddling carefully through the shallow creek connecting Little Rush and Skipper lakes. If you must take the portage, look for it in the small bay about 10 rods north of the creek outlet.

The final portage of your expedition is just as long as the first. Unlike the rugged mile-long trail from Poplar to Meeds Lake, however, this one is predominately downhill, with only 1 short climb after the trail dips through a low, wet drainage. It also has an excellent path, much of it on a carpet of pine needles. After what you've been through on this trip, this is merely a pleasant walk in the woods.

Entry Point 49—Skipper Lake
& Portage Lake

SEASONAL PERMITS: 121

POPULARITY RANK: 38th

DAILY QUOTA: 2

LOCATION: Skipper Lake is located 23 airline miles northwest of Grand Marais and 1 *long* portage south of Poplar Lake. From Highway 61 in Grand Marais, follow the Gunflint Trail northwest for 32 miles, past Poplar Lake, to County Road 92 on the south (left) side of the road. Watch carefully for the USFS sign 1.8 miles past Windigo Lodge. Turn left there and follow the county road ½-mile west to its intersection with a 1-lane gravel road (left). Drive 1 mile south on this good, but narrow gravel road to the Poplar Lake boat landing.

DESCRIPTION: Near the end of the road, you'll see a spur road that leads right 0.2 mile to the boat landing. Parking is not permitted at the landing. Instead, proceed 0.1 mile past that corner to a large parking lot that accommodates 50-60 vehicles. A 15-rod path leads from the parking lot down to the west end of Poplar Lake, on wooden stairs part of the way.

There are 2 good campgrounds located close to Poplar Lake. The Iron Lake Campground is the closer, as well as the smaller, located about 4 miles west of the Poplar Lake boat landing via County Road 92. The 7 campsites are available by reservation and operated by a concessionaire, Way of the Wilderness Outfitters. The narrow county road is recommended for high-clearance vehicles but, if you drive slowly and carefully, any car should make it without difficulty. If that campground is filled up, another convenient place to spend the night before your canoe trip is at the Flour Lake Campground. Operated by Golden Eagle Lodge, the 35 campsites there may also be reserved in advance. It is located 2½ miles east of the Gunflint Trail on County Road 66 (see Entry Point 62). Reservations for either of the campgrounds may be

made by calling the National Recreation Reservation Service (see Chapter 2). A camping fee is charged at both campgrounds.

Skipper and Portage lakes afford access to the same chain of lakes lying just south of the Gunflint Trail, so they are grouped together for the purpose of quota restrictions. Few canoeists penetrate the region between Poplar and Long Island lakes, just south of Portage Lake. Consequently you're in for a high-quality wilderness experience, as you quickly—though not easily—enter into wilderness solitude and Northwoods isolation, regardless of whether you enter the BWCAW at Skipper Lake or Portage Lake. Entry at Skipper is a little easier, even though the portage is longer. Both routes described in this book enter the Wilderness through Skipper Lake. You could access both routes via Portage Lake, but an extra day should be added to your itinerary to make them complete loops. Otherwise, you'll have to shuttle vehicles from Iron Lake to Poplar Lake.

This is one of the most readily available entry points for the Boundary Waters. Only 40% of the overnight camping permits were issued to visitors during the summer of 1997. Only 6 other entry points in all of the BWCAW had a lower percentage of permits used. Also, very few day-use permits were issued. On busy weekends and holidays, when most other entry points are booked up, you may still be able to enter the Wilderness here.

In addition to Skipper Lake, the Meeds Lake and Lizz-Swamp entry points are also accessible from Poplar Lake. Lizz Lake is the most popular of the 4 lakes, as it offers the easiest entry into the Boundary Waters. Meeds Lake is the most challenging of these entry points, and Skipper Lake is a close second—both requiring a mile-long portage from Poplar Lake.

Poplar Lake lies entirely outside the BWCA Wilderness. There are numerous private cabins and several resorts along the northeast shore of the lake. But you won't see many en route to this entry point. The public landing is at the end of a quiet bay in the lake's northwest corner and the portage to Skipper Lake is not far away—only ½-mile down the south shore of the 3½-mile-long lake. Motorboats are permitted on Poplar Lake, of course, but they are not allowed to enter the Wilderness here.

ROUTE #49-1: The Cave Swallow Loop

3 Days, 26 Miles, 16·Lakes, 1 Creek, 17 Portages

DIFFICULTY: Most rugged

FISHER MAP: F-13

INTRODUCTION: This difficult route is recommended for the experienced tripper who values isolation and doesn't mind working hard to achieve it. After the mile-long portage from Poplar Lake, you'll paddle west on a chain of lightly traveled lakes leading to the east end of popular Long Island Lake. Then you'll plot an eastbound course on a chain of small, slender lakes leading to Meeds Lake. Another mile-long portage will transport you back to Poplar Lake.

En route, you will cross the Laurentian Divide twice. The western third of this loop lies north of the continental divide, where water flows ultimately into the Arctic Ocean. Water on the south side of the divide eventually flows into the Atlantic Ocean.

Most of your time will be spent on lakes and portages that receive very light use—particularly the westbound route from Poplar to Long Island Lake. While the southern part of the loop entertains more visitors, you shouldn't feel crowded anywhere along the route. Quiet paddlers have a good opportunity to view moose throughout the loop. Motorboats are permitted only on Poplar Lake, which lies entirely outside the Wilderness. The only sounds of civilization that you might hear on a still night are from trucks on the Gunflint Trail, which parallels the loop about 2 miles north of Skipper Lake.

Although this route is not popular among avid anglers, there are good populations of northern pike in most of the lakes. Walleyes may also be pulled from Skipper and Meeds lakes. There are lake trout in the depths of Long Island Lake, but you'll be crossing only the far-eastern corner of that lake.

Nevertheless, on this rugged loop, you may want to leave the fishing gear at home to keep your pack as light as possible on the exhausting portages. Five portages each exceed 160 rods (½-mile), including 2 that each measures a mile in length. This is not a good route for weak or inexperienced parties—unless you add an extra day or two to your itinerary and leave the kitchen sink at home. For seasoned trippers who travel lightly and want a challenge, however, here it is.

Day 1 (7 miles): Poplar Lake, p. 320 rods, **Skipper Lake,** p. 21 rods, **Little Rush Lake,** p. 50 rods, **Rush Lake,** p. 10 rods, **Banadad Lake.** Even with a mile-long portage, this will be the easiest day of your trip. If you're starting your journey on a crispy cool morning, it won't take long to warm up. That first long portage begins with a fairly steep climb and continues gradually uphill for much of the first 200 rods. It has an excellent path, much of it on a carpet of pine needles, but a trail of this length is a rugged start for any expedition.

All 3 of the short portages are flat, but quite rocky with some potentially wet spots. When the water is high enough, the 21-rod portage can be avoided by paddling carefully through the shallow creek connecting Skipper and Little Rush lakes. The 10-rod portage then crosses the Banadad Ski Trail, and there is a wooden bridge across the creek for skiers. It also crosses the Laurentian Divide.

You may see evidence of fairly recent logging activity along the shore of Rush Lake. Much of this region was logged extensively from 1954 to 1972. The terrain is fairly low and the forest has a boreal appearance. You probably won't see many (if any) other canoeists this day, but you could see a moose. This is an area with a high moose population, so keep a watchful eye.

There is a very nice, elevated campsite with tall pines and birch trees near the west end of Banadad Lake. That destination will put you about 7 miles from your origin. If that site is taken, retreat to one of the vacant sites you passed earlier. Do not forge on. There are no more USFS campsites until you reach Long Island Lake.

Day 2 (10 miles): Banadad Lake, p. 95 rods, **Sebeka Lake,** p. 180 rods, **Ross Lake,** p. 195 rods, **Cave Lake,** p. 109 rods, **Long Island Lake,** p. 20 rods, **Muskeg Creek,** p. 13 rods, **Muskeg Lake,** p. 185 rods, **Kiskadinna Lake,** p. 35 rods, **Omega Lake.** With over 2½ miles of portages, this day is mighty rough. If you need 2 trips to get your gear across, you'll be hiking nearly 8 miles. If that is the case, you may want to spread this part of the route over 2 full days.

Fortunately, the 4 portages between Banadad and Long Island lakes are mostly downhill. But 3 of them have rough paths and the fourth (180 rods) has a path with some sloping rocks that are quite slippery when wet. You'll pass through some wet and muddy marshy areas on the 95-rod and 195-rod trails. Windfalls could also block any of the trails, since this region does not see many visitors and trail maintenance is not a priority by USFS portage crews.

Unfortunately, your roughest portage is yet to come. (See comments for Day 4, paragraphs 1-3, Route #43-2.) At the east end of long, slender Kiskadinna Lake is another steep—but much shorter—climb over a small hill that separates Kiskadinna and Omega lakes. That short trek will put you back on the southeast side of the Laurentian Divide. Omega is a pretty little lake with some small rock cliffs along the shoreline and a couple of nice campsites that are large enough to accommodate larger groups. It is also a very good place to see moose.

Day 3 (9 miles): Omega Lake, p. 32 rods, **Hensen Lake,** p. 58 rods, **Pillsbery Lake,** p. 93 rods, **Swallow Lake,** p. 110 rods, **Meeds Lake,** p. 320 rods, **Poplar Lake.** Though not as rough as the previous day, this day is still far from easy. If you need 2 trips to get your gear across the portages, you'll be walking nearly 6 miles. The short portage leading to Hensen Lake is flat but rocky, and it could be wet. (Also see comments for Day 3, Route #47-1.)

ROUTE #49-2: The Banadad Duck Loop

7 Days, 65 Miles, 41 Lakes, 3 Rivers, 5 Creeks, 49 Portages

DIFFICULTY: Most Rugged

FISHER MAPS: F-5, F-12, F-13

INTRODUCTION: Like the previous loop, this difficult route is recommended for the seasoned tripper who is willing to work hard to achieve a high-quality wilderness experience. After the mile-long portage from Poplar Lake, you'll paddle west on a chain of lightly traveled lakes leading to Long Island Lake. After crossing the full length of that popular lake and up the Long Island River to Gordon Lake, you will then enter the wild and winding wilderness of the Frost River. From Fente Lake a long portage leads south to Hub Lake and the route continues southbound to Sawbill Lake. From the north end of that heavily traveled lake, you will then follow a chain of creeks and tiny lakes leading northeast to beautiful Cherokee and North Temperance lakes. After portaging to South Temperance Lake, you will head east and cross much of big Brule Lake en route to a chain of smaller lakes that will carry you north to Winchell and Omega lakes. Finally, you'll plot an eastbound course on a chain of small, slender lakes leading to Meeds Lake. Another mile-long portage will transport you back to Poplar Lake.

For those who seek canoe-country variety, derive satisfaction from hard work, and prefer to travel where few others dare to go, this rugged loop has got it all. Much of this interesting route will be through parts of the BWCAW that receive very light use—even during the busiest summer periods. Only in the vicinities of Long Island, Sawbill, Cherokee and Brule lakes are you likely to encounter wilderness "crowds."

Although you'll average "only" 7 portages per day, each day includes at least 1 long and exhausting carry. If you need 2 trips to get your gear across the 49 portages, you'll be walking over 39 miles during this week in the Wilderness—an average of over 5½ miles per day. In my book, that's a rugged canoe trip. If you're not ready for such a challenge, either spread this route over 8 or 9 days or consider a different route.

Big-game hunters (with a camera) will be delighted with the opportunities. Moose, in particular, are plentiful in much of this region. Anglers with energy to spare should also be delighted with the opportunities along this route. Most types of BWCAW game fish can be found at some point in the loop, including northern pike, walleyes, smallmouth bass and even brook trout.

Day 1 (7 miles): Poplar Lake, p. 320 rods, **Skipper Lake,** p. 21 rods, **Little Rush Lake,** p. 50 rods, **Rush Lake,** p. 10 rods, **Banadad Lake.** (See comments for Day 1, Route #49-1.)

Day 2 (9 miles): Banadad Lake, p. 95 rods, **Sebeka Lake,** p. 180 rods, **Ross Lake,** p. 195 rods, **Cave Lake,** p. 109 rods, **Long Island Lake, Long Island River,** p. 5 rods, **river,** p. 28 rods, **Gordon Lake,** p. 140 rods, **Unload Lake, creek, Frost Lake.** The 4 portages between Banadad and Long Island lakes are mostly downhill. But 3 of them have rough paths and the fourth (180 rods) has a path with some sloping rocks that are quite slippery when wet. You'll pass through some wet and muddy marshy areas on the 95-rod and 195-rod trails. Windfalls could also block any of the trails, since this region does not see many visitors and trail maintenance is not a priority by USFS portage crews.

There is a good chance that you'll see more people on Long Island Lake than on all of the other lakes so far. Enjoy the respite from long and frequent portages during the 3½-mile stretch across Long Island and Gordon lakes and the Long Island River.

The 140-rod trail leading west from Gordon Lake climbs over a fairly steep hill, but then levels off on a good, smooth path to Unload Lake. The shallow creek joining Unload and Frost lakes may be blocked by a beaver dam that requires a lift-over. Or you can bypass the creek on a 40-rod portage to Frost Lake. It is a rough path that is not often used. But it may be necessary during late summer or an unusually dry year, when the connecting creek is too shallow for a loaded canoe.

There are a couple of excellent campsites on the north shore of Frost Lake. Three other sites are also available. There are some fine sand beaches along the north shore of the lake, while some small cliffs adorn the south shore of this interesting lake. Watch for moose along the sandy shoreline at dawn and dusk.

Day 3 (9 miles): Frost Lake, p. 130 rods, **Frost River, Octopus Lake,** p. 18 rods, **Frost River,** p. 25 rods, **river,** p. 5 rods, **river,** p. 30

rods, **Chase Lake,** p. 20 rods, **Pencil Lake,** p. 60 rods, **Frost River,** p. 10 rods, **river,** p. 5 rods, **river,** p. 12 rods, **river,** p. 20 rods, **river, Afton Lake,** p. 20 rods, **Frost River, rapids, Fente Lake,** p. 300 rods, **Hub Lake.** (See comments for Day 3, Route #40-2.)

Day 4 (10 miles): **Hub Lake,** p. 105 rods, **Mesaba Lake,** p. 80 rods, **Hug Lake,** p. 3 rods, **Duck Lake,** p. 80 rods, **Zenith Lake,** p. 460 rods, **Lujenida Lake, Kelso River, Kelso Lake, Kelso River,** p. 13 rods, **Sawbill Lake.** (See comments for Day 4, paragraphs 1-3, Route #40-2.) Plan to camp in the north end of Sawbill Lake for a 10-mile day of travel. Sawbill is the third most popular entry point for the BWCAW and canoeing traffic is heavy throughout the lake. If you're running late, it might be wise to claim the first available campsite you see after the long portage from Zenith Lake.

Day 5 (9 miles): **Sawbill Lake,** p. 80 rods, **Ada Creek,** p. 80 rods, **Ada Lake, Skoop Creek,** p. 12 rods, **Skoop Lake,** p. 180 rods, **Cherokee Creek, Cherokee Lake,** p. 140 rods, **Sitka Lake,** p. 105 rods, **North Temperance Lake.** (See comments for Day 1, Route #38-1.) The 140-rod carry is the most exhausting portage of the day. It is a hilly trail that rises over 90 feet in elevation before dropping to the north shore of Sitka Lake. The next trail also has its ups and downs, as it crosses the Laurentian Divide.

North Temperance Lake is a scenic place to spend your night. Steep hills rising more than 200 feet above the water border the north end of the lake. Don't delay in claiming your campsite, as this part of the Wilderness entertains visitors from several popular entry points.

Day 6 (10 miles): **North Temperance Lake,** p. 55 rods, **South Temperance Lake, creek,** p. 10 rods, **Brule Lake,** p. 37 rods, **Lily Lake,** p. 32 rods, **Mulligan Lake,** p. 40 rods, **Grassy Creek,** p. 200 rods, **Wanihigan Lake,** p. 14 rods, **Winchell Lake.** The region lying east of South Temperance Lake was scarred by a large wildfire that burned 4,450 acres of timber in June of 1996. It was started by lightning and cost $1.5 million to fight. Unlike other "prescribed" natural fires that are allowed to burn in the Wilderness, the South Temperance Fire threatened areas lying outside the BWCAW and was, therefore, not allowed to burn freely. (Also see comments for Day 2, Route #39-1, and for Day 1, Route #41-1.)

Day 7 (11 miles): **Winchell Lake,** p. 44 rods, **Omega Lake,** p. 32 rods, **Hensen Lake,** p. 58 rods, **Pillsbery Lake,** p. 93 rods, **Swallow Lake,** p. 110 rods, **Meeds Lake,** p. 320 rods, **Poplar Lake.** The first portage has a level but rocky path between Winchell and Omega lakes. (Also see comments for Day 3, Route #49-1.)

Entry Point 50—Cross Bay Lake

SEASONAL PERMITS: 337

POPULARITY RANK: 24th

DAILY QUOTA: 3

LOCATION: Cross Bay Lake is 31 airline miles northwest of Grand Marais. From Highway 61 in Grand Marais, follow the Gunflint Trail 48 miles northwest to County Road 47, marked by a sign pointing left to Tuscarora Lodge. Turn left there and drive 0.7 mile south on this good gravel road to the Cross River boat landing on the left side of the road. Cross Bay Lake is 3 portages southeast of the access, via the Cross River and Ham Lake.

DESCRIPTION: A parking lot is located just past where the road skirts the bank of the Cross River. It is large enough to accommodate at least a dozen vehicles. From the north end of the lot, there is a 5-rod trail that leads down some steps to a fine boat dock on the river's edge.

There are no public campgrounds in the immediate vicinity of the boat landing. Trail's End Campground, at the end of the Gunflint Trail (9 miles to the north) is the closest USFS facility at which to camp the night before your trip. The Iron Lake Campground is more convenient, however, located just a mile off the Gunflint Trail from a point 10 miles closer to Grand Marais. The 32 campsites at Trail's End and the 7 campsites Iron Lake are all available by reservation and operated by a concessionaire, Way of the Wilderness Outfitters. Make your reservation by calling the National Recreation Reservation Service (see Chapter 2). Camping fees are charged at both campgrounds. More convenient than either campground is Tuscarora Lodge, located just ½-mile southwest of the boat landing via County Road 47. There you can find clean, dry bunkhouse accommodations, breakfast on the morning of your trip, a hot shower after the trip, and complete or partial outfitting, if needed.

Cross Bay Lake offers a lovely entry into the BWCA Wilderness for those who prefer small, narrow lakes and river-like settings. It affords rather easy access to 2 popular lakes—Long Island and Cherokee—as well as more challenging access to some seldom-visited regions that require long or frequent portages. Many of the visitors who enter the Wilderness here go no farther than Long Island Lake—an easy destination for anglers and families with small children.

It is a good idea to make a reservation for an overnight permit. Cross Bay Lake ranks high among entry points with quotas filled the greatest number of days each summer. In 1997, nearly ¾ of the available permits were issued. You can be sure that most weekends and holidays were booked up, as well as the peak season from late July through late August.

ROUTE #50-1:	The Snipe Tuscarora Loop
	2 Days, 12 Miles, 8 Lakes, 1 River, 9 Portages
DIFFICULTY:	Challenging
FISHER MAPS:	F-12
INTRODUCTION:	This good weekend loop actually has 3 phases of difficulty. From the boat landing, you'll paddle southeast up the Cross River to Ham Lake and then south to Cross Bay Lake (easier). From there you will turn to the west and negotiate the narrow lakes and frequent portages that lead to Tuscarora Lake (challenging). You will then portage more than a mile northeast to Missing Link Lake and another half-mile to Round Lake (most rugged). The route ends at the north end of Round Lake, about 1 mile by road from your origin.

This loop is a good choice for paddlers who want to enjoy a good taste of the Boundary Waters in just 2 short days—a river, several small lakes and 1 large lake, and portages ranging from short and easy to long and rugged. Much of the route receives moderate use by canoeists throughout the summer. You'll probably encounter the fewest other people between Snipe and Tuscarora lakes. Motorboats are permitted at the beginning and end of this loop, on Ham and Round lakes and on the Cross River, which lie completely outside the BWCAW. The entire route contained within the Wilderness, however, is reserved strictly for paddlers.

Although strong, experienced canoeists should have no trouble completing this route in 2 days, Northwoods neophytes might enjoy it even more by stretching it over 3 full days, with nights on Snipe and

Tuscarora lakes. That would also allow more time for the anglers in your group to search the depths of both lakes for the lake trout that reside there.

Day 1 (8 miles): Cross River, p. 68 rods, **river,** p. 40 rods, **Ham Lake,** p. 24 rods, **Cross Bay Lake,** p. 47 rods, **Snipe Lake,** p. 100 rods, **Copper Lake,** p. 69 rods, **Hubbub Lake,** p. 255 rods, **Tuscarora Lake.** Cedar and spruce trees characterize much of the forest along this route. It's truly a boreal forest, with few hardwoods to provide colorful contrast in autumn. The portages are well used and relatively easy at the beginning of this day, as you gain less than 50 feet elevation from the launching site to Cross Bay Lake.

Elongated Cross Bay Lake is essentially a continuation of the Cross River—long and narrow, with a marshy shoreline. Watch for moose throughout this region, which harbors a good population of these gangly critters. You may also encounter a beaver dam in the narrow channel leading toward Snipe Lake.

The 47-rod portage climbs rather steeply from the west bay of Cross Bay Lake, but it has a good path to Snipe Lake. The trail could be wet at the top, however. Snipe is a pretty little lake, with a rocky shoreline populated mostly by spruce trees and occasional jack pines. Should you wish to spend the night here, you'll find a nice campsite on a pine-covered rocky point facing the northwest end of the lake. The first site you'll see near the east end of the lake is also a good one, but the other 2 leave more to be desired.

The 100-rod portage first surmounts a small hill. After passing through a lovely stand of large spruce trees, the trail skirts the grassy edge of a large swamp that drains the northeast end of Copper Lake. The portage at the other end of the lake (69 rods) climbs abruptly during the first 15 rods but then descends the rest of the way to Hubbub Lake.

The 255-rod portage between Hubbub and Tuscarora lakes is not the challenge that it might appear on the map to be. Indeed, it has a few ups and downs at each end, but most of the trail is level to gently rolling and has a good path. About half way across, the trail passes right through the middle of Howl Swamp on a boardwalk that was in need of repairs in 1998. Watch your step!

Tuscarora is another pretty lake, with an abundance of exposed rock along the shoreline. There are some steep ledges as well as sloping outcrops. Eight miles of travel will place you near the center of the lake, where there are several good campsites.

Day 2 (4 miles): Tuscarora Lake, p. 366 rods, **Missing Link Lake,** p. 142 rods, **Round Lake.** Rest up on Tuscarora Lake. You will need all the energy you can muster up for the long portage to Missing Link

Lake. It is one of the roughest portages in the BWCA Wilderness—especially going this way. During the first half of the portage, the trail climbs steeply in 3 places, including a steep climb right at the beginning that gains over 100 feet of elevation during the first 80 rods. Whenever the trail descends, expect wet, muddy ground. Fortunately, there is a boardwalk across the east end of Wish "Lake" (actually more of a swamp than a lake). About ⅔ of the way across the portage, you'll skirt the north edge of Contest Lake and then gradually ascend about 70 feet over the ensuing 80 rods, before descending to the south end of Missing Link Lake. The path is narrow and rocky much of the way, but well beaten.

Fortunately, the final portage to Round Lake is downhill, descending nearly 100 feet from the northwest corner of Missing Link Lake. The rocky trail first skirts the edge of a beaver pond and then follows a creek all the way to Round Lake, crossing the creek about half way down. Expect some mud at the crossing.

If you need 2 trips to carry all of your gear across these 2 portages, you will spend most of this day walking, not paddling—nearly 5 miles in all and over 3 miles with gear. And, if you didn't leave a car at the Round Lake parking lot, you'll end this trip with one more walk—nearly 1 mile via Forest Route 1495 and County Road 47 back to your origin at the Cross River. But that walk is quite easy compared to the 2 portages you just endured.

ROUTE #50-2: The Cherokee Pan Loop

7 Days, 60 Miles, 35 Lakes, 5 Rivers, 5 Creeks, 48 Portages

DIFFICULTY: Challenging

FISHER MAPS: F-5, F-11, F-12

INTRODUCTION: This delightful loop will take you all the way to the south edge of the BWCA Wilderness and return you via some lovely streams and smaller lakes in the central part of the Boundary Waters. You will first follow the Cross River and a chain of small lakes southeast to Long Island Lake and then veer toward the southwest to cross beautiful Cherokee Lake en route to Sawbill Lake. From that popular lake, you'll steer west through Alton, Grace and Phoebe lakes to the Phoebe River, which will transport you onward to Lake Polly.

The Kawishiwi River system will then lead you north to Malberg Lake. From there a chain of small lakes leads northeast to Little Saganaga Lake, at which point you'll steer eastward to cross Mora and Crooked lakes en route to Tuscarora Lake. You will then portage more than a mile northeast to Missing Link Lake and another half-mile to Round Lake. The route ends at the north end of Round Lake, about 1 mile by road from your origin.

This is a wonderful route for seasoned trippers who prefer paddling most of the time on small lakes and streams and who can tolerate frequent portages, including a few rugged carries. Averaging nearly 7 portages per day, including several at more than ½-mile in length and 22 during a 2-day span, it is not a route for everyone. You must be willing to work hard to enjoy a high-quality wilderness experience.

Strong groups of experienced paddlers should have no difficulty completing this loop in just 7 days. A group of weak or inexperienced trippers, however, should consider adding a day or two to their itinerary, especially if 2 trips are needed to get all gear across the portages.

You may encounter moderately heavy canoe traffic on much of the route, including the southbound journey from the Cross River to Phoebe Lake. But you are certain to see fewer people on your northbound return, particularly along the scenic Phoebe River and north of

Scenic portage from Mora Lake to Little Saganaga Lake

Malberg Lake. Probably the most congested areas will be on Long Island, Cherokee and Little Saganaga lakes, from Sawbill Lake to Phoebe Lake and from Lake Polly to Malberg Lake. The only places where motorboats are permitted are the beginning and the end, on Ham and Round lakes and the Cross River.

Anglers will find walleyes and northern pike along much of this route. Lake trout are also known to inhabit several of the lakes. If the fish aren't biting, you won't starve in mid-summer, as blueberries grow abundantly along the midsection of the route. Throughout the loop, you'll also have good opportunities to view wildlife. The moose population, in particular, is abundant in this part of the BWCA Wilderness.

Day 1 (8 miles): Cross River, p. 68 rods, **river,** p. 40 rods, **Ham Lake,** p. 24 rods, **Cross Bay Lake,** p. 56 rods, **Rib Lake,** p. 37 rods, **Lower George Lake,** p. 28 rods, **Karl Lake, Long Island Lake.** You will surely look back at this as your easiest day of the trip. The portages are well worn, well maintained and not difficult, although you will be traveling generally uphill all day. Paddle quietly and watch for moose along the way. This is a good area in which to see them.

Plan to camp near the southwest corner of Long Island Lake for an 8-mile day of travel. If your arrival is late in the day during peak season, on the other hand, you should probably claim the first suitable site you see. This is a popular route, and during the peak periods of summer all 14 campsites on the lake could be occupied. So try to make camp early. If you don't mind one extra, short portage, you can save over a mile of paddling by portaging 35 rods directly from Karl Lake to the northwest bay of Long Island Lake, where you'll find a nice, large campsite on an island.

Day 2 (10 miles): Long Island Lake, Long Island River, p. 5 rods, **river,** p. 28 rods, **Gordon Lake,** p. 13 rods, **Cherokee Lake, Cherokee Creek,** p. 180 rods, **Skoop Lake,** p. 12 rods, **Skoop Creek, Ada Lake,** p. 80 rods, **Ada Creek,** p. 80 rods, **Sawbill Lake.** You'll be traveling through a lovely part of the BWCAW this day, including one of the prettiest and most popular lakes in this part of the Wilderness. Like travel on the previous day, travel is quite easy from Long Island Lake to Cherokee Lake.

Island-studded Cherokee Lake is nearly as popular as it is beautiful, and the route south from there receives a great deal of traffic from the Sawbill Lake entry point. Cherokee Creek is a dependable waterway, even during drought years and late in the summer. Moose are often seen along the banks of the creek at dawn and dusk but, unfortunately, mid-day is not the best time to see them. Nevertheless, paddle quietly, keep a watchful eye, and you just might be rewarded.

At the west end of the creek, you'll confront your biggest challenge of the day—a half-mile carry across the Laurentian Divide. Fortunately, you'll be hiking on a good path that receives a considerable amount of use.

When the water level is low during a year of drought, as it was in 1998, Skoop Creek may nearly dry up. When that happens, you may have to carry your canoe and gear all the way from Ada Lake to Skoop Lake, which adds about 100 rods to the designated 12-rod portage. The last 2 quarter-mile portages along Ada Creek are not difficult.

Plan to camp in the north end of Sawbill Lake, and try to claim your campsite as early as possible. Sawbill is the third most popular entry point for the BWCA Wilderness. A busy outfitter and a campground are located at the south end of the lake. So there is plenty of competition for the campsites on this lake.

Day 3 (10 miles): Sawbill Lake, p. 13 rods, **Kelso River, Kelso Lake,** p. 10 rods, **Alton Lake,** p. 140 rods, **Beth Lake,** p. 285 rods, **Grace Lake.** This is the "scenic route" from Sawbill to Alton Lake via the Kelso River. It also avoids the busiest part of Sawbill Lake, near the campground. If you prefer to save time, the most direct route is via a 30-rod portage from Sawbill to Alton Lake and requires about 1½ miles less paddling and one fewer portages.

Regardless of how you get there, the easiest part of this weeklong route ends at the southwest corner of Alton Lake. The 140-rod portage from Alton starts out easy enough, but eventually gains about 85 feet elevation as the trail surmounts the Laurentian Divide en route to Beth Lake. The long portage from Grace to Beth Lake, on the other hand, is not as bad as it looks on the map. It's not a difficult carry as you gradually descend on a well-worn path that drops about 70 feet elevation en route. (An alternate route through Ella Lake may appear on the map to be easier, with shorter carries of 80 and 130 rods. But it's not. The shorter path may be wet and muddy and the longer trail is quite rocky, with poor landings at both ends. Perhaps the only reason to visit Ella Lake is to escape from other visitors in this area.)

Plan to camp near the east end of Grace Lake for a 10-mile day of travel (via the Kelso River). Don't expect a night alone. The "lady lakes" attract nearly as many visitors from Sawbill Lake as do the lakes north of that popular entry point.

Day 4 (9 miles): Grace Lake, p. 15 rods, **Phoebe River,** p. 15 rods, **river,** p. 5 rods, **river,** p. 85 rods, **river, Phoebe Lake, Phoebe River, Knight Lake, Phoebe River,** p.140 rods, **Hazel Lake,** p. 59 rods, **Phoebe River,** p. 25 rods, **river,** p. 92 rods, **river,** p. 16 rods, **river,** p. 97 rods, **Lake Polly.** All 10 of the portage this day are basically downhill, as you drop a total of 192 feet from Grace to Lake Polly. The Phoebe River region is quite scenic, and a place where moose, beaver, mink and other types of wildlife abound. Besides the designated portages, you may also encounter a few beaver dams along the way that necessitate quick lift-overs.

You should encounter far fewer people between Phoebe Lake and Lake Polly than during the previous days of this route. On Lake Polly, however, you'll probably be joined by an influx of paddlers who entered the BWCAW at Kawishiwi Lake, the 10th most popular entry point. Do your best—again—to make camp early.

Hang your food pack well this evening. While camping on popular lakes, like Polly, it is not uncommon to encounter bears at campsites. Rather intelligent creatures, black bears learn to associate food with campers. And where campsites are plentiful, bears often "make the rounds" in search of food. If you keep a clean campsite and hang your food pack safely between trees at night and when you are away from the site during the day, however, the chances are slim that you will have any problems.

For a 9-mile day of travel, plan to camp at one of the sites in the northern part of Lake Polly. Anglers should find good walleye fishing nearby. At dusk, keep a watchful eye for moose along the shoreline. This is another good area in which to see them.

Day 5 (10 miles): Lake Polly, p. 19 rods, **Kawishiwi River,** p. 48 rods, **river,** p. 127 rods, **Koma Lake,** p. 24 rods, **Malberg Lake,** p. 48 rods, **Kawishiwi River,** p. 42 rods, **Kivaniva Lake, creek,** p. 18 rods, **Anit Lake,** p. 65 rods, **Pan Lake,** p. 50 rods, **Panhandle Lake,** p. 90 rods, **pond,** p. 60 rods, **Makwa Lake,** p. 55 rods, **Elton Lake.** With 12 portages lying in wait, you are in for another big day on the trail. Fortunately, most of the portages have very good, fairly level paths that were well constructed years ago when labor-intensive trail work was feasible. Nevertheless, the cumulative length of these trails is more than 2 miles. That means more than 6 miles of walking if you need 2 trips to get your gear across.

A small beaver dam is located in Kivaniva Lake, just after the first put-in at a scenic spot across from a steep rock ledge. You can easily lift over the dam. It's easier, however, to simply extend the portage another 8 rods (to 42 rods) and put in just past the beaver dam.

Low water levels can cause problems at some of the portage landings. The portage to Anit Lake can vary from 13 to 25 rods, depending on the water level in the creek draining Kivaniva Lake. A large beaver dam maintains the depth in Anit Lake. As long as it holds tight, the water level should not be a problem in that lake.

The unnamed "pond" showing on the map between Anit and Pan lakes is no longer a pond (in 1998). It dried to a grassy bog. What was once a 15-rod portage plus a 20-rod portage, separated by a small

Striped cliff on Makwa Lake

pond, is now a 65-rod portage. The beginning and end are on good, dry paths. In the middle, however, you will be skirting the west end of the bog on a soft, grassy path that may also be wet and muddy at times.

Elton is a pretty lake, with rock outcrops along its shores. There are a couple of nice campsites near the middle of the lake. Northern pike is the only game fish you'll find there. The lake is known to harbor some big ones.

Day 6 (9 miles): Elton Lake, p. 19 rods, **creek,** p. 19 rods, **Little Saganaga Lake,** p. 45 rods, **Mora Lake,** p. 10 rods, **Tarry Lake,** p. 50 rods, **Crooked Lake,** p. 55 rods, **Owl Lake,** p. 63 rods, **Tuscarora Lake.** On this day you will paddle on a chain of very pretty lakes, each bordered by mixed forest habitat with some exposed rock along the shoreline, and hike again on good, well-constructed portage trails. Little Saganaga, with its many islands and peninsulas, is a popular destination for many BWCAW visitors. There are 2 dozen campsites on the lake to accommodate them, so expect to see people there. As you depart from the southeast corner of the lake, you'll be walking on one of the most scenic portages in the BWCA Wilderness—a good 45-rod path that closely follows a small stream draining Mora Lake.

At the north end of Tarry Lake the smoothest place to take out is 3 rods east of a boulder field where many start the 50-rod portage. The 55-rod trail to Owl Lake is uphill most of the way and quite rocky (large boulders) for about 10 rods where the path crosses a creek. The next portage (63 rods) is also uphill for all but the final 25 rods to Tuscarora Lake.

Tuscarora is yet another pretty lake, with numerous rock outcrops and low cliffs, surrounded by low hills. It has several nice campsites that are large enough to accommodate larger groups. Nine miles of travel should place you near the middle of this big lake.

Day 7 (4 miles): Tuscarora Lake, p. 366 rods, **Missing Link Lake,** p. 142 rods, **Round Lake.** (See comments for Day 2, Route #50-1.)

Entry Point 51—Missing Link Lake

SEASONAL PERMITS: 429

POPULARITY RANK: 17th

DAILY QUOTA: 5

LOCATION: Missing Link Lake is accessible from Round Lake, which is 32 airline miles northwest of Grand Marais. From Highway 61 in Grand Marais, follow the Gunflint Trail 48 miles northwest to County Road 47, marked by a sign pointing left to Tuscarora Lodge. Turn left there and drive ¾ mile south on this good gravel road to Forest Route 1495. Turn right and follow this narrow gravel road another ¾ mile to its end. There you will find a parking lot large enough to accommodate 40-50 vehicles. Access to Round Lake is 5 rods downhill from the end of the parking lot.

DESCRIPTION: There are no public campgrounds in the immediate vicinity of the boat landing. Trail's End Campground, at the end of the Gunflint Trail (9 miles to the north) is the closest USFS facility at which to camp the night before your trip. The Iron Lake Campground is more convenient, however, located just a mile off the Gunflint Trail from a point 10 miles closer to Grand Marais. The 32 campsites at Trail's End and the 7 campsites at Iron Lake are all available by reservation and operated by a concessionaire, Way of the Wilderness Outfitters. Make your reservation by calling the National Recreation Reservation Service (see Chapter 2). Camping fees are charged at both campgrounds. More convenient than either campground is Tuscarora Lodge, located at the east end of Round Lake, just a mile by road from the public landing (¼-mile southwest of the junction of County Road 47 and F.R. 1495). There you can find clean, dry bunkhouse accommodations, breakfast on the morning of your trip, a hot shower after the trip, and complete or partial outfitting, if needed.

Don't worry if you see a nearly full parking lot. It serves the visitors to both Missing Link and Brant lakes, as well as anglers who go no farther than Round Lake itself. The canoe traffic is fairly evenly split between the 2 entry points. Although the 2 entry points do channel traffic initially in different directions, much of that canoe traffic converges on Gillis Lake and/or Little Saganaga Lake. So, when one of those lakes is your destination, make camp early or you may not find a vacant campsite.

Missing Link and Brant lakes provide BWCAW access to nearly the same number of visitors each year. Because the quota is one permit larger for Missing Link Lake, there are more permits available there. Only 56% of the available permits were actually issued to visitors in 1997, while 69% of the Brant Lake permits were issued. It's easier to get a permit for Missing Link Lake. Motorboats are not permitted through either entry point, but they are allowed on Round Lake, which lies entirely outside the BWCA Wilderness.

Missing Link Lake provides access to a lovely part of the Boundary Waters for canoeists with strength and stamina. This is one of the most physically challenging entry points in the entire Wilderness. Regardless of the route you take, Day 1 will always be *rugged*. With 508 rods of portaging in less than a 2-mile span from Round Lake to Tuscarora Lake, there is no other word to describe it than *tough*. The beauty of Tuscarora Lake, however, should make the work seem worthwhile. And farther to the west of that large lake is some of the prettiest scenery in all of the Boundary Waters.

Either of the routes suggested below may be reversed by entering the BWCAW through Brant Lake or Cross Bay Lake. For additional route suggestions, see both of those entry points.

ROUTE #51-1: **The Crooked Bat Loop**

2 Days, 13 Miles, 13 Lakes, 13 Portages

DIFFICULTY: Most Rugged

FISHER MAP: F-12

INTRODUCTION: This weekend outing will take you across several pretty lakes and a few long, steep portages. From Round Lake you will portage southwest to Missing Link and Tuscarora lakes. With the roughest part of the route behind you, you will continue westbound through Owl Lake to Crooked Lake and then portage north to Gillis Lake. From the northeast corner of Gillis you will paddle through a chain of pretty little lakes leading east to your origin at Round Lake.

Avid anglers may want to schedule 3 days for this loop and go no farther than Tuscarora Lake on the first day. That's only 4 miles, but it may feel like 40 miles after those first 2 portages. In spite of the rough start, most groups of experienced trippers should have no difficulty completing this route in 2 days.

The entire loop receives moderately heavy use throughout much of the summer. Don't expect total escape from other people anywhere along this route. Motorboats are allowed only on the last 3 lakes of the route, which are outside the BWCAW.

Day 1 (6 miles): Round Lake, p. 142 rods, **Missing Link Lake,** p. 366 rods, **Tuscarora Lake,** p. 63 rods, **Owl Lake,** p. 55 rods, **Crooked Lake.** This is one of the roughest starts to any canoe trip in the BWCA Wilderness. If you need 2 trips to get your gear across the portages, you'll be walking more than 6½ miles this day, including 4½ miles with gear. Right away you'll confront an uphill portage from Round Lake. It has a rocky path that gains nearly 100 feet in elevation. The trail follows a creek that drains Missing Link Lake and skirts the edge of a beaver pond near the top. Expect some mud where the trail crosses the creek about half way across the portage.

The long trail to Tuscarora Lake has another rocky, narrow path but, fortunately, you'll be hiking mostly downhill. After a short climb at the beginning, the trail descends a total of 160 feet en route to Tuscarora Lake. You'll pass over low hills with gradual slopes or fairly level terrain for the first half-mile. Then you'll encounter the steepest part of the trail, first down and then back up. About ⅓ of the way across the portage, you'll skirt the north edge of Contest Lake. Near the end (just before the steep descent to Tuscarora Lake) you'll cross the east end of Wish "Lake" (actually more of a swamp than a lake) on a boardwalk. Expect wet, muddy ground in the low areas before each climb. Over the final 100 rods you will descend steeply to a nice sandy beach at the shore of Tuscarora Lake.

Tuscarora is a pretty lake, with lots of exposed rock on the shoreline. There are some steep ledges, as well as sloping outcrops. While resting after the long portage, anglers may want to troll slowly for one of the luscious lake trout inhabiting the depths of that scenic lake. The deepest hole (130 feet down) is in the west end of the lake, not far from the Owl Lake portage.

Gillis Lake

The final 2 portages leading to and from Owl Lake are mostly downhill and much easier than the first two. Near the end of the final trail (55 rods) the path is littered with large boulders for about 10 rods where it crosses a small creek. The footing is tricky, so use caution, especially when the rocks are wet.

Crooked is another lovely lake with several nice campsites, some of which can accommodate larger groups with several tents. Two of the best are near the south end of the lake. With time and patience, anglers will find lake trout in the deep, clear water nearby.

Day 2 (7 miles): Crooked Lake, p. 82 rods, **Gillis Lake,** p. 25 rods, **Bat Lake,** p. 20 rods, **Green Lake,** p. 70 rods, **Flying Lake,** p. 10 rods, **Gotter Lake,** p. 100 rods, **Brant Lake,** p. 35 rods, **Edith Lake,** p. 50 rods, **West Round Lake,** p. 85 rods, **Round Lake.** The portage from Crooked Lake has a rocky path and may be wet and muddy in a few places. Ten rods from the beginning of the trail, you will see the dilapidated remains of an old log cabin that was once used by a trapper. There is still an old dock (in disrepair, but usable) at the landing. After passing the old cabin, the trail skirts the edge of a pond for 23 rods. Those who prefer 2 short carries to a longer one can paddle across the pond and have carries of 13 rods and 46 rods at either end. It is probably quicker to simply portage the entire 82 rods, but the middle stretch that skirts close to the pond may be quite wet when the water level is high.

Gillis is another very nice, clear lake with many scenic rock out-croppings along the shoreline. There are several excellent campsites, all on rocky ledges or sloping rock outcroppings. This is a good alternate destination if the campsites on Crooked Lake are filled up, or if you find yourself ahead of schedule.

The portages between Gillis and Brant lakes are well worn and not very long—but they are *not easy*, with some steep climbs along the way. The 25-rod portage starts in a cedar grove and climbs abruptly to more than 50 feet above Gillis Lake. The 70-rod trail surmounts a 100-foot hill that separates Green and Flying lakes. Before loading up with gear, make certain that you are on the correct portage—not on an old 75-rod trail to Crag Lake, which starts nearby to the southeast. The next short portage starts on a wooden stairway with 28 steps to assist you with the steep ascent. Just beyond the top of the stairs, you can drop down to the far-western end of Gotter Lake when the water level is high enough in that shallow bay to float your canoe. If not, a good path continues for a total of 50 rods to a better landing along the north shore of the lake. The 100-rod portage climbs over a big hill, with short, steep segments up and down.

The last 3 portages are virtually flat, but the paths are littered with rocks and roots. The final trail also has muddy spots, but there is a 4-rod boardwalk over the wettest spot near West Round Lake.

ROUTE #51-2: **The Louse River Knight Loop**

7 Days, 64 Miles, 38 Lakes, 1 Pond, 6 Rivers, 3 Creeks, 57 Portages

DIFFICULTY: Most Rugged

FISHER MAPS: F-5, F-11, F-12

INTRODUCTION: This fascinating loop will take you through some of the most attractive scenery in the central part of the BWCA Wilderness. From Round Lake you will portage southwest to Missing Link and Tuscarora lakes. With perhaps the roughest part of the route behind you, you will continue west-bound through Owl Lake to Crooked Lake and then steer south through Mora and Hub lakes to Mesaba Lake. The Louse River will carry you through the most isolated part of the loop, west to Malberg Lake. Then the Kawishiwi and Phoebe rivers will be your paths southeast to the "Lady

Lakes" and on to Alton Lake. From busy Sawbill Lake you will begin a northeast journey through beautiful Cherokee and Gordon lakes to Long Island Lake, at which point you'll veer northwest to exit the BWCAW at Cross Bay Lake. Your expedition will end at the Cross River landing, about a mile by road from your origin.

This is a wonderful route for seasoned trippers who prefer paddling on smaller lakes and streams, who want to escape from most other travelers, and who don't mind working hard to achieve a high-quality wilderness experience. Averaging more than 8 portages per day, including 2 that exceed a mile in length, it's not a suitable route for everyone. A few days are downright rugged (one with 14 portages). Groups of weaker or less experienced paddlers would surely be happier spreading the route over at least 8 full days. Fortunately, more than half of the carries measure less than 50 rods.

Although you will enjoy stretches of this route where few other people venture, you will probably share some of the lakes with many other travelers, at least during the peak of the canoeing season. Along the route, you'll spend 1 night on a lake served by the 10th busiest entry point (Kawishiwi Lake) and another night close to the 3rd most popular entry point in the Boundary Waters (Sawbill Lake). You'll also camp on one of the most popular lakes in the BWCAW (Cherokee Lake). There are numerous campsites in the popular areas, but there is also plenty of competition for them. Start your days early and try to find your campsites as early in the afternoons as possible. You'll find the most seclusion while paddling on the Louse and Phoebe rivers. Motorboats are prohibited from the entire loop, except for the parts that lie outside the Wilderness at the start and end of the route.

Anglers should have plenty of opportunities to wet their lines. Northern pike and walleyes are found in many of the lakes along this route. Lake trout inhabit Little Saganaga, Alton, Cherokee and Long Island lakes. Smallmouth bass and bluegills may also be found in some of the water along the way.

At dawn and dusk, watch for moose—almost anywhere along this route. They are most often seen in the areas south of Malberg Lake and north of Cherokee Lake. Beaver, mink and other types of Northwoods fauna are also common along parts of the route.

Note: This route is most favorable during spring or early summer, when water levels are normally the highest. During late summer or dry years, you may find the shallow streams to be a drag in places—literally. Consult with a USFS ranger in the Tofte District before heading out. Ask specifically about the Louse River.

Day 1 (6 miles): Round Lake, p. 142 rods, **Missing Link Lake,** p. 366 rods, **Tuscarora Lake,** p. 63 rods, **Owl Lake,** p. 55 rods, **Crooked Lake.** (See comments for Day 1, Route #51-1.)

Day 2 (9 miles): Crooked Lake, p. 50 rods, **Tarry Lake,** p. 10 rods, **Mora Lake,** p. 100 rods, **Whipped Lake,** p. 15 rods, **Fente Lake,** p. 300 rods, **Hub Lake,** p. 105 rods, **Mesaba Lake,** p. 20 rods, **Chaser Lake,** p. 7 rods, **pond,** p. 130 rods, **Dent Lake.** This day starts and ends with fairly easy portages, but you'll have a serious challenge in the middle of the day. Near the end of the first portage, bear left on a trail that passes to the east of a field of boulders to end at a smoother landing. From then onward, you will surely see few, if any, canoeists as you penetrate a more remote area where few others venture. You'll soon see why, when you confront the longest and most exhausting carry of the day. The 300-rod trail gains nearly 130 feet in elevation during the first 80 rods. Fortunately, the rest of the trail is fairly level and has a decent path.

After a fairly level trek from Hub to Mesaba Lake, you'll encounter a rather steep climb on the short portage from Chaser Lake to the small pond just west of Chaser Lake. The first half of the final carry of the day is over a hill, but the path then levels off en route to the narrow east end of Dent Lake.

There are just 2 campsites on Dent Lake. If you know (or suspect) that 2 groups are a short distance in front of you, you'd be wise to stop on Mesaba Lake and make camp early. Then, if blueberries are ripe, take time to explore the east shore of Mesaba Lake where the berries grow in abundance. There are no other campsites after Dent Lake until you reach Trail Lake, 4 portages away.

Day 3 (8 miles): Dent Lake, p. 45 rods, **Bug Lake,** p. 115 rods, **Louse River,** p. 50 rods, **river,** p. 130 rods, **Trail Lake,** p. 21 rods, **Louse River,** p. 56 rods, **river,** p. 41 rods, **river,** p. 20 rods, **river,** p. 100 rods, **river,** p. 60 rods, **Boze Lake,** p. 11 rods, **Louse River,** p. 21 rods, **river, Frond Lake, Louse River,** p. 15 rods, **Malberg Lake,** p. 24 rods, **Koma Lake.** (See comments for Day 5, Route #37-2.)

Day 4 (10 miles): Koma Lake, p. 127 rods, **Kawishiwi River,** p. 48 rods, **river,** p. 19 rods, **Lake Polly,** p. 97 rods, **Phoebe River,** p. 16 rods, **river,** p. 92 rods, **river,** p. 25 rods, **river,** p. 59 rods, **Hazel Lake,** p. 140 rods, **Phoebe River, Knight Lake, Phoebe River, Phoebe Lake.** All 9 of the portages this day are basically uphill, as you first head up the Kawishiwi River to Lake Polly and then navigate upstream on the Phoebe River. You'll gain 175 feet of elevation throughout the day. After what you've already experienced, however, none of the portages should seem too challenging. Once you "turn the corner" at Lake Polly, you should leave the "Kawishiwi crowd" behind. (Also see comments for Day 2, Route #37-1.)

Day 5 (9 miles): Phoebe Lake, Phoebe River, p. 85 rods, **river,** p. 5 rods, **river,** p. 15 rods, **river,** p. 15 rods, **Grace Lake,** p. 285 rods, **Beth Lake,** p. 140 rods, **Alton Lake.** (See comments for Day 3, Route #37-1.) For a 9-mile day of travel, plan to camp at the north end of Alton Lake, and expect company. Sawbill Lake, the BWCAW's 3rd busiest entry point, is just a short portage away. Find your campsite early in the afternoon. Then try your luck at catching some of the lake trout, walleyes, smallmouth bass or northern pike that lurk beneath the surface of this deep, clear lake.

Day 6 (10 miles): Alton Lake, p. 10 rods, **Kelso Lake, Kelso River,** p. 13 rods, **Sawbill Lake,** p. 80 rods, **Ada Creek,** p. 80 rods, **Ada Lake, Skoop Creek,** p. 12 rods, **Skoop Lake,** p. 180 rods, **Cherokee Creek, Cherokee Lake.** This is the more scenic and quieter, albeit longer, route from Alton Lake to Sawbill Lake. You can also portage directly from Alton to Sawbill Lake, but that will take you to the busy south end of Sawbill Lake, which lies outside the BWCA Wilderness, near the Sawbill Campground and public landing. I prefer the Kelso River route. (Also see comments for Day 1, Route #38-1.) For a 10-mile day of travel, plan to camp near the center of beautiful Cherokee Lake.

Day 7 (12 miles): Cherokee Lake, p. 13 rods, **Gordon Lake,** p. 28 rods, **Long Island River,** p. 5 rods, **river, Long Island Lake, Karl Lake,** p. 28 rods, **Lower George Lake,** p. 37 rods, **Rib Lake,** p. 56 rods, **Cross Bay Lake,** p. 24 rods, **Ham Lake,** p. 40 rods, **Cross River,** p. 68 rods, **river.** This is the longest, yet perhaps the easiest, day of your trip, as you descend 128 feet from Cherokee Lake to the Cross River landing on County Road 47. All of the portages are well worn, well maintained and, for the most part, downhill.

Like Cherokee, Long Island is also a very popular lake that attracts visitors from several directions. You are bound to see numerous other people throughout the day as you progress toward the Cross Bay Lake entry point. In spite of the canoeing traffic, however, this is good moose country. So keep a watchful eye along the way.

Entry Point 52—Brant Lake

SEASONAL PERMITS: 420

POPULARITY RANK: 19th

DAILY QUOTA: 4

LOCATION: Brant Lake is accessible from Round Lake, which is 32 airline miles northwest of Grand Marais. From Highway 61 in Grand Marais, follow the Gunflint Trail 48 miles northwest to County Road 47, marked by a sign pointing left to Tuscarora Lodge. Turn left there and drive ¾ mile south on this good gravel road to Forest Route 1495. Turn right and follow this narrow gravel road another ¾ mile to its end. There you will find a parking lot large enough to accommodate 40-50 vehicles. Access to Round Lake is 5 rods downhill from the end of the parking lot.

DESCRIPTION: There are no public campgrounds in the immediate vicinity of the boat landing. Trail's End Campground, at the end of the Gunflint Trail (9 miles to the north) is the closest USFS facility at which to camp the night before your trip. The Iron Lake Campground is more convenient, however, located just a mile off the Gunflint Trail from a point 10 miles closer to Grand Marais. The 32 campsites at Trail's End and the 7 campsites at Iron Lake are all available by reservation and operated by a concessionaire, Way of the Wilderness Outfitters. Make your reservation by calling the National Recreation Reservation Service (see Chapter 2). Camping fees are charged at both campgrounds. More convenient than either campground is Tuscarora Lodge, located at the east end of Round Lake, just a mile by road from the public landing (¼-mile southwest of the junction of County Road 47 and F.R. 1495). There you can find clean, dry bunkhouse accommodations, breakfast on the morning of your trip, a hot shower after the trip, and complete or partial outfitting, if needed.

Don't worry if you see a nearly full parking lot. It serves the visitors to both Missing Link and Brant lakes, as well as anglers who go no farther than Round Lake itself. The canoe traffic is fairly evenly split between the 2 entry points. Although the 2 entry points do channel traffic initially in different directions, however, much of that canoe traffic converges on Gillis Lake or Little Saganaga Lake. So, when one of those lakes is your destination, try to make camp early or you may not find a vacant campsite.

Brant Lake and Missing Link Lake entry points provide BWCAW access to nearly the same number of visitors each year, though the quota is 1 permit fewer for Brant Lake. 69% of the available Brant Lake permits were actually issued to visitors in 1997, while only 57% of the Missing Link Lake permits were issued. It's harder to get a permit for Brant Lake, so make your reservation early, especially if your trip will start on a weekend or during the peak summer period. Motorboats are not permitted through either entry point, but they are allowed on Round Lake, which lies entirely outside the BWCA Wilderness.

Brant Lake provides access to essentially the same lovely part of the BWCA Wilderness as Missing Link. But this is a much easier way to get there. Nevertheless, routes entering the Boundary Waters at Brant Lake are generally not easy. Any way you go, you'll encounter some challenging portages—just not as long and rugged as those at both ends of Missing Link Lake.

If this entry point is booked on the preferred day for your trip, either of the routes suggested below may be reversed by entering the BWCAW through Missing Link Lake. For additional route suggestions, see entry points 50 and 51.

ROUTE #52-1: **The Flying Seahorse Loop**

3 Days, 16 Miles, 17 Lakes, 1 River, 2 Creeks, 18 Portages

DIFFICULTY: Most Rugged

FISHER MAP: F-12

INTRODUCTION: This interesting little route will take you off the beaten path to an area visited perhaps more by hikers than by paddlers. From Round Lake you will first paddle west through Brant to Flying

Lake and then north to Bingshick Lake. From there you will again follow a westbound course, paralleling the famed Kekekabic Trail through a chain of small, shallow, peacefully secluded lakes to Seahorse Lake. After portaging south to French Lake, you will continue paddling southwest through Gillis Lake to Crooked Lake. On your third day, then, you will return to Round Lake via Tuscarora Lake and 2 of the roughest portages of the entire route.

After veering north from Flying Lake, you should have the first day mostly to yourself. While a good deal of canoe traffic from Round Lake is channeled through Gillis and Crooked lakes, very little of it wanders north into the quiet waters between Flying and French lakes. That is where you'll find the most seclusion and tranquility. The rest of the route is lovely, even if it's not only yours to enjoy. Motorboats are permitted only on the first 3 lakes, which lie entirely outside the Wilderness. The entire route contained in the BWCAW is strictly for paddlers.

Strong and experienced trippers would have no trouble completing this loop in just 2 days with a night on French Lake, but that would be an extremely rugged expedition for most paddlers, who will find enough challenge in 3 days of travel. For Northwoods neophytes, weaker groups and avid anglers, this route might be more enjoyable if spread over 4 days, with nights spent at Bingshick, French and Tuscarora lakes—about 4 miles of travel and 3 to 7 portages per day.

Anglers will have opportunities to catch a variety of Northwoods game fish. Northern pike inhabit most of the lakes along the route and lake trout are found in several of them. Brook trout may also be found in Bingshick Lake.

Day 1 (4 miles): Round Lake, p. 85 rods, **West Round Lake,** p. 50 rods, **Edith Lake,** p. 35 rods, **Brant Lake,** p. 100 rods, **Gotter Lake,** p. 10 rods, **Flying Lake, Flying Creek, Bingshick Creek,** p. 15 rods, **creek,** p. 13 rods, **Bingshick Lake.** The first part of this day could be shared with several other groups and there could even be congestion at the portages between Round and Flying lakes. Brant, Gotter and Flying lakes are pretty little lakes, with rock cliffs along the shores and mixed forest vegetation surrounding the water.

The first 3 portages are virtually flat, but the paths are littered with rocks and roots. The first portage also has muddy spots, but there is a 4-rod boardwalk over the wettest part of the trail near West Round Lake, where the trail skirts a swampy area—a good place to watch for moose browsing. The first real test of strength and endurance is at the

100-rod portage. It climbs over a steep hill separating Brant and Gotter lakes. It's a rocky and rooty trail that drops most steeply at the west end.

Gotter Lake is unique—little more than a shallow pond in which there are many standing dead trees. When the lake is too shallow or obstructed by logs to paddle into the southwest end, where the 10-rod portage begins, you must use a 50-rod trail. It follows a low ridge bordering the north shore of the lake. The 10-rod portage joins the end of the 50-rod trail and drops steeply to Flying Lake. A wooden stairway with 28 steps will assist you with the steep descent.

Elevating food pack at Bingshick Lake

After completing the 15-rod portage on Flying Creek, bear right when the creek joins Bingshick Creek. The start of the 13-rod trail to Bingshick Lake is but a few rods to the northeast.

The 2 campsites along the north shore of Bingshick Lake are accessible to backpackers using the Kekekabic Trail, and the sites are situated more for the convenience of hikers than canoe campers. In addition to the designated USFS campsites, you may see several other sites along the north shore where hikers have settled down for the night. There isn't a lot of competition for the sites, however. Only 37 overnight permits were issued in 1997 to backpackers using the Kekekabic Trail—East entry point. You're more likely to see day-hikers passing by. For the anglers in your group, Bingshick is known to harbor some nice brook trout.

Day 2 (6 miles): Bingshick Lake, p. 53 rods, **Glee Lake,** p. 27 rods, **Fay Lake,** p. 45 rods, **Chub River, Warclub Lake,** p. 13 rods, **Chub River, Seahorse Lake,** p. 13 rods, **French Lake,** p. 25 rods, **Gillis Lake,** p. 82 rods, **Crooked Lake.** This is likely to be a quiet day shared by few, if any, other people until you reach Gillis Lake. You will cross the Kekekabic Trail at each of the first 4 portages. Watch carefully to make certain that you don't wander off on the hiking trail. The portage trails are lightly traveled, not well worn and not marked, but common sense should guide you appropriately.

The 45-rod portage from Fay Lake can be broken into 2 portages of 15 rods each when the water level is sufficiently high on the Chub River. But the 45-rod trail is certainly not difficult in one piece. After 20 rods, the portage joins the Kekekabic Trail and they share the same path to the end of the portage. The Kekekabic Trail crosses the 13-rod portage on a beaver dam at the beginning of the portage.

Warclub and Seahorse lakes and the Chub River are very shallow. In late summer or during a dry year, paddling a heavily loaded canoe there could be difficult. Watch for pitcher plants along the boggy south shore of Seahorse Lake. The 13-rod portage from Seahorse is downhill all the way to French Lake. The trail skirts close to scenic rapids and a small waterfall draining Seahorse Lake.

The last and longest portage of the day (82 rods) has a rocky path and may be wet and muddy in places. After 46 rods, the trail skirts the edge of a pond for 23 rods. For those who prefer 2 short carries to a longer one, you can paddle across the pond and have carries of 46 rods and 13 rods at either end. It is probably quicker to simply portage the entire 82 rods, but the middle stretch that skirts close to the pond may be quite wet when the water level is high. Ten rods from the end of the trail, you will see the dilapidated remains of an old log cabin that was once used by a trapper. There is still an old dock (in disrepair, but usable) at the landing on Crooked Lake.

French, Gillis and Crooked are pretty lakes, with a variety of exposed rocks along their shorelines—including a dramatic cliff at the east end of French Lake and numerous scenic outcroppings on Gillis and Crooked lakes. There are several excellent campsites in this area, including a couple at the south end of Crooked Lake that can accommodate larger groups with more tents.

Day 3 (6 miles): Crooked Lake, p. 55 rods, Owl Lake, p. 63 rods, Tuscarora Lake, p. 366 rods, Missing Link Lake, p. 142 rods, Round Lake. The final day of this loop is, by far, the most rugged. If you need 2 trips to get your gear across the portages, you'll be hiking nearly 6 miles, including nearly 4 miles with gear. The 55-rod trail to Owl Lake is uphill most of the way and quite rocky (large boulders) for about 10 rods where the path crosses a creek. The next portage (63 rods) is also uphill for all but the final 25 rods to Tuscarora Lake.

Tuscarora is yet another pretty lake, with numerous rock outcrops and low cliffs, surrounded by low hills. (Also see comments for Day 2, paragraphs 1 and 2, Route #50-1.)

ROUTE #52-2: The Kekekabic Beaver Loop

7 Days, 57 Miles, 45 Lakes, 2 Rivers, 3 Creeks, 6 Ponds, 54 Portages

DIFFICULTY: Challenging

FISHER MAPS: F-11, F-12

INTRODUCTION: This route has a dichotomy. It includes some of the easiest portages and most visited lakes in the east-central part of the BWCA Wilderness. But it also includes some of the most difficult portages and the least visited parts of the Wilderness. From Round Lake you will first paddle west through Brant, Flying, Fay and Peter lakes to Gabimichigami Lake. Then you'll veer northwest to Ogishkemuncie Lake, stopping along the way to view lovely Mueller Falls. A chain of small lakes and scenic ponds will carry you even farther west to Kekekabic Lake. From the south end of that beautiful, big lake, the route zigzags southward through a pleasant variety of lakes and creeks that penetrate the most remote interior part of the BWCA Wilderness. Then, from the northeast corner of the Kawishiwi River system, you'll follow a chain of small lakes and good portage trails that lead northeast to Little Saganaga Lake. After crossing one of the most scenic portages in the Boundary Waters, you'll proceed from Mora Lake north to Tuscarora Lake. Finally you'll hike across the roughest portage of the entire route to exit the Boundary Waters from Missing Link Lake and return to your origin on Round Lake.

This route is an excellent choice for experienced trippers who seek canoeing variety, outstanding scenery, and pockets of solitude that lie deep within the Wilderness—but only if you are up to the challenge of frequent portages, including one that exceeds a mile in length. Averaging nearly 8 portages per day, the trip has 2 days with 10 carries each. While strong canoeists should have no problem completing the loop in a week, those with less strength or experience should stretch the route over 8 or 9 days.

Anglers will have opportunities to catch most types of game fish found in the Boundary Waters. Northern pike and lake trout are found in many of the lakes along this route. Walleyes and bluegills also occupy some of the water.

Day 1 (7 miles): Round Lake, p. 85 rods, **West Round Lake,** p. 50 rods, **Edith Lake,** p. 35 rods, **Brant Lake,** p. 100 rods, **Gotter Lake,** p. 10 rods, **Flying Lake,** p. 90 rods, **Fay Lake,** p. 45 rods, **Chub River, Warclub Lake,** p. 13 rods, **Chub River, Seahorse Lake,** p. 13 rods, **French Lake.** With 9 portages totaling 441 rods on the first day out, this is a challenge that not everyone should accept. (See comments for Day 1, paragraphs 1-3, and for Day 2, paragraphs 2-3, Route #52-1.) The 90-rod portage from Flying to Fay Lake seems longer. The first 30 rods are level, but far from smooth, as the trail skirts the edge of a bog. Then the trail veers north, away from the bog, and climbs over a steep hill. In 1998, the trail was enveloped by dense underbrush that made it difficult to see the path. The end of the portage was partially under water. Watch your step! This is not a well-traveled portage, and it is apparently low on the priority list for trail maintenance. (If you prefer, you can bypass this challenging carry by taking an alternate route from Flying Lake through Bingshick and Glee lakes to Fay Lake, with 4 short portages along the way. See comments for Day 1, paragraph 4, Route #52-1.)

There is a nice lunch site on a rock outcrop along the north shore of Fay Lake, just west of the Glee Lake portage. There are no USFS

Kekekabic Trail bridge spans creek below Mueller Falls

campsites, however, on ANY of the lakes between Brant and French lakes. So if you think this delicious taste of the Wilderness is too much to bite off on your first day, consider heading north from Flying Lake to camp on Bingshick Lake (see comments for Day 1, paragraphs 4-5, Route #52-1.)

The campsite at the north end of French Lake has a nice rock outcrop for swimming and sunbathing. There are 2 fair tent sites. If it's hot, and you prefer shade, the campsite at the southwest end of the lake is more suitable, without the good rock outcrop. Access to it is on a steep rock slope that makes a precarious landing, however.

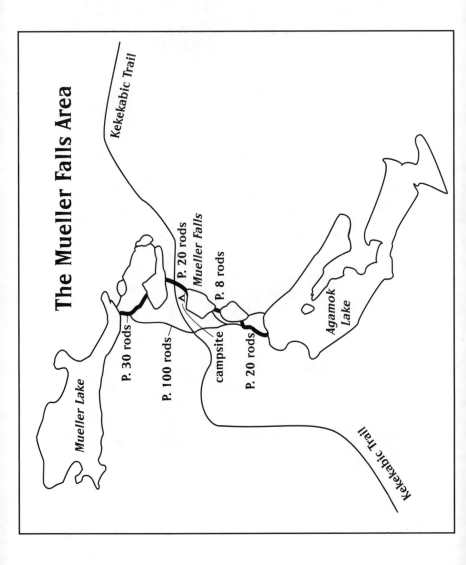

The Mueller Falls Area

Kekekabic Trail

Mueller Lake

P. 30 rods

P. 100 rods

P. 20 rods

Mueller Falls

P. 8 rods

campsite

P. 20 rods

Agamok Lake

Kekekabic Trail

Day 2 (8 miles): French Lake, p. 130 rods, **Peter Lake,** p. 39 rods, **Gabimichigami Lake,** p. 15 rods, **Agamok Lake,** p. 100 rods, **Mueller Lake,** p. 100 rods, **Ogishkemuncie Lake.** This day leads to one of the most scenic places in the central part of the BWCAW—Mueller Falls— but it doesn't come easily. The first and longest portage of the day starts out level for 13 rods, as the trail first skirts and then crosses a bog on logs that should keep your feet dry. Then you'll climb to higher ground to the midpoint of the portage, where the trail descends steeply for a few rods, before continuing on a gentler downhill slope to Peter Lake—descending more than 80 feet in all.

The next portage (39 rods) requires another fairly steep climb and descent over a small hill. The path is plagued with rocks, roots and boulders. Watch your step!

At the 15-rod portage from Gabimichigami Lake to Agamok Lake, there are actually 2 paths from which to choose. They are short, virtually flat, and easy. The one on the right is muddier and grassier than the left alternative. The left choice is rockier, but a bit shorter. Take your pick.

Paddle cautiously through Agamok Lake. It is a pretty little lake but, at the narrow parts of the lake, it is very shallow. There are rocks lurking just below the surface that may "grab" your canoe.

The next 100-rod portage bypasses Mueller Falls and a scenic series of pools and rapids that drain from Agamok to Mueller Lake. The quickest way through is the one long portage. But you can also divide the stretch into 3 or 4 short carries, separated by brief paddles on small pools between the rapids (see Sketch opposite). Regardless of your choice, start your portage at the same good landing on Agamok Lake. You can bypass the first 2 rapids and the small pool in between by veering off the main portage trail (right) 35 rods from the beginning. If you stay on the long portage (left), you will encounter a couple of small hills with 2 steep descents as well as a couple of wet spots bridged by logs. It's not the easiest of portages, but at least it's mostly downhill this way, descending nearly 50 feet to Mueller Lake. To view Mueller Falls, watch for the intersection of the Kekekabic Trail about midway across the portage. The Kekekabic Trail leads east (right) 45 rods to a good wooden bridge that spans the stream and affords a great view of the falls. A campsite for backpackers is located nearby.

At the west end of Mueller Lake, another 100-rod portage first climbs for 18 rods, then descends steeply for 19 rods, before leveling off most of the rest of the way to Ogishkemuncie Lake (with one more short descent along the way).

In spite of numerous campsites on Ogishkemuncie Lake, don't wait too late to claim one. They are in great demand. Those who arrive late in the day are often disappointed to find no vacancies. Back when the Forest Service kept travel zone statistics, Ogishkemuncie had the distinction of having the highest campsite occupancy rate of all the lakes in the Boundary Waters. It is still a very popular destination. Anglers are attracted to the lake because of the walleyes and lake trout that reside there.

Day 3 (9 miles): Ogishkemuncie Lake, p. 15 rods, **Annie Lake,** p. 15 rods, **Jenny Lake,** p. 15 rods, **Eddy Lake,** p. 22 rods, **Kekekabic Pond,** p. 3 rods, **pond,** p. 27 rods, **pond,** p. 18 rods, **pond,** p. 3 rods, **Kekekabic Lake,** p. 85 rods, **Strup Lake,** p. 10 rods, **Wisini Lake.** On this day, you will paddle across one of the prettiest lakes in the BWCA Wilderness—big Kekekabic Lake. To get there you must first cross 8 short portages. All are well worn, and most are quite easy. Beware the trail between Jenny and Eddy lakes, however. It bypasses rather scenic rapids in a narrow gorge populated with tall cedar trees. The path is rocky and treacherous where it descends steeply toward Eddy Lake. Use caution! It's better to make 2 trips on this one, even if you normally take all your gear in just one trip.

All 5 portages connecting Eddy and Kekekabic lakes via the Kekekabic Ponds are uphill, but none is difficult. The first 3-rod carry may be eliminated altogether when the water level is high enough to walk or line your canoe up the shallow rapids. When such is the case, the next portage (27 rods) may be reduced to only 16 rods. After completing the 18-rod portage, hike back a few rods to view the lovely waterfall and rapids that parallel the trail.

Kekekabic Lake is nothing less than spectacular when you enter it from the ponds. As you emerge from the narrow east end, majestic bluffs tower above your canoe, and along the distant south shoreline pine-covered hills rise 400 feet above the lake. Ahead of you lie 4½ miles of scenic lakeshore—most impressive after the chain of little ponds.

If time permits and you feel like stretching your legs in the middle of this long day, you can access the Kekekabic Trail on the south shore of Kekekabic Lake, about a mile from its east end. The spur trail starts at an old USFS ranger cabin (not clearly visible from the lake) and leads 190 rods uphill to the junction of the Kekekabic Trail and the site of the former Kekekabic lookout tower, 425 feet above the lake.

Save some strength for the next portage. The 85-rod trail gains over 100 feet of elevation. Fortunately, it has an excellent path that passes through a lovely aspen forest.

Don't delay in claiming your campsite on Wisini Lake. The 3 choices often fill up early. The best choice is on an elevated rock ledge near the middle of the lake. It is terraced and has sufficient space for at least 4 tents. The only drawback is that there is no good boat landing.

Day 4 (8 miles): Wisini Lake, p. 90 rods, **Ahmakose Lake,** p. 30 rods, **Gerund Lake,** p. 15 rods, **Fraser Lake,** p. 11 rods, **Shepo Lake,** p. 22 rods, **Sagus Lake,** p. 42 rods, **Roe Lake, creek,** p. 65 rods, **Cap Lake,** p. 220 rods, **Boulder Lake, Boulder Creek,** p. 15 rods, **creek,** p. 10 rods, **creek, Adams Lake.** You will see an interesting variety of lakes this day, joined for the most part by rather easy portages, with one noteworthy exception. Throughout much of the morning, you will witness the results of a forest fire that consumed over 1000 acres in 1976. Charred pillars tower above the new growth as reminders of the former 100-year-old pine forest that once dominated the landscape—all the way from the southeast shore of Wisini Lake to the north shore of Sagus Lake.

The first portage (90 rods) goes over a small hill on a good path. At the end of the carry, look up to see an osprey nest in a tall, dead tree (active in 1998). The next short portage (30 rods) starts out on a good, level path. But it soon turns "ugly." It descends rather steeply on a very rocky, deeply eroded path that may also be a streambed during and after heavy rains.

The short portages leading to and from Fraser Lake are both quite easy. The 22-rod path from Shepo Lake is level, but plagued with roots that will slow your pace. If there is a northeast wind and you prefer to not paddle the whole length of Sagus Lake, you can eliminate paddling on all but the north end of Sagus Lake by taking a 65-rod portage from Fraser Lake directly to Sagus Lake. The trail has an excellent path that climbs to a ridge overlooking a scenic bog and pond to the north of the portage.

Both portages to and from Roe Lake have good, dry paths that climb over low hills. The boggy east end of Roe Lake is a bit confusing. Contrary to the map, you must paddle about 40 rods into a small creek before you will see the portage landing on the north (left) side of the creek. Aquatic weeds and muskeg conceal the outlet to the creek, but if you maintain an eastbound course as you proceed toward the east end of the lake, you should find the creek without too much difficulty.

Finding the correct long portage from Cap to Boulder Lake is somewhat confusing. There are 3 portage landings near the southeast end of Cap Lake. The first one you will see and arrive at is NOT the one you want (see the Sketch on page 164). It does lead to Boulder Lake—eventually—but it first takes you on a longer path through a grassy bog. The landing you want is farther east, near the easternmost tip of the lake, on the *south* shore. Another portage landing for a trail to Ledge Lake is nearby on the *north* side of the east tip of the lake.

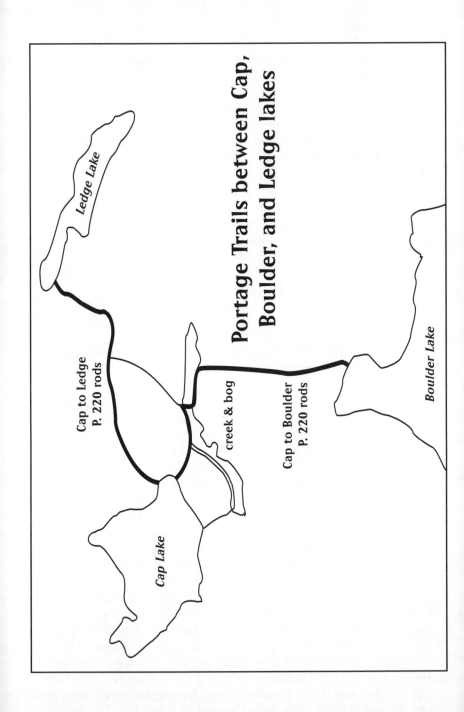

The 220-rod portage intersects 2 other trails along the way. It first climbs over a low, brushy hill and then descends into a creek valley (35 rods). It then follows the north edge of a grassy bog (a meadow during dry years) for 55 rods to intersect a trail leading north to the Ledge Lake portage. After crossing a creek on rocks and boulders, it continues along the south side of the grassy bog for 20 more rods on a rocky, winding path. Then the trail leads south, away from the creek and bog, gradually rises to higher and drier ground, and then levels off for the next 95 rods on a good path. The final 25 rods are downhill to Boulder Lake.

Boulder is a pretty lake with a couple of excellent campsites. If you've had enough for one day and the sites are vacant, you might want to settle here for the night.

If the water level is high enough in Boulder Creek, only 2 short portages (15 rods and 10 rods) are needed en route to Adams Lake. But, if the water level is low late in the summer or during a dry year, it may be necessary to walk nearly the whole distance between Boulder and Adams lakes—about 100 rods on a soft, grassy path that parallels the creek.

Adams is another pretty lake with numerous rock outcrops and several good campsites. If you are traveling with a large group, head for the island site in the middle of the lake. It has 4-5 good tent sites shaded by a cedar forest, as well as a large rock outcrop on the south side of the island.

Day 5 (9 miles): Adams Lake, p. 90 rods, **Beaver Lake**, p. 30 rods, **Trapline Lake**, p. 22 rods, **Kawishiwi River**, p. 18 rods, **river**, p. 42 rods, **Kivaniva Lake, creek**, p. 18 rods, **Anit Lake**, p 65 rods, **Pan Lake.** If you could make a beeline for your next campsite, you'd find it just 2 miles east of Adams Lake. But you'll be taking the long way to Pan Lake on a route that passes through a chain of lovely lakes separated, for the most part, by short and easy carries. The first and longest portage at the southwest end of Adams Lake follows an excellent path downhill to Beaver Lake. It goes through a scenic narrow, deep gorge that is lined with steep rock slopes.

As you approach the portage connecting Trapline Lake with the Kawishiwi River, you may have to lift over a couple of small beaver dams before you reach the 22-rod trail. Or you could take out earlier on a longer portage that bypasses the whole area. (Also see comments for Day 5, paragraphs 2-4, Route #50-2.)

There is a nice campsite on the north shore of Pan Lake, with 2 good tent sites nestled in a lovely forest of birch and jack pines. For the anglers in your group, there are walleyes, northern pike and bluegills swimming nearby.

Day 6 (10 miles): Pan Lake, p. 50 rods, **Panhandle Lake,** p. 90 rods, **pond,** p. 60 rods, **Makwa Lake,** p. 55 rods, **Elton Lake,** p. 19 rods, **creek,** p. 19 rods, **Little Saganaga Lake,** p. 45 rods, **Mora Lake,** p. 10 rods, **Tarry Lake,** p. 50 rods, **Crooked Lake.** On this day, you will pass through a chain of lovely lakes with numerous rock outcrops and occasional cliffs. Portages are generally quite easy, and most have fairly good paths that are well constructed, well worn and well maintained.

Little Saganaga, with its many islands and peninsulas, is a popular destination for many BWCAW visitors. There are 2 dozen campsites on the lake to accommodate them, so expect to see people there. As you depart from the southeast corner of the lake, you'll be walking on one of the most scenic portages in the BWCA Wilderness—a good 45-rod path that closely follows a small stream draining Mora Lake.

At the north end of Tarry Lake the smoothest place to take out is 3 rods east of a boulder field where many start the 50-rod portage to Crooked Lake. Crooked is another pretty lake that entertains numerous visitors from the Round Lake entry points. There are several excellent campsites, including a couple at the south end of the lake that can accommodate larger groups with more tents. Try to claim your site as early as possible during the peak summer season. Then, if fresh fish sounds good for your final supper on the trail, see if you can entice a lake trout or northern pike onto your hook.

Day 7 (6 miles): Crooked Lake, p. 55 rods, **Owl Lake,** p. 63 rods, **Tuscarora Lake,** p. 366 rods, **Missing Link Lake,** p. 142 rods, **Round Lake.** (See comments for Day 3, Route #52-1.)

Entry Point 54—Seagull Lake

SEASONAL PERMITS: 1,311

POPULARITY RANK: 6th

DAILY QUOTA: 13

LOCATION: Seagull Lake is located 38 airline miles northwest of Grand Marais, near the end of the Gunflint Trail. There are 2 good public accesses to the lake. The first is 54 miles up the Gunflint Trail from Highway 61 in Grand Marais. The public landing is at the end of a ¼-mile access road leading west (left) from the Gunflint Trail. There are outhouses, a telephone and a picnic area adjacent to the large parking area.

Continue driving past this turnoff for 3 miles to Trail's End Campground, where there is a large parking lot that serves public accesses to both Gull Lake (north of the parking lot) and Seagull Lake (south of the lot). A map and directory at the entrance to the campground will show you the way. Both of the routes described below start and end at Trail's End Campground.

DESCRIPTION: Trail's End Campground is a fine place to camp the night before your trip. The 32 campsites are available by reservation and operated by a concessionaire, Way of the Wilderness Outfitters. Make your reservation by calling the National Recreation Reservation Service (see Chapter 2). Camping fees are charged. Or to ensure that you start the canoe trip with a dry tent, you could rent bunkhouse accommodations from Way of the Wilderness Outfitters, located adjacent to the campground. There you can also get a hot shower, breakfast on the morning of your trip departure day and complete or partial outfitting, if needed.

Seagull Lake is the third most popular entry point in the Eastern Region of the BWCAW. In spite of its high daily quota, don't expect to simply drop by and pick up a permit during the busiest parts of the summer. Permits may be hard to come by. Of the 13 daily permits, 2 are restricted to travel only on Seagull Lake (Entry Point 54A). Eleven are available for parties traveling beyond the lake itself (Entry Point 54). Seagull ranks among the top 20 entry points with quotas filled the greatest number of days. So it is a good idea to make a permit reservation in advance of your arrival.

Motorboats not exceeding 10 horsepower are permitted in the BWCAW at the east end of Seagull Lake, east of Threemile Island, and motors of any size are allowed on the part of the lake lying outside the Wilderness boundary. You may also see day-trippers. Seagull ranks 8th among all entry points for the number of day-use permits issued during the summer season.

The Roy Lake fire of 1976 scarred much of the area immediately north of Seagull Lake. West of Trail's End Campground, across the Seagull River, you can still see evidence of that destructive blaze. The forest has rapidly recovered, however, and very little evidence of that wildfire is visible from the lakes and streams on which you will be paddling. Seagull Lake grants easy access to one of the loveliest parts of the Boundary Waters, and the entry lake itself is an island-studded spectacle to behold.

ROUTE #54-1: The Eddy Falls Loop

3 Days, 35 Miles, 15 Lakes, 1 River, 1 Creek, 13 Portages

DIFFICULTY: Easier

FISHER MAPS: F-11, F-19

INTRODUCTION: This popular loop is a good introduction to the BWCA Wilderness, leading to several lovely lakes that are separated, for the most part, by easy portages. From the public access at Trail's End Campground, you will paddle southwest across Seagull, Alpine and Jasper lakes to Ogishkemuncie Lake. From there, you'll cross a chain of smaller lakes leading northwest to the scenic South Arm of Knife Lake. After viewing Eddy Falls, then, you will steer northeastward to cross Hanson and Ester lakes en route to the Canadian border at Ottertrack Lake. After crossing tiny Swamp Lake, a long paddle across big Saganaga Lake will lead to Gull Lake, where you'll end this journey at a public landing near the entrance to Trail's End campground.

If your #1 goal is to escape from all other people for 3 days of wilderness isolation, choose another route. This entire route is heavily traveled and motorboats are permitted at the beginning and end of the loop (on Seagull, Saganaga and Gull lakes). On the other hand, if scenic lakes with crystal-clear water, easy portages and a lovely waterfall appeal to you, you are sure to love this easy loop.

Try to get an early start every day, so you can do most of your paddling in the morning hours when wind is normally the lightest. That will also afford you an opportunity to claim your campsite early in the afternoon, while there is still a choice. Furthermore, it will allow plenty of time for the anglers in your group to wet their lines. Walleyes, northern pike, lake trout and smallmouth bass inhabit most of the lakes on which you'll be paddling.

Day 1 (11 miles): Seagull Lake, p. 105 rods, **Alpine Lake,** p. 45 rods, **Jasper Lake,** p. 25 rods, **Kingfisher Lake,** p. 38 rods, **Ogishkemuncie Lake.** If wind is not a problem on the wide expanse of Seagull Lake, this should be a delightfully easy day, with good, well worn and well maintained portages. Although you will be gaining elevation throughout the day, your destination is only 32 feet higher than your origin.

The only challenge at all is at the first trail, which climbs over a small hill en route to Alpine Lake. If you prefer getting your feet wet to portaging 105 rods, you can avoid that first long carry by paddling up the channel connecting Seagull and Alpine lakes. You'll encounter 3 short sets of rapids, up which you can easily walk or line your canoe (given normal-to-low water level). You may find it quicker to take the 105-rod portage, however. The shallow rapids connecting Kingfisher and Ogishkemuncie lakes may also be walked without much difficulty, if the water level is not too high and the opposing current is not too swift, to eliminate the 38-rod carry.

Plan to camp near the center of Ogishkemuncie Lake for 11 miles of travel. Although there are several fine campsites on Ogishkemuncie Lake, don't wait too late to claim one. They are in great demand. Those who arrive late in the day are often disappointed to find no vacancies. Back when the Forest Service kept travel zone statistics, Ogishkemuncie had the distinction of having the highest campsite occupancy rate of all the lakes in the Boundary Waters. It is still a very popular destination. Anglers are attracted to the lake because of the walleyes and lake trout that reside there.

Day 2 (10 miles): Ogishkemuncie Lake, p. 15 rods, **Annie Lake,** p. 15 rods, **Jenny Lake,** p. 15 rods, **Eddy Lake,** p. 25 rods, **South Arm**

Bunkhouse at Way of the Wilderness Outfitters

of Knife Lake, p. 120 rods, **Hanson Lake, creek, Ester Lake.** All of the portages have well worn paths and most are quite easy again this day. Beware the short trail between Jenny and Eddy lakes, however. It bypasses rather scenic rapids in a narrow gorge populated with tall cedar trees. The path is rocky and treacherous where it descends steeply toward Eddy Lake. Use caution! It's better to make 2 trips on this one, even if you normally take all your gear in just one trip.

After the steep descent from Eddie Lake to the South Arm of Knife Lake (a 75-foot drop over 25 rods), take time to enjoy the scenic waterfall on the connecting stream. The best view of lower Eddy Falls can be found by paddling away from the portage to the creek's outlet (right) and then hiking up a trail on the *east* side of the creek. That also leads you away from any congestion on the portage. Then enjoy paddling across the scenic South Arm of Knife Lake, where steep ridges, rising as much as 200 feet above the water, border the shoreline. It's obvious why Knife Lake is such a popular destination for Wilderness paddlers.

The longest and most challenging portage on this route (120 rods) gains nearly 100 feet of elevation from the shore of Knife Lake before descending gradually to the southwest end of Hanson Lake. At the opposite end of the lake, then, you will simply paddle through the shallow, sandy-bottom creek leading to Ester Lake (unless a beaver dam there necessitates a quick lift-over). There you'll find 4 nice campsites clustered together near the south end of the lake. Ester is a very clear, deep lake that harbors lake trout.

Day 3 (14 miles): Ester Lake, p. 80 rods, **Ottertrack Lake,** p. 80 rods, **Swamp Lake,** p. 5 rods, **Saganaga Lake, Seagull River, rapids, river, Gull Lake.** If there is a westerly breeze, the final day should be quite easy. If there is a brisk wind from the northeast, however, look out! Most of the day (more than 10 miles of paddling) will be spent on enormous Saganaga Lake.

The 3 portages are nothing to worry about. On the first 80-rod trail, after a short climb, you'll descend over 90 feet to Ottertrack Lake. The next 80-rod trail (Monument Portage) doesn't require a monumental effort. It merely passes over a low hill shared by the United States and Canada. At the summit of the hill is a large steel monument that marks the international boundary.

In the narrow south end of Saganaga Lake, just before entering the Seagull River, you will see a charred, barren landscape along the shorelines. That's where a massive fire consumed 12,600 acres of dense forest during August of 1995. Most of the destruction was on the Canadian side of the border. Yet the fire-fighting effort cost the United States alone $2,650,000—all because of a careless camper who left an unattended campfire on Romance Lake, half a mile west of the Saganaga narrows.

Soon after entering the mouth of the Seagull River, you'll have to paddle up through some small rapids. Though the water is swift, the channel is deep if you stay in the center. At the Gull Lake boat landing, hike ¼-mile northeast (left) to find your vehicle at the parking lot.

ROUTE #54-2:	The Adams Knife Loop
	7 Days, 70 Miles, 39 Lakes, 2 Rivers, 4 Creeks, 41 Portages
DIFFICULTY:	Challenging
FISHER MAPS:	F-11, F-12, F-19
INTRODUCTION:	This outstanding loop will take you to some of the prettiest scenery in the BWCA Wilderness. From the public landing at Trail's End Campground, you will paddle southwest across Seagull, Alpine and Jasper lakes to Ogishkemuncie Lake. From there, you'll steer toward the southeast and work your way toward Gabimichigami and Little Saganaga lakes, while stopping along the way to view picturesque Mueller Falls. A chain of small lakes and short

portages will then lead you southwest to the Kawishiwi River. Then another chain of lovely lakes will carry you north to Boulder Lake. After hiking the longest portage on this route, you will plot a course from Cap Lake to Fraser Lake and then veer north to Kekekabic and Knife lakes. There you will enjoy a panoramic view across the Canadian border from Thunder Point before paddling east on the South Arm of Knife Lake. After viewing Eddy Falls, then, you will cross Hanson and Ester lakes en route to the Canadian border at Ottertrack Lake. Beyond tiny Swamp Lake, a long paddle across big Saganaga Lake will lead to Gull Lake, where you'll end this journey at a public landing near the entrance to Trail's End campground.

When your expedition is complete, you will have seen some of the prettiest lakes in the BWCAW and visited one of the most isolated interior parts of the Wilderness. Much of the route is quite popular and entertains many visitors each summer, particularly at the start and end of this loop. Nevertheless, you will have a good opportunity to seek respite from the summer "crowds" near the middle of the loop.

Although you will average nearly 6 portages per day, only 9 exceed 80 rods in length and only 1 is longer than half a mile. Most are much shorter and quite easy. About half are each less than 40 rods long. A strong group of experienced paddlers should have no problem completing the route in 7 days. But groups of anglers and less experienced trippers should consider stretching the route over 8 days, especially if 2 trips are needed to get gear across the portages.

Anglers will have plenty of good opportunities to wet their lines. Walleyes, northern pike and lake trout are found in many of the lakes and rivers along the way. Smallmouth bass and bluegills are also found in some.

Day 1 (11 miles): Seagull Lake, p. 105 rods, **Alpine Lake,** p. 45 rods, **Jasper Lake,** p. 25 rods, **Kingfisher Lake,** p. 38 rods, **Ogishkemuncie Lake.** (See comments for Day 1, Route #54-1.)

Day 2 (9 miles): Ogishkemuncie Lake, p. 100 rods, **Mueller Lake,** p. 100 rods, **Agamok Lake,** p. 15 rods, **Gabimichigami Lake,** p. 25 rods, **Rattle Lake,** p. 30 rods, **Little Saganaga Lake,** p. 19 rods, **creek,** p. 19 rods, **Elton Lake.** This area is one of the most beautiful parts of canoe country—from island-studded Little Saganaga Lake, to the wide-open expanse of Gabimichigami Lake, to the sheltered little pools and rapids between Mueller and Agamok lakes.

There are 2 challenging portages right away to get your heart pumping. The first 100-rod trail starts on a good, level path, but it climbs over a steep hill during the second half of the portage. The second 100-rod trail is mostly uphill, but more gradual than the previous climb. The portage bypasses Mueller Falls and a scenic series of pools and rapids that drain from Agamok to Mueller Lake. The quickest way through is the one long portage. But you can also divide the stretch into 3 or 4 short carries, separated by brief paddles on small pools between the rapids (see the Sketch on page 160). Regardless of your choice, start your portage at the same rocky landing on Mueller Lake, about 10 rods west of the creek's outlet. Bear left immediately if you want to take the "rapids route" with the shorter carries. This is the more scenic route, but all of the short trails around the rapids are rocky and rather steep in places. The paths can be quite slippery when wet. Use caution! If you stay on the long portage, you will encounter a couple of hills with 2 steep ascents as well as a couple of wet spots bridged by logs. To view Mueller Falls, watch for the intersection of the Kekekabic Trail about midway across the portage. The Kekekabic Trail leads east (left) 45 rods to a good wooden bridge that spans the stream and affords a great view of the falls. A campsite for backpackers is located nearby. This side trip is well worth the extra time and effort required.

Use caution paddling through pretty, little Agamok Lake. At the narrow parts of the lake, it is very shallow. There are rocks lurking just below the surface to grab your canoe. The remaining short portages this day are quite easy, and they all have good paths. At the 15-rod trail from Agamok to Gabimichigami Lake, there are actually 2 paths from which to choose. Both are virtually flat. The one on the left is muddier and grassier than the right alternative. The "right" choice is rockier, but a bit shorter. Take your pick.

Little Saganaga, with its many islands and peninsulas, is a lovely lake and a popular destination for many BWCAW visitors. There are 2 dozen campsites on the lake to accommodate them. Expect to see people here. An old rock-and-gravel dam maintains the water level in the creek connecting Little Saganaga and Elton lakes. After leaving Little Saganaga Lake, you will again be entering a part of the Wilderness that receives lighter use during much of the summer.

Elton is another pretty lake, with rock outcrops along its shores. There are a couple of nice campsites near the middle of the lake. Northern pike is the only game fish you'll find there. The lake is known to harbor some big ones.

Day 3 (8 miles): Elton Lake, p. 55 rods, **Makwa Lake**, p. 60 rods, **pond**, p. 90 rods, **Panhandle Lake**, p. 50 rods, **Pan Lake**, p. 65 rods, **Anit Lake**, p. 18 rods, **creek**, **Kivaniva Lake**, p. 42 rods, **Kawishiwi**

Anit Lake

River, p. 18 rods, **river.** (See comments for Day 5, paragraphs 1-4, Route #38-2.) For an 8-mile day of travel, plan to camp near the "Y" in the Kawishiwi River, south of the Trapline Lake portage. There are several good campsites in this vicinity, including one on each end of a pine-covered long island with rock outcrops. The Kawishiwi River is part of a fairly popular route, so don't delay in claiming your campsite.

Day 4 (7 miles): Kawishiwi River, p. 22 rods, **Trapline Lake,** p. 30 rods, **Beaver Lake,** p. 90 rods, **Adams Lake, Boulder Creek,** p. 10 rods, **creek,** p. 15 rods, **creek, Boulder Lake,** p. 220 rods, **Cap Lake.** You will surely see fewer people after you steer away from the Kawishiwi River into an area characterized by scenic lakes and some interesting portages. How easy this day is will depend, in large part, on the water levels. Most of the portages have good paths, but you'll be hiking generally uphill throughout the day. Immediately after the 22-rod portage, there were a couple of small beaver dams across a creek that required lift-overs in 1998.

The 90-rod portage from Beaver Lake has an excellent path that gradually ascends to Adams Lake. It is a rather scenic trail that passes through a narrow gorge with steep rock slopes. Along Boulder Creek there may be a couple of beaver dams that require lift-overs in addition to the 2 short portages. When the creek is nearly dry, it might be necessary to portage nearly all of the way from Beaver Lake to Boulder Lake—a total distance of nearly 150 rods—by walking along the soft, grassy bank of the creek.

Boulder and Adams are both pretty lakes, with rock outcrops along their shores. There are several very nice campsites, including a large site in a cedar grove on the island in the middle of Boulder Lake. If you are ready for an easy day with a peaceful afternoon of R&R, this would be a good place to stop for the night.

The only difficult portage this day is the long trail from Boulder Lake. Not only is it exhausting, it is also confusing because of intersecting trails along the way. (See the Sketch on page 164.) The trail starts on a good path that gradually climbs during the first 25 rods and then continues on a level-to-gently-sloping path for 95 more rods until it reaches an unnamed creek (it looks like a narrow lake on the map). For the next 15 rods, the trail skirts the edge of the grassy creek bog on a rocky, winding path, until it crosses the creek on rocks and boulders. On the north side of the creek is the first intersection. The path that heads northward up a steep incline is not the shortest route to Cap Lake. It joins the Cap-to-Ledge lakes portage. Instead of that trail, you should continue along the north edge of the grassy creek bog and meadow for 55 more rods to another intersection. At that point, the best trail to Cap Lake veers northwest, away from the creek valley, and passes over a low ridge toward the east tip of Cap Lake.

There is a nice campsite on an elevated rock outcrop on the north shore of Cap Lake—the only campsite on this little lake. Unfortunately, there is only 1 good tent site. So, if you are traveling with a larger group, it's best to stop for the night on Boulder Lake. Then plan to get a very early start the next morning to make up the difference.

Day 5 (10 miles): Cap Lake, p. 65 rods, **creek, Roe Lake,** p. 42 rods, **Sagus Lake,** p. 65 rods, **Fraser Lake,** p. 15 rods, **Gerund Lake,** p. 30 rods, **Ahmakose Lake,** p. 90 rods, **Wisini Lake,** p. 10 rods, **Strup Lake,** p. 85 rods, **Kekekabic Lake,** p. 80 rods, **Pickle Lake,** p. 25 rods, **Spoon Lake,** p. 25 rods, **Bonnie Lake,** p. 33 rods, **South Arm of Knife Lake.** With 12 portages, this day is a challenge. Fortunately, none of the trails is difficult. If you need 2 trips to get your gear across each trail, however, you'll be walking more than 5 miles.

At the north end of Sagus Lake, the northeast shore of Fraser Lake and the southeast shore of Wisini Lake, you'll witness the site of a forest fire that burned over a thousand acres in 1976. Charred pillars from the former 100-year-old pine forest still tower above the surrounding new growth.

The 65-rod portage from Sagus Lake to the east end of Fraser Lake has an excellent path that gradually descends along a ridge overlooking a rather scenic bog and pond to the north. It is an easy portage. If you prefer 2 shorter trails (22 rods and 11 rods), however, you could take an alternate route to Fraser Lake via Shepo Lake.

The steepest climb you'll encounter is at the short portage connecting Gerund and Ahmakose lakes (30 rods), where the rocky path is deeply eroded. The trail is a streambed during heavy rains and the spring runoff. Look up to see an osprey nest near the start of the next portage on the north shore of Ahmakose Lake. It was an active nest in 1998. The trail (90 rods) passes over a small hill on a good path. The 85-rod portage passes through a lovely aspen forest on an excellent path that drops over 110 feet to the south end of Kekekabic Lake. The remaining portages are nothing to worry about. All 4 of them are generally downhill, dropping a total of 112 feet from Kekekabic Lake to Knife Lake. The well-used paths are well maintained and easy to negotiate.

Plan to camp near where the South Arm of Knife Lake joins the main part of the lake—a half-mile *west* of the final portage. After setting up camp, eating dinner and completing all the evening chores, try to muster up energy for a short side trip: at the westernmost end of the long island that separates the branches of Knife Lake is Thunder Point. There you'll find a ¼-mile trail that leads to an overlook. A hike to the top is rewarded by a panoramic view of the Canadian border country from 150 feet above the lake. This is a great place to watch the sun set. Then, while paddling back to your campsite, try your luck at catching one of the walleyes, northern pike, lake trout or smallmouth bass that inhabit this big, beautiful lake.

Day 6 (11 miles): South Arm of Knife Lake, p. 120 rods, **Hanson Lake, creek, Ester Lake.** Unless there is a strong wind out of the east, this will be a very easy day of paddling with just 1 portage to break up the routine. (See comments for Day 2, paragraphs 2-4, Route #54-1.)

Day 7 (14 miles): Ester Lake, p. 80 rods, **Ottertrack Lake,** p. 80 rods, **Swamp Lake,** p. 5 rods, **Saganaga Lake, Seagull River, rapids, river, Gull Lake.** (See comments for Day 3, Route #54-1.)

Entry Point 55—Saganaga Lake

SEASONAL PERMITS: 1,651

POPULARITY RANK: 4th

DAILY QUOTA: 20

LOCATION: Saganaga Lake is located 40 airline miles northwest of Grand Marais, near the end of the Gunflint Trail. There are 3 public accesses to the lake. The first 2 are north of the Gunflint Trail, about 56 miles from Highway 61 in Grand Marais. Both Saganaga Landing and End of the Trail Landing have Cook County parking lots where a fee is charged ($3 per day in 1998). They afford the most direct access to Saganaga Lake.

For the routes described in this book, however, continue driving past these turnoffs (¾-mile past County Road 11) to Trail's End Campground. There you'll find a large *free* parking lot that serves public accesses to both Gull Lake (north of the parking lot) and Seagull Lake (south of the lot). A map and directory at the entrance to the campground will show you the way. Saganaga Lake lies 2 miles north of the campground via Gull Lake and the Seagull River.

DESCRIPTION: Trail's End Campground is an excellent place to camp the night before your trip. The 32 campsites are available by reservation and operated by a concessionaire, Way of the Wilderness Outfitters. Make your reservation by calling the National Recreation Reservation Service (see Chapter 2). Camping fees are charged. Or to ensure that you start your canoe trip with a dry tent, you could rent bunkhouse accommodations from Way of the Wilderness Outfitters, located adjacent to the campground. There you can also get a hot shower, breakfast on the morning of your departure day and complete or partial outfitting, if needed.

The Roy Lake fire of 1976 scarred much of the area immediately north of Seagull Lake. West of Trail's End Campground, across the Seagull

River, you can still see evidence of that destructive blaze. The forest has rapidly recovered, however, and very little evidence of that wildfire is visible from the lakes and streams on which you will be paddling.

Saganaga Lake, part of the international boundary, is the busiest lake in the eastern region of the BWCAW. Motorboats with up to 25 horsepower motors are permitted on the US side of the lake (banned west of American Point), and many of the BWCAW permits issued here are to groups using motorized craft. There are no motor restrictions on the Canadian side of the border. Saganaga is also the starting point for paddlers en route to Canada's Quetico Provincial Park, which is accessible from the west end of the lake. You may see towboats race past you on their way to the park with canoeists preferring to save time by not paddling across big Saganaga Lake. Summer residents with cabins on the Canadian side of the border also access their properties from US boat landings. Several private cabins, lodges and canoe trip outfitters are located at the southernmost end of Saganaga Lake. But the rest of this mammoth lake (on the US side of the boundary) is contained within the BWCA Wilderness, where there are no other monuments to civilization.

In spite of all the activity on Saganaga Lake, it is actually one of the easier BWCAW entry points for which to get a permit. Only 54% of the available permits were actually issued to visitors in 1997. Of the 20 overnight permits available each day, 3 are restricted to use only on Saganaga Lake (Entry Point 55A) and are, therefore, not suitable for the routes described below. But that still leaves 17 permits per day for canoe trippers wanting to travel beyond the big lake. While a reservation is always advised for trips starting on weekends and during the peak of the summer season, this is an entry point that you may be able to use at the last minute on a weekday throughout the summer.

Saganaga Lake is a lovely entry point that provides relatively easy access to some of the most beautiful scenery in the BWCA Wilderness. Although wind could be a problem on parts of the big lake, this is generally a good starting point for inexperienced groups of Wilderness neophytes looking for a good introduction to the Boundary Waters.

ROUTE #55-1: The Red Rock Lake Loop

2 Days, 18 Miles, 5 Lakes, 1 River, 4 Portages

DIFFICULTY: Easier

FISHER MAPS: F-19

INTRODUCTION: This is an excellent weekend route for anyone who would rather paddle than portage, with only 3 carries totaling 163 rods during the entire loop. From the Gull Lake landing, you will first paddle north to the main part of Saganaga Lake. Then you will follow its southern shoreline southwest through Red Rock Bay to Red Rock and Alpine lakes. From Alpine Lake you will portage east to Seagull Lake and then paddle across that lovely, island-studded lake to the public landing at the northeast end of the lake. You will end your trip at Trail's End Campground, ¼ mile south of your starting point and just a short walk back to the parking lot, which is situated between the 2 boat landings.

This loop circumnavigates the vast area burned by the Roy Lake fire of 1976. Only in a few spots, however, will you witness evidence of that fire. All 5 lakes on the route are quite pretty, with countless islands, bays and peninsulas scattered throughout them. They create a lovely scene that may confuse the inexperienced navigator. Don't expect solitude anywhere along the route. Find your campsite early in the afternoon while there is still a choice of sites.

Because of all the human activity in the area, ground-dwelling fauna may seldom be seen—except for the black bears that are sometimes attracted by messy visitors who leave food scraps and garbage lying around their campsites. The observant paddler, however, should see bald eagles, ospreys and a variety of waterfowl and other birds. Anglers will find walleyes, northern pike, smallmouth bass and lake trout along most of the route.

Day 1 (9 miles): Gull Lake, Seagull River, rapids, river, Saganaga Lake, p. 10 rods, Red Rock Lake. There is swift current in the small rapids in the Seagull River. You'll be headed downstream, so if you stay in the center of the deep channel, you should have no problem getting through.

In the narrow south end of Saganaga Lake, soon after entering the lake from the Seagull River, you will see a charred, barren landscape along the shorelines. That's where a massive fire consumed 12,600 acres of dense forest during August of 1995. Most of the destruction was on the Canadian side of the border. Yet the fire-fighting effort cost the United States alone $2,650,000—all because of a careless camper who left an unattended campfire on Romance Lake, half a mile west of the Saganaga narrows.

Beware the wakes from motorboats and the waves from potentially strong winds on big Saganaga Lake. Also keep your compass and map in front of you at all times. Navigation is quite confusing on large lakes with many islands and peninsulas.

If the water level is not too low, the only portage of the day may be avoided by paddling through the short, shallow creek connecting Saganaga and Red Rock lakes. Plan to camp in the north end of Red Rock Lake for 9 miles of travel.

Day 2 (9 miles): Red Rock Lake, p. 48 rods, **Alpine Lake,** p. 105 rods, **Seagull Lake.** The 2 portages this day have good well-worn paths that are well maintained and not difficult. They both pass over small hills. If you prefer to bypass the 105-rod carry, paddle into the channel leading north from the east end of Alpine Lake. It loops around to the southeast and then constricts into 3 short sets of shallow rapids that drain into Seagull Lake. A 20-rod portage goes around the first rapids on the right (west) side, but there are not paths around the last 2 rapids. If the water level is not too low, you can probably run them easily. Otherwise, walk or line your canoe between the boulders. Scout the rapids first. If you have any doubts about your ability to safely run, walk or line these rapids, use the 105-rod portage. You should never take unnecessary risks in a wilderness setting.

Enjoy paddling across the scenic northern part of Seagull Lake where numerous islands make navigation confusing. See if you can find the Palisades—steep cliffs on a peninsula that juts into the lake. Just before reaching the landing, you might also enjoy a short side trip to Seagull Falls. You can view the scene from a 38-rod portage that passes through the campground. Or complete your canoe trip, and then walk over to the falls before heading home.

ROUTE #55-2:	**The Knife and Hatchet Loop**
	7 Days, 70 Miles, 33 Lakes, 5 Ponds, 2 Rivers, 2 Creeks, 38 Portages
DIFFICULTY:	Easier
FISHER MAPS:	F-11, F-19
INTRODUCTION:	This outstanding route slices right through the heart of the BWCA Wilderness on a chain of lovely lakes that are joined, for the most part, by relatively easy portages. First you'll follow the international boundary southwest from Saganaga Lake all the way through Ottertrack and Knife lakes and down the Knife River to Carp and Birch lakes. Then you'll steer toward the southeast to

cross Ensign and Ima lakes and a chain of much smaller lakes that leads to Thomas Lake. From the east end of Thomas Lake, you will head north through Fraser Lake to Kekekabic Lake. After a night on that awesome lake, you'll cross the Kekekabic Ponds en route to Ogishkemuncie Lake, enjoying a short side trip to Eddy Falls along the way. From the northeast end of popular Ogishkemuncie Lake, then, you'll head east to Seagull Lake. This incredible journey will end at Trail's End Campground, ¼ mile south of your starting point and just a short walk back to the parking lot, which is situated between the 2 boat landings.

This is a terrific route for a group of canoeists looking for their first long adventure through the Boundary Waters. While it does loop through the heart of the Wilderness, the entire route is well traveled during the summer months. The portage trails are well worn, well maintained and not too difficult. You'll probably never be too far from another party—even in the most remote interior part of the loop. That is comforting to less experienced groups, while it may be a drawback to those in search of solitude. This is not a route for "escapists."

Some of the finest scenery in the BWCAW is found along this route, from slender Ottertrack Lake to cliff-lined Kekekabic Lake. You'll also have opportunities to enjoy a panoramic overlook, 2 small waterfalls, numerous rapids, 2 former homestead sites and sections of landscape that were scoured by wildfire. It's a fun route, with plenty of variety—big lakes, tiny ponds, narrow streams, and attractive scenery everywhere you look.

How can a route with 38 portages be rated "easier," you ask? Indeed, the route could well be labeled "challenging" if covered in fewer days. Spread over 7 full days, however, these 38 portages should pose no problems to even a rookie crew of overweight desk jockeys. None of the carries is long enough to worry about, and only a few have steep gradients. If the water level is suitable, you may be able to eliminate several of the carries by walking, lining or running some of the rapids along the route.

As for any route of this length, it's a good idea to schedule an extra layover day for rest and relaxation midway through the journey. This will also provide a "cushion" in the event that you encounter strong winds or nasty weather that slows your progress and puts you behind schedule.

Anglers will have plenty of opportunities to wet their lines. Virtually all of the common canoe-country fish species are found in the lakes along this route, including lake trout, walleyes, northern pike, smallmouth bass and pan fish.

Day 1 (10 miles): Gull Lake, Seagull River, rapids, river, Saganaga Lake. (See comments for Day 1, Route #55-1.) You can pack your portage boots away and lather up with sun block, since you won't have a single portage this day. Plan to camp in the protected southwest end of the lake, where motorboats are not permitted west of American Point. You'll be a stone's throw from Canadian soil, but don't set foot on that soil. Camp only at one of the designated USFS campsites on American soil.

Day 2 (13 miles): Saganaga Lake, p. 5 rods, **Swamp Lake,** p. 80 rods, **Ottertrack Lake,** p. 12 rods, **Knife Lake.** Though not as easy as the previous day, the 3 portages are nothing to worry about. The 80-rod "Monument Portage" doesn't require a monumental effort—it merely passes over a low hill shared by the United States and Canada at the summit of which is a large steel monument that marks the international boundary.

Ottertrack is a very scenic lake—long, narrow and lined with bluffs and a rocky shore. Watch for a plaque cemented to the base of a cliff on the Canadian shoreline, about ½-mile after the lake's 2 arms join together. The plaque commemorates "Ben Ambrose 1896-1982." Benny was a prospector who sought gold for more than 60 years in this area. His homestead once occupied the property across the lake, on the US shore.

For a 12-mile day of travel, plan to camp near the center of Knife Lake, about a mile before you reach where the north and south arms of the lake merge. For more seclusion and privacy, paddle away from the international border and into one of the protected bays between the two arms.

After setting up camp, eating dinner and completing all the evening chores, you might want to muster up energy for a short side trip. At the westernmost end of the long island that separates the branches of Knife Lake, is Thunder Point. There you'll find a ¼-mile trail that leads to an overlook. A hike to the top is rewarded by a fabulous panorama of the Canadian border country from 150 feet above the lake. This is a great place to watch the sun set. Then, while paddling back to your campsite, try your luck at catching one of the walleyes, northern pike, lake trout or smallmouth bass that inhabit this big, beautiful lake.

Day 3 (10 miles): Knife Lake, p. 75 rods, **Knife River,** p. 15 rods, **Seed Lake,** p. 15 rods, **Melon Lake,** p. 25 rods, **Carp Lake,** p. 48 rods,

Birch Lake, p. 100 rods, **Frog Lake,** p. 70 rods, **Trident Lake.** About a mile east of "Big Knife Portage" (75 rods), in a cluster of 3 small islands in Knife Lake, is the site of the BWCAW's last permanent resident. Dorothy Molter sold homemade rootbeer to canoeing passersby for nearly half a century. She called her home Isle of Pines. She passed away in December 1986. Two of her log cabins were then moved, log by log, to Ely and reconstructed as a memorial to her near the International Wolf Center.

If the water level is high enough (but not too high) and you don't mind wet feet, you could eliminate all of the portages along the Knife River by walking, lining or running your canoe down the series of gentle rapids around which the portages pass. Scout them first. Only on one occasion must you lift your canoe and gear—around a low falls. The final rapids (at the 25-rod portage) is the swiftest and most difficult to negotiate. Use caution! Visibility in rapids is restricted, and there may be sharp rocks or deep holes between the rocks. If you have any doubts about your ability to safely walk, line or run these rapids, use the portages. You should never take unnecessary risks in a wilderness setting. On a warm, sunny day, when the river is not too swift, however, it's a refreshing way to avoid 4 portages.

The final 2 portages are the biggest challenges so far, but nothing to fear. The 100-rod trail from Birch Lake will transport you away from the busy border route on a path that gains about 60 feet of elevation en route to Frog Lake. It has a muddy spot near the middle of the trail, followed by a short, but rather steep climb. There is a campsite at the far-eastern end of Frog Lake if you are ready for a night of total solitude. Otherwise, continue onward to Trident Lake, where there are 2 campsites. The 70-rod portage climbs a small hill and then descends more than 80 feet to the north shore of Trident Lake. The path is mostly dry, but the put-in at the mouth of a small creek could be muddy when the water level is low.

Day 4 (10 miles): Trident Lake, p. 100 rods, **Ensign Lake,** p. 53 rods, **Ashigan Lake,** p. 105 rods, **Gibson Lake,** p. 25 rods, **Cattyman Lake,** p. 55 rods, **Jordan Lake,** p. 5 rods, **Ima Lake,** p. 50 rods, **Thomas Creek, Hatchet Lake,** p. 10 rods, **Thomas Creek,** p. 10 rods, **creek,** p. 10 rods, **Thomas Pond,** p. 5 rods, **Thomas Lake.** This may be the busiest part of a route that is well traveled throughout. Served by the most popular entry point in the entire BWCA Wilderness (Moose Lake), Ensign is a very popular lake, and the flow of canoe traffic often continues all the way to Thomas Lake.

With 11 portages, this day is also the most challenging of the route—so far. The first and longest carry of the day will get your blood circulating. The trail passes over a big hill, gaining more than 90 feet of

Kekekabic Lake

elevation above Trident Lake, before descending more than 100 feet to Ensign Lake. From Ensign all the way to Thomas Lake, then, you'll be portaging uphill, gaining 186 feet of elevation along the way. The 53-rod portage is a gradual climb all the way from Ensign to Ashigan Lake, gaining 56 feet along the way. The next trail (105 rods) is also uphill for the first 90 rods—a gradual climb over a 75-foot-high hill between Ashigan and Gibson lakes. At the next portage (25 rods), you'll find a scenic little waterfall on the creek draining Cattyman into Gibson Lake. If the day is warm, a cooling hydro-massage in the cascading stream might be in order.

Access to the 50-rod portage is quite limited at the rocky landing on Ima Lake. With heavy canoe traffic in this area, you may have to wait in line for your turn to cross the portage. Don't crowd the party in front of you. Hopefully, the group behind you won't crowd you.

Under normal water conditions, you can probably pull your canoe up through the first 2 shallow rapids in the creek between Hatchet and Thomas lakes, eliminating 2 10-rod portages. The third 10-rod trail crosses the famed Kekekabic Trail, a 40-mile footpath that connects the Fernberg Road with the Gunflint Trail.

Plan to camp at the northeast end of Thomas Lake for a 10-mile day of travel. If the anglers in your party have any energy remaining at the end of this long day, they may find lake trout, walleyes and northern pike in the clear, deep lake.

Day 5 (9 miles): Thomas Lake, creek, Fraser Lake, p. 15 rods, **Gerund Lake,** p. 30 rods, **Ahmakose Lake,** p. 90 rods, **Wisini Lake,** p. 10 rods, **Strup Lake,** p. 85 rods, **Kekekabic Lake.** This is a relatively easy day through an area that receives moderate use during the canoeing season, highlighted by a night on one of the prettiest lakes in the BWCA Wilderness. At the northeast end of Fraser Lake and along the southeast shore of Wisini Lake, you'll witness the site of a forest fire that burned over a thousand acres in 1976. Charred pillars from the former 100-year-old pine forest still tower above the surrounding new growth.

The portages are well worn and well maintained. The steepest climb you'll encounter is at the short portage connecting Gerund and Ahmakose lakes (30 rods). The rocky path is deeply eroded because the trail is a streambed during heavy rains and the spring runoff. Look up to see an osprey nest near the start of the next portage on the north shore of Ahmakose Lake. It was an active nest in 1998. The 90-rod trail passes over a small hill on a good path. The 85-rod portage penetrates a lovely aspen forest on an excellent path that drops over 110 feet to the south end of Kekekabic Lake.

The west end of Kekekabic Lake is nothing to write home about. The scene improves dramatically, however, as you work your way to the east end of the lake, where majestic bluffs tower above your canoe, and along the distant southern shoreline pine-covered hills rise 400 feet above the lake. There are a couple of wonderful, large campsites along the north shore, toward the east end of the lake.

If you feel like stretching your legs at the end of this day, you can access the Kekekabic Trail on the south shore of Kekekabic Lake, about a mile from its east end. It starts at an old USFS ranger cabin (not clearly visible from the lake) and leads 190 rods uphill to the site of the former Kekekabic lookout tower, 425 feet above the lake.

Day 6 (10 miles): Kekekabic Lake, p. 3 rods, **Kekekabic Pond,** p. 18 rods, **pond,** p. 27 rods, **pond,** p. 3 rods, **pond,** p. 22 rods, **Eddy Lake,** p. 15 rods, **Jenny Lake,** p. 15 rods, **Annie Lake,** p. 15 rods, **Ogishkemuncie Lake,** p. 38 rods, **Kingfisher Lake,** p. 25 rods, **Jasper Lake.** Most of the 10 short portages this day are easy, but their frequency will slow your progress, especially if 2 trips are needed to get your gear across them. The first 5 trails will transport you to and from a chain of tiny lakes called the Kekekabic Ponds. All 5 are essentially downhill, but you'll descend only 37 feet from Kekekabic Lake to Eddy Lake. Before starting across the 18-rod portage, take a few minutes to view the lovely waterfall and rapids that parallel the trail a few rods down the path. If the water level is high enough, you may paddle past the start of the next 27-rod portage to another landing that will reduce the length of the portage to just 16 rods. Likewise, the next 3-rod carry may be eliminated altogether when the water is high enough to walk, line or run your canoe down the shallow rapids.

When you reach Eddy Lake, before heading on to Jenny Lake, take a short side trip to Eddy Falls. You'll find it on the creek, which parallels the 25-rod portage and plunges 75 feet from Eddy Lake down to the South Arm of Knife Lake. The best view of lower Eddy Falls can be found by paddling away from the portage on Knife Lake to the creek's outlet (right) and then hiking up a trail on the east side of the creek. If you'd rather not take that steep portage, however, you can also enjoy the view from the west side of the falls. Leave your canoe at the top of the trail, off to the side of the path to not block the landing from use by other paddlers.

The only portage this day that is tricky to negotiate is between Eddy and Jenny lakes. It bypasses rather scenic rapids in a narrow gorge populated with tall cedar trees. The path is rocky and treacherous where it ascends steeply from Eddy Lake. Use caution! It's better to make 2 trips on this one, even if you normally take all your gear in just 1 trip.

Jasper is a pretty lake with several campsites. Don't wait too late to claim one. Jasper is on a very popular route, just 2 carries away from the busy Seagull Lake entry point. Anglers may find lake trout, walleyes, smallmouth bass and northern pike in the deep, clear water.

Day 7 (8 miles): Jasper Lake, p. 45 rods, **Alpine Lake,** p. 105 rods, **Seagull Lake.** (See comments for Day 2, Route #55-1.)

5

Entry from the **Gunflint Trail** **—East** and **Arrowhead Trail**

The Tip of the Arrowhead Area

The "Tip of the Arrowhead" lies to the east of Cook County Road 12—the Gunflint Trail—in the easternmost point of the Minnesota Arrowhead region. The 11 entry points in this area include a few of the busiest and some of the least used entry points in the BWCA Wilderness, but most receive moderate to heavy use throughout the summer months. Eight entry points are accessible from the Gunflint Trail, while 3 are served by the Arrowhead Trail (Cook County Road 16).

The Gunflint Trail begins in the center of Grand Marais, on the North Shore of Lake Superior. It leads north for 25 miles, then veers west for another 25 miles, and finally heads north again to its end at Gull Lake, 57 miles northwest of Grand Marais. All of the road is black-top and it's normally in good condition. Resorts, outfitters and public campgrounds are located intermittently along the road's entire course. Traffic is fairly heavy during the summer months (of course, "heavy traffic" to those of us living Up North may not mean what it does to folks from The City).

The Arrowhead Trail begins at the tiny village of Hovland, 20 miles northeast of Grand Marais via Highway 61, and leads 18 miles north to McFarland Lake. It is a gravel road for all but the first 2½ miles from Lake Superior. Eight miles up the trail you'll drive through a stand of old white pines that date back to the early 1800's.

Grand Marais is the commercial center for all of Cook County. It is a small but bustling community that is supported mostly by the tourism and logging industries. For canoe trippers in need of refuge before or after their trips, a municipal campground is located near the center of the village. Adjacent to the campground is a municipal indoor swimming pool where a grimy tourist may purchase an inexpensive shower and sauna—as well as soak in the whirlpool bath and swimming pool.

BWCAW overnight permits are issued at the USFS Visitors Center at the southwest edge of town, 1 mile from the municipal campground on Highway 61. It is a newer facility that was opened in May of 1996. If you know that you'll be passing through town late at night, after office hours, you can make prior arrangements to pick up your permit at one of several cooperating outfitters located along the Gunflint Trail. For trips starting far up the Trail, that may be a practical alternative. That's not an option, however, for those heading up the Arrowhead Trail, where there are no USFS "cooperators." If you're headed there, be sure to pick up your permit in Grand Marais.

Entry Point 80—Larch Creek

SEASONAL PERMITS: 87

POPULARITY RANK: 50th

DAILY QUOTA: 1

LOCATION: Larch Creek is located 35 airline miles northwest of Grand Marais. From Highway 61 in Grand Marais, drive 51 miles to the north and west on County Road 12. Watch for a turnoff on the right side of the road. It is just past the Seagull Guard Station, on the *north* side of unmarked Larch Creek.

DESCRIPTION: There is parking space large enough for only a couple of vehicles in a clearing next to the road. Access to the creek is at the bottom of a small hill, just below an old beaver dam.

The closest public campground for this access is at the end of the Gunflint Trail, 6 miles beyond Larch Creek. Trail's End Campground is a fine place to camp the night before your trip. Thirty-two campsites are available by reservation and operated by a concessionaire, Way of the Wilderness Outfitters. Make your reservation by calling the National Recreation Reservation Service (see Chapter 2). Camping fees are charged.

Larch Creek is a delightful entry point for paddlers who like to "sneak" quietly into the BWCA Wilderness. At the boat landing, the creek is barely wide enough for one canoe and, in places, it winds so sharply that you may have difficulty negotiating some of the turns in a canoe longer than 16 feet. Near the end of its mile-and-a-half course to Larch Lake, however, the stream expands to nearly 2 rods in width.

Although there are no bona fide portages along Larch Creek, there will likely be several obstructions (beaver dams or logs) that necessitate lift-overs. The creek is usually navigable, but during dry periods you may find yourself dragging the bottom at times. Be prepared for wet feet. People who go to great lengths to avoid getting their feet wet will probably not enjoy this Wilderness entry point.

Larch Creek provides a tranquil access to the famed and popular Granite River route between Gunflint and Saganaga lakes. Besides the

2 routes suggested below, you can also "plug into" route #57-1 or #57-2 by starting at Larch Creek instead of at Magnetic Lake. Only the first day will be different. For a pleasant day trip or a very easy overnight outing, you can also combine the first day described below with the reverse of the first day on Route #57-1, starting at Larch Creek and ending at Magnetic Lake. Regardless of the route you select, be prepared to either shuttle vehicles between entry and exit points, or hike a few miles back to your origin. None of the routes is a complete loop.

ROUTE #80-1: The Devil's Elbow Route

3 Days, 21 Miles, 7 Lakes, 3 Rivers, 1 Creek, 7 Portages

DIFFICULTY: Easier

FISHER MAPS: F-12, F-19 and F-20

INTRODUCTION: This short route offers a wonderful introductory taste of the Wilderness, including a tiny creek, a scenic river, several small lakes and one of the largest lakes in the BWCAW. From the Gunflint Trail you will first paddle east on tiny Larch Creek to Larch and Clove lakes. Then you'll turn to the north and follow the Granite River flowage through Gneiss, Devil's Elbow and Maraboeuf lakes to Saganaga Lake. From near the east end of that gigantic lake, you will navigate carefully through a maze of islands, bays and peninsulas en route to the narrow channel leading to the south end of the lake. The Seagull River will then lead you to the public landing at Gull Lake. The route ends at Trail's End Campground, 6 miles northwest of your starting point, at the end of the Gunflint Trail.

You'll be following the US-Canadian boundary from Clove Lake to Saganaga Lake. Keep that in mind when searching for campsites. Those on the east shoreline rest on Canadian soil and are, therefore, off limits to campers without clearance from Canada Customs. The sites on the west side of the route lie in the BWCA Wilderness, on US soil.

Although you may have Larch Creek all to yourself, don't expect to escape from other people on the rest of this popular route. You may see motorboats anywhere on the Canadian side of the border, as well as on the US side of Saganaga Lake. Most of the canoeing traffic on the

Granite River system comes from the Magnetic Lake entry point. Three parties per day may enter the Wilderness there.

Anglers will find walleyes, northern pike and smallmouth bass in most of the water along this route. Lake trout also inhabit the depths of Gneiss and Saganaga lakes. With only 21 miles to cover in 3 days, you should have plenty of time to cast your line.

Day 1 (7 miles): Larch Creek, Larch Lake, p. 25 rods, **Larch Creek, Clove Lake,** p. 48 rods, **Pine River, Granite River,** p. 72 rods, **river,** p. 25 rods, **Granite River, rapids, river,** p. 25 rods, **Gneiss Lake.** Allow plenty of time for that first 1½-mile stretch on Larch Creek to Larch Lake. Don't let the small obstacles, like recurring beaver dams, be an annoyance. Consider them an integral part of a unique wilderness environment that makes this type of BWCAW entry far more appealing (to this author) than entries on most lakes. Larch is a lovely lake, with some low rock outcroppings along its shoreline and hills rising nearly 100 feet around it.

After entering Clove Lake, you'll be paddling along the Canadian border on a popular route that is rich in Voyageur history. An expert whitewater canoeist could probably eliminate all of the portages along the scenic Granite River. A novice and anyone who is not absolutely confident of having the necessary whitewater skills, however, should definitely use the portages.

The portages are neither long nor difficult. At the 48-rod portage, there are trails on both sides of the rapids. Use the US portage (left side) which is well maintained and follows closely to the scenic rapids. The Canadian path is not as well maintained. The 72-rod "Swamp Portage" is virtually level, but it is indeed swampy—wet and muddy. Soon after the 25-rod "Granite River Portage," there are 2 short rapids around which there is no portage. They can be easily run, lined or walked when the water level is low, and you may not even notice them when the water level is high. The final 25-rod "Gneiss Lake Portage" is quite easy.

If the 3 campsites on Gneiss Lake are occupied, you'll find more choices a short distance farther along the route on both Devil's Elbow and Maraboeuf lakes.

Day 2 (7 miles): Gneiss Lake, Devil's Elbow Lake, rapids, Maraboeuf Lake, p. 27 rods, **Granite River,** p. 36 rods, **Saganaga Lake.** The small rapids separating Devil's Elbow and Maraboeuf lakes is little more than swift current and can be easily run. No portage is necessary. If there is a strong north wind, however, and you prefer to shorten the paddling distance on Maraboeuf Lake, you may choose the 40-rod "Maraboef Lake Portage" that leads north from Devil's Elbow Lake across a Canadian peninsula. It will save about 1½ miles of paddling.

Saganaga Falls

You will see a scorched shoreline at the north end of Gneiss Lake, along both sides of Maraboeuf Lake and (on Day 3) in the narrows at the south end of Saganaga Lake. That's where a massive fire consumed 12,600 acres of dense forest during August of 1995. The conflagration started in the US but most of the destruction was on the Canadian side of the border. The fire-fighting effort cost the United States alone $2,650,000—all because of a careless camper who left an unattended campfire on Romance Lake, half a mile west of the Saganaga narrows. The "upside" to the story is that there is now superb habitat for a thriving moose population, as well as for wild flowers and blueberries.

The 27-rod portage is around Horsetail Rapids, which are not safe to run. Old relics of the 18th Century Voyageurs have been found at the base of these rapids. Don't let your gear add to the debris. The trail on the Canadian shore has a treacherous path alongside the rapids. Watch your step.

The final portage bypasses Saganaga Falls, a picturesque 6-foot cascade that attracts picnickers and anglers from Saganaga Lake. There are portages on both the US and the Canadian shorelines. When the water level is high and the current is swift above the falls, the safest landing is on the Canadian (right) side, which is located well away from the top of the falls. On the US (left) side, there are 2 options, both of which start very close to the top of the falls. One is a short 8-rod descent to the base of the falls. The 36-rod trail extends farther downstream to a point below any protruding rocks in low water or swift current in high water (the best choice for those paddling upstream).

During the summer season, you'll likely be sharing Saganaga Lake with many other people. Motorboats are permitted on both sides of the border, and there are numerous cabins on the Canadian side of the lake. Plan to camp in the vicinity of Conners Island for 7 miles of travel.

Day 3 (7 miles): Saganaga Lake, Sea Gull River, rapids, river, Gull Lake. Beware a strong west or southwest wind on big Saganaga Lake. Allow plenty of time if you're paddling out on a windy day.

As you exit the BWCAW via the Seagull River, you will encounter some small rapids. Stay near the center of the deep channel and paddle hard up through the swift current. Or, if necessary, you could walk or line your canoe up the rapids. There is no portage around the rapids.

The Trail's End parking lot is a short walk to the left of the public landing on Gull Lake (past the entrance to Way of the Wilderness Outfitters). If you didn't leave a car there, you'll have to end this journey with a walk of nearly 6 miles back to Larch Creek.

Route #80-2: The Ester Lake Route

5 Days, 48 Miles, 19 Lakes, 2 Rivers, 2 Creeks, 19 Portages

Difficulty: Easier

Fisher Maps: F-11, F-19, F-20

Introduction: This is a wonderful route for paddlers who like variety and good scenery and who don't want to work too hard to enjoy it all. From the Gunflint Trail you will first paddle east on tiny Larch Creek to Larch and Clove lakes. Then you'll turn north and follow the Granite River flowage through Gneiss, Devil's Elbow and Maraboeuf lakes to big Saganaga Lake. From near the east end of that gigantic lake, you will paddle all the way to its west end. Continuing along the Canadian border to Ottertrack Lake, you will then veer south to cross Ester and Hanson lakes en route to the beautiful South Arm of Knife Lake. After stopping to view Eddy Falls, you will plot a southeast course to Ogishkemuncie Lake. From there you will follow a chain of lakes that leads northeast to Seagull Lake. This route ends at Trail's End Campground, 6 miles northwest of your starting point, at the end of the Gunflint Trail.

You'll be following the US-Canadian boundary from Clove Lake to Ottertrack Lake. Keep that in mind when searching for campsites. Those on your right lie on Canadian soil and are, therefore, off limits to campers without clearance from Canada Customs. The sites on the left side of the boundary lie in the BWCA Wilderness, on US soil.

Even novice paddlers with little or no previous experience in the Boundary Waters should have no problem completing this route in just 5 days. Portages average less than 4 per day. The longest trail measures only 120 rods and most are less than 40 rods long. All are well maintained, well worn and frequently used. Nevertheless, you might consider adding a layover day to your trip itinerary. A gale wind blowing across Saganaga Lake could whip up treacherous waves, and you could find yourself wind-bound for awhile. A planned layover day takes the worry out of unanticipated events, like gale winds and thunderstorms.

You'll be paddling through a very popular region. Don't expect wilderness solitude anywhere along this route, except on Larch Creek. Motorboats without restrictions are permitted on the Canadian side of the border, and motors with less than 25 horsepower are allowed in the BWCAW on Saganaga Lake east of American Point. You'll also see private cabins on the Canadian side of Saganaga. In spite of all the activity, this is a beautiful route that is sure to please.

Anglers will find walleyes, northern pike and smallmouth bass in much of the water along this route. Lake trout also inhabit the depths of several lakes. With only 48 miles to cover in 5 days, there should be plenty of time to cast a line.

Note: If you can't get a permit for Larch Creek on your preferred day of entry, you could also take this route from Entry Point 57. Simply substitute Day 1 of Route #57-1 for the first day described below.

Day 1 (7 miles): Larch Creek, Larch Lake, p. 25 rods, **Larch Creek, Clove Lake,** p. 48 rods, **Pine River, Granite River,** p. 72 rods, **river,** p. 25 rods, **Granite River, rapids, river,** p. 25 rods, **Gneiss Lake.** (See comments for Day 1, Route #80-1.)

Day 2 (10 miles): Gneiss Lake, Devil's Elbow Lake, rapids, Maraboeuf Lake, p. 27 rods, **Granite River,** p. 36 rods, **Saganaga Lake.** (See comments for Day 2, Route #80-1.) Plan to camp in the vicinity of Voyageurs Island for 10 miles of travel. Or, if it's early in the afternoon, big Saganaga Lake is smooth, you've got energy to burn and you would prefer to camp in a quieter part of the lake, continue onward for 3 more miles. Motorboats are not permitted west of American Point. There are 4 campsites located just west of the point.

Putting in at Larch Creek

Day 3 (11 miles): Saganaga Lake, p. 5 rods, **Swamp Lake,** p. 80 rods, **Ottertrack Lake,** p. 80 rods, **Ester Lake.** If the winds are calm and the lake is smooth, this will be a very easy morning of paddling. If there is a strong west wind and the waves are running, however, the first part of this day could be both frustrating and treacherous. Use caution on "big water" and stay close to the shoreline. Not only is it safer, that's also where the wildlife is.

Much of the canoe traffic you see on this part of Saganaga Lake will be heading toward Cache Bay, the southeastern entry point for Ontario's Quetico Provincial Park. Like the BWCAW, Quetico is a paddler's paradise with about a million acres of protected wilderness.

The 80-rod "Monument Portage" from Swamp Lake to Ottertrack Lake doesn't require a monumental effort—it merely passes over a low hill shared by the United States and Canada at the summit of which is a large steel monument that marks the international boundary. The second 80-rod trail is more of a challenge. It gains nearly a hundred feet of elevation on a path that climbs most of the way.

You'll find 4 nice campsites clustered together near the south end of Ester Lake. Ester is a very clear, deep lake that harbors lake trout.

Day 4 (10 miles): Ester Lake, creek, Hanson Lake, p. 120 rods, **South Arm of Knife Lake,** p. 25 rods, **Eddy Lake,** p. 15 rods, **Jenny Lake,** p. 15 rods, **Annie Lake,** p. 15 rods, **Ogishkemuncie Lake.** You should be able to paddle through the shallow, sandy-bottom creek leading to Hanson Lake. A beaver dam, however, could necessitate a quick lift-over.

The longest portage on this route (120 rods) isn't too bad when you are headed in this direction. The trail climbs gradually for the first 80 rods, and then descends more than 100 feet of elevation en route to the shore of Knife Lake.

The South Arm of Knife Lake is quite scenic, where steep ridges, rising as much as 200 feet above the water, border the shoreline. It's obvious why Knife Lake is such a popular destination for Wilderness paddlers. Before starting the 25-rod portage to Eddy Lake, take time to enjoy the scenic waterfall on the connecting stream. The best view of lower Eddy Falls can be found by paddling away from the portage landing to the creek's outlet and then hiking up a trail on the east side of the creek. That also leads you away from any congestion on the portage. Then take a deep breath before embarking on the short portage. The trail gains 75 feet from Knife Lake to Eddy Lake.

The only portage this day that is really tricky to negotiate is between Eddy and Jenny lakes. It bypasses rather scenic rapids in a narrow gorge populated with tall cedar trees. The path is rocky and treacherous where it ascends steeply from Eddy Lake. Use caution! It's better to make 2 trips on this one, even if you normally take all your gear in just one trip.

In spite of numerous campsites on Ogishkemuncie Lake, don't wait to claim one. They are in great demand. Those who arrive late in the day are often disappointed to find no vacancies. Back when the Forest Service kept travel zone statistics, Ogishkemuncie had the distinction of having the highest campsite occupancy rate of all the lakes in the Boundary Waters. It is still a very popular destination. Anglers are attracted to the lake because of the walleyes and lake trout there. Plan to camp in the northeast part of the lake, just past the narrows, for 10 miles of travel.

Day 5 (10 miles): Ogishkemuncie Lake, p. 38 rods, **Kingfisher Lake,** p. 25 rods, **Jasper Lake,** p. 45 rods, **Alpine Lake,** p. 105 rods, **Seagull Lake.** The portages this day have good well-worn paths that are well maintained and not difficult. To eliminate the 38-rod carry, the shallow rapids connecting Ogishkemuncie and Kingfisher lakes can be lined or walked without much difficulty, if the water level is not too high and the current is not too swift.

If you prefer to bypass the 105-rod carry, paddle into the channel leading north from the east end of Alpine Lake. It loops around to the southeast and then constricts into 3 short sets of shallow rapids that drain into Seagull Lake. A 20-rod portage goes around the first rapids on the right (west) side, but there are no paths around the last 2 rapids. If the water level is not too low, you can probably run them easily. Otherwise, walk or line your canoe between the boulders. Scout the rapids first. If you have any doubts about your ability to safely run, walk or line these rapids, use the 105-rod portage. You should never take unnecessary risks in a wilderness setting.

Enjoy paddling across the scenic northern part of Seagull Lake, where numerous islands make navigation confusing. See if you can find the Palisades—steep cliffs on a peninsula that juts into the lake. Just before reaching the landing, you might also enjoy a short side trip to Seagull Falls. You can view the scene from a 38-rod portage that passes through the campground. Or complete your canoe trip, and then walk over to the falls before heading home.

Entry Point 57—Magnetic Lake

SEASONAL PERMITS: 302

POPULARITY RANK: 27th

DAILY QUOTA: 3

LOCATION: Magnetic Lake is located 32 airline miles northwest of Grand Marais, accessible by boat from Gunflint Lake. From Highway 61 in Grand Marais, drive 45 miles on the Gunflint Trail to County Road 50. Turn right and follow this hilly gravel road ½-mile to the public landing for Gunflint Lake on the left side of the road. The outlet to Magnetic Lake is straight across the west end of Gunflint Lake, 1 mile north of the landing.

DESCRIPTION: A small parking area at the access will accommodate half a dozen vehicles. The Iron Lake Campground, 8 miles closer to Grand Marais via the Gunflint Trail and County Road 92, is the closest USFS facility. It's a very quiet little campground with only 7 campsites, operated by a concessionaire, Way of the Wilderness Outfitters. A camping fee is charged. Make your reservation by calling the National Recreation Reservation Service (see Chapter 2). A more convenient place to camp the night prior to your trip is at Gunflint Pines Resort and Campground, about a half-mile east of the public landing via County Road 50. The private campground has a shower house with indoor toilets. The lodge there has a snack bar where you can buy pizzas, burgers, pop and beer, as well as some grocery items. Or, if you'd rather not unpack your tent for the night before your canoe trip, you could stay in one of the inexpensive bunkhouses at Gunflint Lodge, located just east of the public landing. There you can have a hot shower and a scrumptious breakfast on the morning of your departure, a sauna after the trip and complete or partial outfitting at Gunflint Northwoods Outfitters, located adjacent to the bunkhouses and just across the road from Gunflint Lodge.

Magnetic Lake got its name from a geologic phenomenon. Magnetic Rock, a glacially deposited block of iron located less than a mile west of the lake, is attractive to magnets. Hence your compass needle may be deflected from magnetic north as you pass through this region.

Magnetic Lake offers canoeists access to one of the most varied and interesting parts of the international boundary—a series of lovely lakes, roaring rapids, beautiful waterfalls and peaceful parts of a river system that stretches from the north end of Magnetic Lake 14 miles north to Saganaga Lake. The Pine and Granite rivers are picturesque, adorned with irregular shorelines of fascinating rock outcroppings and bordered by a mature forest of jack pine, black spruce and occasional patches of paper birch. They are also sprinkled with evidence of a long-gone era in our history, when Voyageurs passed this way en route to the northwestern hinterlands.

A forest fire that consumed 12,600 acres of forested land in August of 1995 charred much of the Granite River region between Gneiss and Saganaga lakes. It started at an unattended campfire on Romance lake (north of the Saganaga Lake access) and quickly spread eastward, across the Seagull River, through the Granite River flowage, and on into Canada. This is a stark reminder of what careless campers can unwittingly do to the wilderness.

During the summer months, use of this area is fairly heavy and reservations are needed. Two-thirds of the available overnight permits were issued to visitors during the summer of 1997. Whitewater enthusiasts are attracted here because of the many fine rapids in the Pine and Granite rivers, ranging in difficulty from easy to dangerous. Novice paddlers and anyone not 100% comfortable navigating through whitewater should use the portages. A wilderness is no place to take unnecessary chances.

Note: For 2 other route suggestions, refer to Entry Point 80—Larch Creek. The routes described for the Larch Creek entry point may also be started at Gunflint Lake by simply substituting Day 1 of Route #57-1 for the first days of Routes #80-1 (3-day trip) and #80-2 (5 days). Regardless of the route you select, be prepared to either shuttle vehicles between entry and exit points, or to hike a few miles back to your origin. None of the routes is a complete loop.

ROUTE #57-1: The Granite Red Rock Route

4 Days, 32 Miles, 10 Lakes, 2 Rivers, 13 Portages

DIFFICULTY: Easier

FISHER MAPS: F-12, F-19, F-20

INTRODUCTION: This fascinating route is a delightful combination of scenic lakes and rivers. From the public landing on Gunflint Lake, you will paddle north through Magnetic Lake and down the Pine River to Clove Lake. You'll continue winding your way northward via the Granite River to Maraboeuf Lake and onward to Saganaga Lake. Then you will follow the south shoreline of that enormous lake southwest through Red Rock Bay to Red Rock and Alpine lakes. From Alpine Lake you will portage east to Seagull Lake and then paddle across that lovely, island-studded lake to the public landing at the northeast end of the lake. You will end your trip at Trail's End Campground, about 12 miles by road from your origin.

If you do not have 2 vehicles for your party, make arrangements with one of the outfitters near the end of the Gunflint Trail to drop you off at Gunflint Lake. By leaving your vehicle at the Trail's End Campground parking lot, you won't need to worry about meeting a pick-up deadline for your return to Gunflint Lake.

Although most folks will agree that this entire route deserves an "easier" rating, be prepared for a rather challenging first day. You'll encounter 8 of the 13 portages during the first 9 miles of travel. None of the portages is very difficult, but the frequency of those carries will slow your progress, especially if you need 2 trips to get your gear across. Consequently, if your group is much better at paddling than portaging, you might prefer to spend your first night on Clove Lake and your second night on Maraboeuf Lake, with just 4 portages on each of the first 2 days. Then split the final 21 miles of mostly paddling over the last 2 days. Or spread the route more evenly over 5 full days, with your campsites on Clove, Maraboeuf, Saganaga and Alpine lakes, about 6 miles apart.

This is one of the prettiest routes in all of the BWCA Wilderness, with 2 lovely waterfalls and many rapids along the way. And it could be one of the most exciting routes, if you choose to test your canoeing skills on some of the whitewater. If you do, always stop to check out the rapids before you plunge into them. Their difficulties vary considerably with the water level. If there is any doubt at all, use the portages. Most of the portages are quite easy, so why take chances? The BWCA Wilderness is no place to take unnecessary risks.

The Granite River system was part of the extensive fur trade route used by Indians and Voyageurs alike. Where 18th Century Voyageurs swamped their canoes, trying to avoid portages around rapids, relics have been found by modern voyagers. Flint chips from old Indian camps and gunflints from muskets have also been found at campsites adjacent to the portages.

You'll be following the US-Canadian boundary from Gunflint Lake through Saganaga Lake. Keep that in mind when searching for campsites. Those on Canadian soil are off limits to campers without prior clearance from Canada Customs. Use only designated USFS campsites. Not all of the red dots on the maps are legal sites for BWCAW visitors.

Don't expect to escape from other people on this popular route. You may see motorboats anywhere on the Canadian side of the border, as well as on the US side of Gunflint, Magnetic and Saganaga lakes. Saganaga is arguably the busiest lake in the eastern region of the BWCA Wilderness.

Anglers will find walleyes, northern pike and smallmouth bass in most of the water along this route. Lake trout also inhabit the depths of Gneiss and Saganaga lakes. With only 32 miles to cover in 4 days, you should have plenty of time to cast your line.

Note: You may shorten this route to 22 miles by ending at Gull Lake. Substitute Day 3 below with Day 3 of Route #80-1. Both routes end at Trail's End Campground, one on the Gull Lake side, the other on the Seagull Lake side.

Day 1 (9 miles): Gunflint Lake, Magnetic Lake, p. 15 rods, **Pine River,** p. 13 rods, **river,** p. 35 rods, **river,** p. 110 rods, **Clove Lake,** p. 48 rods, **Pine River, Granite River,** p. 72 rods, **river,** p. 25 rods, **Granite River, rapids, river,** p. 25 rods, **Gneiss Lake.** The scenery this day is superb, with an abundance of exposed rock along the shores of the Pine and Granite rivers. A narrow, shallow channel separates Gunflint and Magnetic lakes. It should pose no problem to canoeists.

The first 3 portages are on the Canadian (right) side of the river. The landings at both ends of each trail are rocky and rather treacherous, especially when wet. The paths, too, are rather tricky—plagued with rocks and roots and sometimes steep. The second portage goes around a beautiful 15-foot drop in the river called Little Rock Falls—a fine place for a morning rest stop. There are 3 different places to put in at the bottom of the falls, depending on the water level. At the 35-rod "Blueberry Portage" ("Wood Horse Portage" on the Fisher map) the river splits into 3 channels, none of which is navigable. The unmarked portage is on a large rock outcropping on the Canadian shore, difficult to see from the river.

The rest of the portages this day are on US soil and have much better paths. Most travelers enter Clove Lake via the 110-rod carry across Pine Island, called "Pine Portage." The trail climbs at the beginning, but most of the trail is downhill, including a long, steep drop near the end. An alternate route to Clove Lake follows a very scenic section of the Pine River around the north side of Pine Island. Three sets of rapids are bypassed by shorter portages. It's quicker to simply take "Pine Portage."

(Also see comments for Day 1, Route #80-1, paragraphs 3-4.)

Day 2 (7 miles): Gneiss Lake, Devil's Elbow Lake, rapids, Maraboeuf Lake, p. 27 rods, Granite River, p. 36 rods, Saganaga Lake. (See comments for Day 2, Route #80-1.)

Day 3 (8 miles): Saganaga Lake, p. 10 rods, Red Rock Lake. Beware the wakes from motorboats and the waves from potentially strong winds on big Saganaga Lake. Also keep your compass and map in front of you at all times. Navigation is quite confusing on large lakes with many islands and peninsulas.

If the water level is not too low, the only portage of the day can be avoided by paddling through the short, shallow creek connecting Saganaga and Red Rock lakes.

Plan to camp in the south end of Red Rock Lake for 8 miles of travel. This may be your quietest night in the Wilderness, since motorboats are not permitted on Red Rock Lake.

Day 4 (8 miles): Red Rock Lake, p. 48 rods, Alpine Lake, p. 105 rods, Seagull Lake. (See comments for Day 2, Route #55-1.)

ROUTE #57-2: The Thunder Point Route

8 Days, 77 Miles, 41 Lakes, 3 Rivers, 4 Creeks, 49 Portages

DIFFICULTY: Challenging

FISHER MAPS: F-11, F-12, F-19, F-20

INTRODUCTION: This long route is one of the most interesting and varied routes in the BWCA Wilderness. From the public landing on Gunflint Lake, you will paddle north through Magnetic Lake and down the Pine River to Clove Lake. You'll continue winding your way north via the Granite River to

Maraboeuf Lake and onward to Saganaga Lake. You will then continue along the Canadian border in a southwest direction, through Swamp and Ottertrack lakes to Knife Lake. At Thunder Point, the route veers away from the international boundary. It leads south to the heart of the Boundary Waters via Kekekabic and Fraser lakes and a chain of smaller lakes and frequent portages. When you reach the Kawishiwi River, then, you'll steer northeast and follow a chain of small lakes and good portage trails that lead to Little Saganaga Lake. After crossing one of the most scenic portages in the Boundary Waters, you'll proceed from Mora Lake north to Tuscarora Lake. Finally you'll hike across the roughest portage of the entire route to exit the Boundary Waters from Missing Link Lake. This outstanding route ends at the public landing on Round Lake, about 5 miles from your origin at Gunflint Lake. (See Entry Point 52, Location, for directions to Round Lake.)

This route is an excellent choice for trippers who seek canoeing variety, outstanding scenery, and pockets of solitude that lie deep within the Wilderness—but only if you're up to the challenge of frequent portages, including one tough one that exceeds a mile in length. Don't let the beginning of the route fool you. After 2 easy days of paddling with only 4 portages (Days 2 and 3), the route quickly becomes a challenge. You'll average more than 8 portages per day during 5 of the 8 days and, although the final day has only 4 carries, it is the toughest day of all.

Most of the route entertains many visitors throughout the summer months. You may see motorboats on the Canadian side of the border from Gunflint Lake to Saganaga Lake, as well as on the US side of Gunflint, Magnetic and Saganaga lakes. Saganaga is a very busy lake, and canoe traffic may be fairly heavy all along the Canadian border from Saganaga to Knife Lake. The middle part of this route, on the other hand, penetrates the remote central part of the Wilderness, which receives relatively few visitors. Make it a goal throughout your expedition to get started early each morning and make camp as early as possible in the afternoon.

Anglers will find walleyes and northern pike in most of the water along this route. Lake trout and smallmouth bass also inhabit several of the lakes.

Day 1 (9 miles): Gunflint Lake, Magnetic Lake, p. 15 rods, **Pine River,** p. 13 rods, **river,** p. 35 rods, **river,** p. 110 rods, **Clove Lake,** p. 48 rods, **Pine River, Granite River,** p. 72 rods, **river,** p. 25 rods, **Granite River, rapids, river,** p. 25 rods, **Gneiss Lake.** (See comments for Day 1, Route #57-1.)

Day 2 (10 miles): Gneiss Lake, Devil's Elbow Lake, rapids, Maraboeuf Lake, p. 27 rods, **Granite River,** p. 36 rods, **Saganaga Lake.** (See comments for Day 2, Route #80-2.)

Day 3 (13 miles): Saganaga Lake, p. 5 rods, **Swamp Lake,** p. 80 rods, **Ottertrack Lake.** If you're not heading into a strong southwest wind on Saganaga Lake, this will surely be the easiest day of your trip. The 80-rod "Monument Portage" does not require a monumental effort—it merely passes over a low hill shared by the United States and Canada at the summit of which is a large steel monument that marks the international boundary.

Ottertrack is a very scenic lake—long, narrow and lined with bluffs and a rocky shore. Watch for a plaque cemented to the base of a cliff on the Canadian shoreline, about ½-mile after the lake's 2 arms join together. The plaque commemorates "Ben Ambrose 1896-1982." Benny was a prospector who sought gold for more than 60 years in this area. His homestead once occupied the property across the lake, on the US shore.

There is a cluster of campsites at the southwest end of Ottertrack Lake, near "Little Knife Portage." Choose a good site. Then choose your

Gotter Lake

favorite lure and search the lake's depths for the walleyes, northern pike and lake trout that dwell there.

Day 4 (12 miles): Ottertrack Lake, p. 5 rods, **Knife Lake,** p. 33 rods, **Bonnie Lake,** p. 25 rods, **Spoon Lake,** p. 25 rods, **Pickle Lake,** p. 80 rods, **Kekekabic Lake,** p. 85 rods, **Strup Lake,** p. 10 rods, **Wisini Lake.** The westernmost end of the long island that separates the branches of Knife Lake is known as Thunder Point. There you'll find a ¼-mile trail that leads to an overlook. A hike to the top is rewarded by a panoramic view of the Canadian border country from 150 feet above the lake.

Thunder Point is the turning point in your journey—in two ways. In addition to being the westernmost point on this route, it also marks the end of the easiest part of your journey. After Knife Lake, portages are more frequent, and they are all uphill this day. You'll gain over 215 feet of elevation from the shore of Knife Lake to your campsite on Wisini Lake. Fortunately, the trails are well worn, well maintained and easy to negotiate, in spite of the ascent. Over half of the elevation gain is spread over the 4 portages between Knife and Kekekabic lakes. The steepest climb is on the 85-rod trail, which gains over 100 feet of elevation. Fortunately, it has an excellent path that passes through a lovely aspen forest.

Don't delay in claiming your campsite on Wisini Lake. The 3 choices often fill up early. The best choice is on an elevated rock ledge near the middle of the lake. It is terraced and has sufficient space for at least 4 tents. The only drawback is that there is no good boat landing.

Day 5 (8 miles): Wisini Lake, p. 90 rods, **Ahmakose Lake,** p. 30 rods, **Gerund Lake,** p. 15 rods, **Fraser Lake,** p. 11 rods, **Shepo Lake,** p. 22 rods, **Sagus Lake,** p. 42 rods, **Roe Lake, creek,** p. 65 rods, **Cap Lake,** p. 220 rods, **Boulder Lake, Boulder Creek,** p. 15 rods, **creek,** p. 10 rods, **creek, Adams Lake.** (See comments for Day 4, Route #52-2.)

Day 6 (9 miles): Adams Lake, p. 90 rods, **Beaver Lake,** p. 30 rods, **Trapline Lake,** p. 22 rods, **Kawishiwi River,** p. 18 rods, **river,** p. 42 rods, **Kivaniva Lake, creek,** p. 18 rods, **Anit Lake,** p 65 rods, **Pan Lake.** (See comments for Day 5, Route #52-2.)

Day 7 (10 miles): Pan Lake, p. 50 rods, **Panhandle Lake,** p. 90 rods, **pond,** p. 60 rods, **Makwa Lake,** p. 55 rods, **Elton Lake,** p. 19 rods, **creek,** p. 19 rods, **Little Saganaga Lake,** p. 45 rods, **Mora Lake,** p. 10 rods, **Tarry Lake,** p. 50 rods, **Crooked Lake.** (See comments for Day 6, Route #52-2.)

Day 7 (6 miles): Crooked Lake, p. 55 rods, **Owl Lake,** p. 63 rods, **Tuscarora Lake,** p. 366 rods, **Missing Link Lake,** p. 142 rods, **Round Lake.** (See comments for Day 3, Route #52-1.)

Entry Point 58—South Lake

SEASONAL PERMITS: 159

POPULARITY RANK: 35th

DAILY QUOTA: 3

LOCATION: South Lake is located 26 airline miles northwest of Grand Marais, accessible by boat from Gunflint Lake. From Highway 61 in Grand Marais, drive 45 miles on the Gunflint Trail to County Road 50. Turn right and follow this hilly gravel road ½-mile to the public landing for Gunflint Lake on the left side of the road. South Lake is 12 miles (via 4 lakes) east of the Gunflint landing.

DESCRIPTION: A small parking area at the access will accommodate half a dozen vehicles. The Iron Lake Campground, 8 miles closer to Grand Marais via the Gunflint Trail and County Road 92, is the closest USFS facility. It's a very quiet little campground with only 7 campsites. Operated by a concessionaire, Way of the Wilderness Outfitters, a camping fee is charged. Make your reservation by calling the National Recreation Reservation Service (see Chapter 2). A more convenient place to camp the night prior to your trip is at Gunflint Pines Resort and Campground, about a half-mile east of the public landing via County Road 50. The private campground has a shower house with indoor toilets. The lodge there has a snack bar where you can buy pizzas, burgers, pop and beer, as well as some grocery items. Or, if you'd rather not unpack your tent for the night before your canoe trip, you could stay in one of the inexpensive bunkhouses at Gunflint Lodge, located just east of the public landing. There you can have a hot shower and a scrumptious breakfast on the morning of your departure, a sauna after the trip and complete or partial outfitting at Gunflint Northwoods Outfitters, located adjacent to the bunkhouses and just across the road from Gunflint Lodge.

For most paddlers, it takes a full day of paddling along the international boundary just to reach South Lake from Gunflint Lake. Motorboats are permitted on all of the border lakes leading to South Lake, but they cannot enter the BWCAW. Strong winds are a constant threat to paddlers. A gentle west wind, however, will enhance your progress. There are 2 easy portages along the way.

Historic reminders of the 18th and 19th centuries are hidden along this part of the international border. On the north shore of Gunflint Lake, where the town of La Blaine once stood, the ovens used for baking bread can still be seen. Some abandoned remains of the Canadian Northern railroad parallel the Canadian side of the border from the west end of Gunflint Lake to the east end of North Lake—a result of the mining boom that struck northeastern Minnesota in the 1880's. The remnants of an old railroad town (North Lake, Ontario) are situated on the north shore of North Lake. The "Height of Land Portage" between North and South lakes is the place where French-Canadian Voyageurs initiated "rookies" into their fraternity.

Lakes are long and portages are relatively few and far between in this part of the Wilderness. Paddling may approach tedium. But the scenery is outstanding, with steep ridges bordering the lakes. Beginning canoe trippers will be sufficiently challenged, and experienced photographers will be duly rewarded on either of the routes entering the BWCAW at South Lake.

Reservations for overnight travel permits may not be necessary here at times, especially if your trip will start on a weekday. Only 35% of the available permits were issued to visitors during the summer of 1997. If you decide at the last minute to take a canoe trip through the Tip of the Arrowhead region, this may be the only entry point available.

ROUTE #58-1: The Historic Border Route

2 Days, 21 Miles, 9 Lakes, 6 Portages

DIFFICULTY: Easier

FISHER MAPS: F-13

INTRODUCTION: This easy route will take you along part of the historic Voyageurs' Highway. Along the way, you'll enjoy some breathtaking scenery, including steep ridges rising as high as 400 feet above the water, a panoramic vista and a lovely waterfall. From the public landing at Gunflint Lake, you will paddle east along the international boundary to Rose Lake, crossing 3 huge lakes and 2 smaller ones en route. Then you will portage south to Duncan Lake and exit the BWCAW at Bearskin Lake. The route ends at the public landing at the west end of Bearskin Lake, 19 miles by road from your origin.

This is not a route for people wanting to escape from all reminders of civilization. Motorboats are permitted on the Canadian side of the border and on the US side of the lakes lying west of South Lake—about half the route. Your first day will be almost entirely outside the BWCAW, while the second day will be on a popular route that entertains almost as many daytime visitors as overnight travelers. Nevertheless, your only night in the Wilderness will be in the quietest part of the route.

Anglers will find smallmouth bass and lake trout along much of the route. Northern pike and walleyes also inhabit some of the lakes.

Have a car waiting at Bearskin Lake. If your group doesn't have 2 vehicles, make arrangements with an outfitter in the area to drop you off at the Gunflint Lake landing. By leaving your vehicle at the *end* of the route, you won't need to worry about meeting a pick-up deadline for your return to Gunflint Lake.

Day 1 (12 miles): Gunflint Lake, Little Gunflint Lake, p. 13 rods, **Little North Lake, North Lake,** p. 80 rods, **South Lake.** If wind is not a problem, this should be a very pleasant day of paddling. But beware the potential for strong wind on big Gunflint Lake—head wind or tail wind. It is best to get an early start, before the wind picks up. Stay close to the shore, in case the wind suddenly picks up. You will see cabins and resorts along the south shore of this clear, deep lake for the first 4 miles. But most of the cabins blend well with the natural environment and should not detract from your first day on the water.

The narrow channel connecting Gunflint and Little Gunflint lakes is quite shallow. When the water level is low, you may have to walk a heavily loaded canoe across the sandy shallows. There is a beautiful, big sand beach on the Canadian shore adjacent to the narrows.

The 13-rod portage connecting Little Gunflint and Little North lakes follows an old rail-car path that was once used to haul motor boats from one lake to the other. Most of the rails are still on the ground, but the old docks at both ends are in disrepair. You can see the

Waterfall at Stairway portage

old rail car submerged in Little North Lake just beyond the end of the portage.

The 80-rod "Height of Land Portage" climbs over a low rise that is part of the Laurentian Divide. North of this continental divide, water flows north to Hudson Bay and the Arctic Ocean. Water on the south side flows southeast to Lake Superior and eventually to the Atlantic Ocean. This portage was a point of great significance to the Voyageurs traveling from Lake Superior. Up to this point they had been paddling against the current and portaging uphill. West of South Lake, they paddled with the current and portaged mostly downhill on their journey to the Great Northwest. There are now international boundary markers at both ends of the trail. It has a good path—sandy at the north end, but rocky at the south end. The border was cleared with a 30-foot-wide right-of-way, and the portage trail follows it closely most of the way across.

You'll be following the US-Canadian boundary throughout the day. Keep that in mind when searching for campsites. Those on Canadian soil are off limits to campers without prior clearance from Canada Customs. Use only designated USFS campsites. Not all of the red dots on the maps are legal sites for BWCAW visitors. Plan to camp near the west end of South Lake where there are 3 campsites located on the north shore of the lake, just west of the "Height of Land Portage".

Day 2 (9 miles): South Lake, p. 57 rods, **Rat Lake,** p. 4 rods, **Rose Lake,** p. 80 rods, **Duncan Lake,** p. 75 rods, **Bearskin Lake,** p. 8 rods. This is another easy morning of paddling along the Canadian border, with an opportunity to enjoy lunch at one of the most scenic places overlooking one of the most photographed lakes in the North Woods.

With one noteworthy exception, the portages are easy and relatively short. The 57-rod "South Lake Portage" has a good path, except where it crosses a rocky creek. The short portage at the other side of this tiny lake is little more than a lift-over. But the 80-rod trail from Rose to Duncan Lake is a horse of a different color. Called "Stairway Portage," it actually has 2 stairways—the first with 90 steps, followed by another with 28 steps. The uphill gradient from Rose Lake is so steep that these wooden stairways were constructed to make the climb safer and easier—as well as to mitigate the erosion that might otherwise occur from all the traffic that this popular trail receives.

At the "Stairway Portage" you'll climb nearly 150 feet en route to a scenic overlook near the top of the stairs. Nearby is a lovely waterfall on the creek draining Duncan Lake. A bridge across the creek is part of the Border Route Trail—a spectacular hiking trail that parallels the international boundary for 70 miles from near Lake Superior to near Gunflint Lake. Take time to hike ¼-mile east from the portage to some high cliffs where there is a breathtaking view across Rose Lake and the Canadian wilderness beyond. The rugged Caribou Rock Trail leads south from the Border Route Trail.

The next portage (75 rods) passes over a low hill on a trail that gains about 60 feet elevation before leveling off and then descending gradually to the northwest corner of Bearskin Lake. It has a good, wide, smooth path that passes through a stand of tall pines.

You may end this route at either the east end of Bearskin Lake (County Road 66) or the portage connecting Bearskin and Hungry Jack lakes (County Road 65). The Hungry Jack portage is the closer and more convenient, both for paddling and for shuttling vehicles from Gunflint Lake. The portage trail passes through a small parking lot on the north side of County Road 65, 2½ miles from the Gunflint Trail. As you drive out, watch for the trailhead for the Caribou Rock Trail. It is just past the turnoff to Hungry Jack Lodge, ½-mile west of the portage.

There is a small parking lot on the south side of the road. The trail starts on the north side of the road and leads uphill for ¼-mile to a beautiful overlook across Bearskin Lake from Caribou Rock, nearly 200 feet above the lake. This 15-minute side trip is well worth the effort.

ROUTE #58-2: **The Canadian Border Route**

6 Days, 61 Miles, 19 Lakes, 1 River, 15 Portages

DIFFICULTY: Challenging

FISHER MAPS: F-13, F-14

INTRODUCTION: This is arguably the most scenic route in the Wilderness—especially in autumn. From the public landing on Gunflint Lake, you will follow historic Canadian border lakes all the way to North Fowl Lake at the east end of the Boundary Waters. Then you'll loop back toward the west via the Royal River and follow a chain of long lakes that parallels the border just a couple of miles to the south. The route ends at the public landing on Clearwater Lake, nearly 24 miles by road from your origin.

Bordering the entire route are steep ridges and mountainous peaks that tower from 300 to 500 feet above the water—the most rugged terrain in the entire BWCA Wilderness. Sheer cliffs overlook many of the lakes, most of which are long, deep and clear.

Because of the size of these lakes, and because of their east-west orientation, wind and waves are a constant threat. Consequently, it's wise to schedule a layover day as part of your itinerary. Allowing 7 full days to complete this route takes the worry out of being wind-bound at various points along the way.

Portages are relatively few and far between, averaging less than 3 per day. But many are long. Eight of the trails are at least 100 rods long. The longest measures just over 2 miles. Fortunately, none passes over a steep ridge.

The only drawback to this route is that the Canadian side of the border is outside the Wilderness. You may see and hear motorboats on any of the border lakes, and you may also hear chainsaws or motor vehicles operating on Canadian soil. Furthermore, the US side of the first 4 lakes on this route lies outside the BWCAW, where there is no restriction on the use of motors. Motors not exceeding 10 horsepower are also allowed on the parts of North Fowl and Clearwater lakes that

Rose Lake

lie within the Wilderness. The only part of the entire route where you can be sure of not seeing or hearing a motorboat is from John Lake to West Pike Lake.

If you are willing to tolerate occasional sounds of civilization, and you enjoy long periods of paddling on big lakes, this route is a "must do." Anglers will have plenty of opportunities to catch walleyes, small-mouth bass and lake trout along the way.

Day 1 (12 miles): Gunflint Lake, Little Gunflint Lake, p. 13 rods, **Little North Lake, North Lake,** p. 80 rods, **South Lake.** (See comments for Day 1, Route #58-1.)

Day 2 (7 miles): South Lake, p. 57 rods, **Rat Lake,** p. 4 rods, **Rose Lake.** This is an easier day than the first, to allow plenty of time to explore —as well as to find a vacant campsite on popular Rose Lake. Find a campsite as early as possible on the south shore of the lake. They tend to fill up early in the day. Then take time to explore on foot the rugged and beautiful ridge accessible from the "Stairway Portage." (See comments for Day 2, Route #58-1, paragraphs 1-3.)

If the immediate vicinity of the "Stairway Portage" isn't enough to satisfy your desire to explore, consider spending your afternoon on the Caribou Rock Trail. It is a rugged trail—steep and demanding—that starts just east of the bridge across the Border Route Trail (east of the portage) and leads 3½ miles to County Road 65 near the northwest corner of Hungry Jack Lake. You should allow plenty of time (5-7 hours is recommended) to hike the entire trail roundtrip, rated "most difficult" by the Forest Service. Overlooks along the trail include some excellent vistas across Duncan, Moss and Bearskin lakes. Hiking only as far as the portage connecting Duncan and Bearskin lakes may be challenge enough for one afternoon.

Day 3 (10 miles): Rose Lake, p. 660 rods, **Rove Lake, Watap Lake,** p. 100 rods, **Mountain Lake.** If you need 2 trips to get your gear across portages, be prepared to spend the first half of this day hiking—more than 6 miles on the first portage. The "Long Portage" is not nearly as bad as it might appear on the map, however. It first follows an old railroad grade that connects Rose and Daniels lakes. For the first 1½ miles, the trail gradually gains about 100 feet of elevation on a good gravel path most of the way. Beavers flooded parts of the trail, however, and a short, steep detour was constructed around one large beaver pond about 150 rods from Rose Lake. It appeared in 1998 that another section of the trail might soon also need a detour. After 460 rods, watch for a turnoff to the left where a sign points east for the Border Route Trail. The portage to Rove Lake shares the path of the Border Route Trail to the west end of Rove Lake. This part of the trail (200 rods) is hilly, rocky, plagued with roots, and muddy in one place. There are a couple of short boardwalks over other wet spots. Along the way, you will see some large white pines atop a high ridge.

Like Rose Lake, Rove, Watap and Mountain are beautiful lakes—bordered by high ridges with occasional sheer cliffs, and mountainous peaks rising as high as 400 feet above the lakes. This is perhaps the prettiest chain of lakes in the entire BWCA Wilderness. The most spectacular cliff is at the southwest end of Watap Lake. It can be seen from Rove Lake, too. The narrow channel between those 2 lakes is quite shallow.

"Watap Portage" (100 rods) follows a good, though somewhat rocky, path over a low hill. It has a short boardwalk over a wet spot. You'll see large international boundary monuments at both ends of the portage.

During the peak of the canoeing season, you would be wise to claim the first vacant campsite you see at the west end of Mountain

Trail signs on the Long Portage

Lake (the south shore, on US soil). Paddlers have easy access to this beautiful lake from Clearwater Lake, just 90 rods to the south. There is also primitive road access to the Canadian shoreline. If the anglers in your group have any energy at the end of this long day, they are likely to find lake trout and smallmouth bass nearby. Mountain is a very clear lake that reaches a maximum of 210 feet deep.

Day 4 (10 miles): Mountain Lake, p. 90 rods, **Fan Lake,** p. 40 rods, **Vaseux Lake,** p. 140 rods, **Moose Lake.** If you're not bucking a strong east wind, this should be another pleasant day of paddling along the scenic Canadian border—much easier than the previous day, but not without some challenges.

The 3 portages through the "Lily Lakes" chain (Fan and Vaseux) are more difficult than most along the Canadian border. The paths are plagued with rocks, roots and muddy spots, and the landings at both ends of Fan Lake are poor. Fortunately, the longest carry of the day (140 rods) is downhill. The trail is fairly steep near the west end.

You should be able to make camp early in the afternoon. Nine miles of travel will put you in the east-central part of the lake at the easternmost campsite on the US shore. Resist the temptation to keep going. There is only one BWCAW campsite on North Fowl Lake, and it's not a particularly desirable site. There are a couple of USFS sites on South Fowl Lake, but they lie outside the Wilderness. To proceed all the way to John Lake would make too long a day of paddling and portaging for most groups.

Day 5 (10 miles): Moose Lake, p. 130 rods, **North Fowl Lake, Royal River,** p. 100 rods, **river, Royal Lake, Royal River,** p. 78 rods, **river, John Lake,** p. 200 rods, **East Pike Lake.** You may see motorboats lined up on the Canadian shoreline at the west end of "Moose Portage" (130 rods). They serve guests staying at resorts on North Fowl Lake, most of which is outside the BWCA Wilderness. The portage has a rocky path on a gradual downhill slope that tends to be muddy and wet early in the canoeing season.

North Fowl is another beautiful lake, with high cliffs on the Canadian shore and steep hills bordering the US shore. Unlike most border lakes, however, it is neither deep nor clear. Its maximum depth is only 10 feet, and most of the lake is even shallower. During late summer, you'll see parts of the lake full of weeds and wild rice. In fact, the grassy bay into which the river flows may conceal the mouth of the Royal River. Expect to see and hear motorboats throughout the lake. There is a small resort (Ron's Lodge) located on the only part of North Fowl Lake's west shore that lies outside the BWCA Wilderness. The Canadian shore of the lake has road access.

Unless the Royal River is running high, you may have to bushwhack 15 to 20 rods along the grassy edge of the river before you get to the start of the actual portage trail, which then has a good path.

Royal Lake may be clogged with reeds, weeds and cattails after mid-summer. Follow the narrow channel that is kept open by the river's current. A steep bluff rises more than 450 feet from the south shore of the little lake. Cliffs also face the Royal River along the mile-long stretch leading northwest to John Lake.

The long, final portage of the day is also the biggest challenge. The trail gradually gains nearly 120 feet elevation during the first 120 rods. At the end there is a short, steep descent to the shore of East Pike Lake. Ten miles of travel puts you near the center of this long lake. A campsite on the north shore of East Pike Lake faces a steep ridge bordering the south shore of the lake.

Day 6 (12 miles): East Pike Lake, p. 177 rods, **West Pike Lake,** p. 214 rods, **Clearwater Lake.** This is another long day of paddling across beautiful lakes that are absolutely stunning in autumn. You'll be flanked on the south by steep ridges towering 300 to 400 feet above the water, and rising as high as 500 feet at one point near the west end of West Pike Lake.

The first long portage is fairly level, but quite rocky. Resist the temptation to put in at a small pond about midway across the portage. The trail veers away from the pond, so there is no place to take out at the other end of the pond. The second portage shares a path used by hikers on the Border Route Trail. It ascends nearly 100 feet during the first 75 rods from the shore of West Pike Lake and then levels off for the rest of the way to Clearwater Lake.

After reaching Clearwater Lake, you will still have over 5 miles to paddle. If there is a brisk west wind, you might want to rest during the afternoon at one of the campsites near the lake's east end, then paddle to the public landing later in the evening after the wind (hopefully) dies. Motorboats that don't exceed 10 horsepower are permitted in the BWCAW on this deep, very clear lake.

Entry Point 60—Duncan Lake

SEASONAL PERMITS: 375

POPULARITY RANK: 21st (tie)

DAILY QUOTA: 4

LOCATION: Duncan Lake is 23 miles northwest of Grand Marais, accessible by boat from Bearskin Lake. From Highway 61 in Grand Marais, drive 27.1 miles to the junction of County Road 66. Turn right onto the "Clearwater Road" and drive 3¼ miles on this winding, hilly gravel road to the public access to Bearskin Lake on the left side of the road. There is a good landing area and a parking lot large enough for 15-20 vehicles.

If there is a strong west wind on the day of your scheduled departure, you may want to begin your trip near the southwest end of Bearskin Lake at the portage from Hungry Jack Lake. This will shorten the paddle across Bearskin Lake from 2½ miles to just ¾ mile. To get there, follow the Gunflint Trail 1¼ miles past the Clearwater Road to the Hungry Jack Road (County Road 65). Drive north (right) on this gravel road 2½ miles to the 21-rod portage between Bearskin and Hungry Jack lakes. A small parking lot on the north (left) side of the road will accommodate half a dozen vehicles. The lake is 8 rods downhill from the north end of the parking lot. Duncan Lake is a ¼-mile portage northwest of Bearskin Lake.

DESCRIPTION: The Flour Lake Campground is a good, convenient place to spend the night before your canoe trip. It is located ½-mile east of County Road 66 via Forest Route 143 from a point on the Flour Lake Road 2.1 miles northeast of the Gunflint Trail. The campground is operated by a concessionaire, Golden Eagle Lodge. A fee is charged to camp at any of the 35 sites. Make your reservation by calling the National Recreation Reservation Service (see Chapter 2). Or, if you'd rather not unpack your tent for the night before your canoe trip, you could stay in an inexpensive bunkhouse, tipi or screenhouse at Clearwater Lodge and Canoe Outfitters. It is located at the west end of Clearwater Lake, less than a mile from the public landing at the east end of Bearskin Lake. There you can have a hot shower and breakfast on the morning of your departure. Complete and partial outfitting services are also available. Bed and breakfast rooms in the historic lodge are discounted for groups that are completely outfitted.

Duncan Lake offers one of the most scenic entries into the BWCAW, as well as quick access to the Canadian border. "Stairway Portage" follows the creek that drains from Duncan Lake to Rose Lake. A lovely waterfall can be seen about midway across the trail. The famed Border Route Trail intersects the portage, and nearby a scenic overlook faces the Canadian shore of Rose Lake from high above its southwest shoreline. The vista rivals any in all of the Quetico-Superior canoe country. Below the overlook, the path descends so steeply that a stairway was constructed to assist visitors with the descent.

Both the Duncan Lake and Daniels Lake entry points provide direct access to this part of the Canadian border region, but 80% of visitors use the Duncan Lake access. Duncan Lake also entertains many daytime visitors—sixth most among all BWCAW entry points. During the summer of 1997 61% of the available overnight permits were issued. If your trip will start on a weekend or during the peak of the canoeing season, it's a good idea to make a reservation for your permit. With 8 canoeing entry points and 4 hiking entry points all serving the same basic area, the "Tip of the Arrowhead" region is often saturated with visitors during the peak of the canoeing season. Get an early start every morning and try to claim your campsite early in the afternoon while there is still a choice.

If you begin your route at the east end of Bearskin Lake, be sure to visit Honeymoon Bluff either before or after your canoe trip. About 6 rods east of the entrance to the Flour Lake Campground, on the north side of County Road 66, is the start of a foot trail that winds its way north to the top of a bluff. There you'll be treated to a breathtaking view of Hungry Jack Lake, nearly 200 feet below, and Bearskin Lake in the distance. Near the top of your 5-minute climb, you'll also enjoy a panoramic view across Wampus Lake, south of County Road 66. The views are especially outstanding in autumn when the leaves have changed color.

If you begin your route at the Hungry Jack Lake portage, there is also a scenic overlook nearby that deserves a visit either before or after your canoe trip. Watch for the trailhead for the Caribou Rock Trail. It is just west of the turnoff to Hungry Jack Lodge, ½-mile west of the portage. There is a small parking lot on the south side of the road. The trail starts on the north side of the road and leads uphill for ¼-mile to a beautiful overlook across Bearskin Lake from Caribou Rock, nearly 200 feet above the lake. This 15-minute side trip is well worth the effort.

In addition to the 2 routes described below, see Entry Point 61 for 2 other routes you could "plug into" after entering the Wilderness at Duncan Lake.

ROUTE #60-1: The Rose Lake Loop

2 Days, 13 Miles, 4 Lakes, 4 Portages

DIFFICULTY: Challenging

FISHER MAPS: F-13

INTRODUCTION: This short, scenic loop may begin at either of the public accesses to Bearskin Lake. After paddling to the northwest corner of Bearskin Lake, you'll portage to Duncan Lake and then again to Rose Lake on the Canadian border. After exploring the fascinating foot trails along the south shore of Rose Lake, you will paddle on to the east end of the lake and then portage over 1½ miles southeast to Daniels Lake. From the west end of Daniels, you'll portage south to Bearskin Lake and then return to your origin at the public landing. If you start at the east end of Bearskin Lake, your route will be 13 miles long. From the Hungry Jack Lake portage, the loop is reduced to 10 miles.

To most experienced trippers, this route should qualify for an "easier" rating. Indeed, a strong crew could surely complete the loop in one long day. Because of the "Long Portage," however, there is sufficient reason for the route to warrant a "challenging" rating for most groups of less experienced or weaker paddlers. With only 10 to 13 miles to cover in 2 full days, take your time and enjoy the outstanding scenery all around you. Anglers will find smallmouth bass and lake trout along most of the route.

The northbound part of the loop receives rather heavy traffic during much of the summer, and even into early autumn when the colors

Bearskin Lake from the Caribou Rock Trail

are spectacular. During your southbound return to Bearskin Lake, however, you should not encounter nearly as many people—any time of
the year.

Day 1 (6 miles): Bearskin Lake, p. 75 rods, **Duncan Lake,** p. 80
rods, **Rose Lake.** This is a much easier day than the next, to allow plenty of time to explore, as well as to find a vacant campsite on popular
Rose Lake. Find a campsite as early as possible on the south shore of
the lake. Then take time to explore on foot the rugged and beautiful
ridge along the south shore of Rose Lake, which rises as high as nearly
500 feet above the water.

The first portage gradually ascends over a low hill on a wide,
smooth path through a nice stand of tall pines. The first half of the 80-
rod portage has a fairly level, good path that is well worn. After crossing the Border Route Trail, the portage trail plunges nearly 150 feet to
the shore of Rose Lake. Called "Stairway Portage," it actually has 2 stair-

ways—the first with 28 steps followed by another with 90 steps. The gradient is so steep that wooden stairways were constructed to make it safer and easier to walk—as well as to mitigate the erosion that might otherwise occur from all the traffic that this popular trail receives.

A lovely waterfall is on the creek draining Duncan Lake. A bridge across the creek is part of the Border Route Trail—a spectacular hiking trail that parallels the international boundary for 70 miles from near Lake Superior to near Gunflint Lake. Take time to hike ¼-mile east from the portage to some high cliffs where there is a breathtaking view across Rose Lake and the Canadian wilderness beyond.

If the immediate vicinity of "Stairway Portage" isn't enough to satisfy your desire to explore, consider spending your afternoon on the Caribou Rock Trail. It is a rugged trail—steep and demanding—that starts just east of the bridge across the Border Route Trail (east of the portage) and leads 3½ miles to County Road 65 near the northwest corner of Hungry Jack Lake. You should allow plenty of time (5-7 hours is recommended) to hike the entire trail roundtrip, rated "most difficult" by the Forest Service. Overlooks along the trail include some excellent vistas across Duncan, Moss and Bearskin lakes. Hiking only as far as the portage connecting Duncan and Bearskin lakes may be challenge enough for one afternoon.

Day 2 (7 miles): Rose Lake, p. 524 rods, **Daniels Lake,** p. 60 rods, **Bearskin Lake.** If you need 2 trips to get your gear across portages, be prepared to spend much of this day hiking—nearly 5½ miles in all, and more than 3½ miles with gear. The first long portage is not nearly as bad as it might appear on the map, however. It follows an old railroad grade that gradually gains 128 feet of elevation on a good gravel path most of the way. Beavers flooded parts of the trail, however, and a short, steep detour was constructed around one large beaver pond about 150 rods from Rose Lake. It appeared in 1998 that another section of the trail might soon also need a detour. After 460 rods, watch for a junction where the "Long Trail" branches east to Rove Lake. The portage to Daniels Lake continues straight ahead. The final portage passes over a couple of small hills en route to Bearskin Lake—merely a hop and a skip compared to the previous carry.

ROUTE #60-2: The Rose Mountain Moose Loop

5 Days, 47 Miles, 15 Lakes, 1 River, 13 Portages

DIFFICULTY: Challenging

FISHER MAPS: F-13, F-14

INTRODUCTION: This is one of the most scenic routes in the Wilderness—especially in autumn. From the public landing at the east end of Bearskin Lake, you'll paddle across Bearskin and Duncan lakes en route to Rose Lake on the Canadian border. After exploring the fascinating foot trails along the south shore of Rose Lake, you will follow the Canadian border lakes all the way to North Fowl Lake at the east end of the Boundary Waters. Then you'll loop back toward the west via the Royal River and follow a chain of long lakes that parallels the border just a couple of miles to the south. The route ends at a public landing on Clearwater Lake, just 2 miles by road from your origin (less than a mile from Clearwater Lodge at the westernmost tip of the lake).

Bordering the entire route are steep ridges and mountainous peaks that tower from 300 to 500 feet above the water—the most rugged terrain in the entire BWCA Wilderness. Sheer cliffs overlook many of the lakes, most of which are long, deep and clear.

Because of the size of these lakes, and because of their east-west orientation, wind and waves are a constant threat. Consequently, it's wise to schedule a layover day as part of your itinerary. Allowing 6 full days to complete this route takes the worry out of being wind-bound at various points along the way.

Portages are relatively few and far between, with only 2 to 4 carries per day. But 6 of those trails are each more than 100 rods long. The longest measures just over 2 miles. Fortunately, none passes over a steep ridge. If you are traveling light and can get all of your gear across the portages in just one trip, and if the wind isn't a significant factor, this should be an "easier" route for you. If you need 2 trips for each of those portages, however, you'll be walking nearly 20 miles on this journey—a challenge to most folks.

The only other drawback to this route is that the Canadian side of the border is outside the Wilderness. You may see and hear motorboats on any of the border lakes, and you may also hear chainsaws or motor vehicles on the Canadian shore. Motors not exceeding 10 horsepower are also allowed on the parts of North Fowl and Clearwater lakes that lie within the Wilderness. The only parts of the entire route where you can be sure of not seeing or hearing a motorboat is on Duncan Lake and from John Lake to West Pike Lake.

If you enjoy long periods of paddling on big lakes surrounded by truly outstanding scenery, and you don't mind taking some long

Resting on the Long Portage between Rose and Rove lakes

portages along the way, this route is sure to please. Anglers will have plenty of opportunities to catch walleyes, smallmouth bass and lake trout.

Day 1 (6 miles): Bearskin Lake, p. 75 rods, **Duncan Lake,** p. 80 rods, **Rose Lake.** (See comments for Day 1, Route #60-1.)

Day 2 (10 miles): Rose Lake, p. 660 rods, **Rove Lake, Watap Lake,** p. 100 rods, **Mountain Lake.** (See comments for Day 3, Route #58-2.)

Day 3 (9 miles): Mountain Lake, p. 90 rods, **Fan Lake,** p. 40 rods, **Vaseux Lake,** p. 140 rods, **Moose Lake.** (See comments for Day 4, Route #58-2.)

Day 4 (10 miles): Moose Lake, p. 130 rods, **North Fowl Lake, Royal River,** p. 100 rods, **river, Royal Lake, Royal River,** p. 78 rods, **river, John Lake,** p. 200 rods, **East Pike Lake.** (See comments for Day 5, Route #58-2.)

Day 5 (12 miles): East Pike Lake, p. 177 rods, **West Pike Lake,** p. 214 rods, **Clearwater Lake.** (See comments for Day 6, Route #58-2.)

Entry Point 61—Daniels Lake

SEASONAL PERMITS: 89

POPULARITY RANK: 49th

DAILY QUOTA: 1

LOCATION: Daniels Lake is 23 miles northwest of Grand Marais, accessible by boat from Bearskin Lake. From Highway 61 in Grand Marais, drive 27.1 miles to the junction of County Road 66. Turn right onto the "Clearwater Road" and drive 3¼ miles on this winding, hilly gravel road to the public access for Bearskin Lake on the left side of the road. There is a good landing area and a parking lot large enough for 15-20 vehicles.

If there is a strong west wind on the day of your scheduled departure, or for Route #61-2, you should begin your trip near the southwest end of Bearskin Lake at the portage from Hungry Jack Lake. This will shorten the paddle across Bearskin Lake from 2½ miles to just ¾ mile. To get there, follow the Gunflint Trail 1¾ miles past the Clearwater Road to the Hungry Jack Road (County Road 65). Drive north (right) on this gravel road 2½ miles to the 21-rod portage between Bearskin and Hungry Jack lakes. A small parking lot on the north (left) side of the road will accommodate half a dozen vehicles. The lake is 8 rods downhill from the north end of the parking lot. Daniels Lake is north of Bearskin Lake by way of a 60-rod portage.

DESCRIPTION: The Flour Lake Campground is a good, convenient place to spend the night before your canoe trip. It is located ½-mile east of County Road 66 via Forest Route 143 from a point on the Flour Lake Road 2.1 miles northeast of the Gunflint Trail. The campground is operated by a concessionaire, Golden Eagle Lodge. A fee is charged to camp at any of the 35 sites. Make your reservation by calling the National Recreation Reservation Service (see Chapter 2). Or, if you'd rather not unpack your tent for the night before your canoe trip, you could stay in an inexpensive bunkhouse, tipi or screenhouse at Clearwater Lodge and Canoe Outfitters. It is located at the west end of Clearwater Lake, less than a mile from the public landing at the east end of Bearskin Lake. There you can have a hot shower and breakfast on the morning of your departure. Complete and partial outfitting services are also available. Bed and breakfast rooms in the historic lodge are discounted for groups that are completely outfitted.

Like its neighboring entry point to the west (#60), Daniels Lake affords quick access to the most beautiful part of the Canadian border region. Long, deep lakes are bordered by steep ridges with occasional sheer cliffs and mountainous peaks that tower as much as 400 feet above the water. Scenes that are awesome any time of the year are nothing less than spectacular in autumn when the dark green pines are highlighted by the yellow and gold hues of the aspen and birch leaves. Like Duncan Lake, Daniels is just one portage away from the Canadian border and lovely Rose Lake. Unlike the Duncan Lake route, however, entry from Daniels Lake is not accompanied by a panoramic vista. Instead, it requires one of the longest portages in the BWCAW—524 rods over a gently sloping path adjacent to the international boundary. That's why most Rose Lake visitors travel through Duncan Lake and why the 2 suggested routes herein avoid the long portage and veer east to Rove Lake, which is *merely* 264 rods away.

Only 58% of the available overnight permits were actually issued to visitors during the summer of 1997. Nevertheless, with a quota of only 1 permit per day, Daniels Lake ranks high among all entry points with quotas filled the greatest number of days. If your trip will start on a weekend or during the peak of the canoeing season, it's a good idea to make a reservation for your permit. With 8 canoeing entry points and 4 hiking entry points all serving the same basic area, the "Tip of the Arrowhead" region is often saturated with visitors during the peak of the canoeing season. Get an early start every morning and try to claim your campsite early in the afternoon while there is still a choice to be made.

If you begin your route at the east end of Bearskin Lake, be sure to visit Honeymoon Bluff either before or after your canoe trip. About 6 rods east of the entrance to the Flour Lake Campground, on the north side of County Road 66, is the start of a foot trail that winds its way north to the top of a bluff. There you'll be treated to a breathtaking view of Hungry Jack Lake, nearly 200 feet below, and Bearskin Lake in the distance. Near the top of your 5-minute climb, you'll also enjoy a panoramic view across Wampus Lake, south of County Road 66. The views are especially outstanding in autumn when the leaves have changed color.

If you begin your route at the Hungry Jack Lake portage, there is also a scenic overlook nearby that deserves a visit either before or after your canoe trip. Watch for the trailhead for the Caribou Rock Trail just west of the turnoff to Hungry Jack Lodge, ½-mile west of the portage. There is a small parking lot on the south side of the road. The trail starts on the north side of the road and leads uphill for ¼-mile to a beautiful overlook across Bearskin Lake from Caribou Rock, nearly 200 feet above the lake. This 15-minute side trip is well worth the effort.

In addition to the 2 routes described below, see Entry Point 60 for 2 other route suggestions. Route #60-1 could simply be reversed by entering the BWCAW at Daniels Lake and exiting at Duncan Lake. You could "plug into" route #60-2 after entering the Wilderness at Daniels Lake by making the second day of that route the first day of this alternate route.

ROUTE #61-1: The Mountain Lake Loop

2 Days, 15 Miles, 6 Lakes, 4 Portages

DIFFICULTY: Challenging

FISHER MAPS: F-13, F-14

INTRODUCTION: This short loop will take you through some of the most outstanding scenery in the BWCA Wilderness. From the public landing at the east end of Bearskin Lake (County Road 66), you will paddle across Bearskin and Daniels lakes en route to the Canadian border. Then you'll follow the border east through scenic Rove and Watap lakes to Mountain Lake. The next morning you will portage south to Clearwater Lake and then paddle to the west end of that lovely lake. The route ends at the public landing on Clearwater Lake, less than 2 miles by road from your origin.

Bordering the entire route are steep ridges and mountainous peaks that tower from 300 to 400 feet above the water—the most rugged terrain in the entire BWCA Wilderness. Sheer cliffs overlook many of the lakes, most of which are long, deep and clear.

To most experienced trippers, this route should qualify for an "easier" rating. Indeed, a strong crew could surely complete the loop in

Watap Lake cliffs

one long day. For most groups of less experienced or weaker paddlers, however, there is sufficient reason for the route to warrant a "challenging" rating. With only 15 miles to paddle and 4 portages to take in 2 full days, however, you'll have plenty of time to enjoy the outstanding scenery all around you. Anglers will find smallmouth bass and lake trout along most of the route.

Day 1 (10 miles): Bearskin Lake, p. 60 rods, **Daniels Lake,** p. 264 rods, **Rove Lake, Watap Lake,** p. 100 rods, **Mountain Lake.** The first portage passes over a couple of small hills as it descends a total of 30 feet from Bearskin to Daniels Lake. Don't be fooled by the easy beginning of the long portage to Rove Lake. The trails to Rose and Rove lakes are the same for the first 64 rods, descending gradually on the smooth path of an old railroad bed. At a junction with the Border Route Trail, the good path to Rose Lake continues straight ahead. The eastbound trail (right) to Rove Lake, on the other hand, is hilly, rocky, plagued with roots, and muddy in one place. There are a couple of short boardwalks over other wet spots. Along the way, you will see some large white pines atop a high ridge.

Rove, Watap and Mountain are beautiful lakes—bordered by high ridges with occasional sheer cliffs, and mountainous peaks rising as high as 400 feet above the lakes. This is perhaps the prettiest chain of lakes in the entire BWCA Wilderness. The most spectacular cliff is at the southwest end of Watap Lake. It can be seen from Rove Lake, too. The narrow channel between those 2 lakes is quite shallow, but a portage should not be necessary.

"Watap Portage" (100 rods) follows a good, though somewhat rocky, path over a low hill. It has a short boardwalk over a wet spot. You'll see large international boundary monuments at both ends of the portage.

Claim the first vacant campsite you see on Mountain Lake. It's about 10 miles to the first campsite on the US shore. There is primitive road access to the Canadian shoreline, so don't be surprised if you hear a motorboat off in the distance. If the anglers in your group have any energy left at the end of this long day, they are likely to find lake trout and smallmouth bass nearby. Mountain is a very clear lake that reaches a maximum depth of 210 feet.

Day 2 (5 miles): Mountain Lake, p. 90 rods, **Clearwater Lake.** This should be an easy day of paddling across another beautiful lake that is absolutely stunning in autumn. You'll be flanked on the south by steep ridges towering as high as 350 feet above the water.

Your only portage of the day will accelerate your heart, as you climb 110 feet over a ridge separating the 2 lakes. At the crest of the hill is an intersection with the Border Route Trail. You can hike along the trail in either direction to the tops of cliffs that afford spectacular views across Mountain Lake. The overlook to the east is closer (about ¼-mile), but the vista from the cliff west of the portage (¾-mile hike) is more impressive.

After reaching Clearwater Lake, you will have about 4 miles to paddle—an easy task if you're not battling the wind. If there is a brisk west wind, you might want to rest during the afternoon at the campsite located ¼-mile from the portage, then paddle to the public landing later in the evening after the wind (hopefully) dies. Motorboats that don't exceed 10 horsepower are permitted in the BWCAW on this deep, very clear lake.

ROUTE #61-2: The Royal Caribou Loop

        5 Days, 48 Miles, 19 Lakes, 1 River, 19 Portages

DIFFICULTY: Challenging

FISHER MAPS: F-13, F-14

INTRODUCTION: Like most of the routes in the Tip of the Arrowhead region, this is a journey through one of the most scenic parts of the Wilderness. Unlike some other routes, however, this one is a complete loop that requires no shuttling or walking between entry points. From the public landing near the west end of Bearskin Lake (County Road 65), you will paddle across Bearskin and Daniels lakes en route to the Canadian border. Then you'll follow the scenic border eastward, all the way to North Fowl Lake at the east end of the Boundary Waters. From there you'll loop back toward the west via the Royal River and follow a chain of long lakes that parallels the border just a couple of miles to the south. At the east end of Clearwater Lake you will then portage south to Caribou, Deer and Moon lakes. After exiting the BWCA Wilderness to Flour Lake, you'll paddle and portage northwest to the parking lot north of Hungry Jack Lake.

Bordering the entire route are steep ridges and mountainous peaks that tower from 300 to 500 feet above the water—the most rugged terrain in the entire BWCA Wilderness. Sheer cliffs overlook many of the lakes, most of which are long, deep and clear.

Because of the size of these lakes, and because of their east-west orientation, wind and waves are a constant threat. Consequently, it's wise to schedule a layover day as part of your itinerary. Allowing 6 full days to complete this route takes the worry out of being wind-bound at various points along the way.

Portages are relatively few and far between, with only 3 to 5 carries per day. But 9 of those trails are each more than 100 rods long, including 5 that exceed ½-mile in length. The longest measures 264 rods. Two pass over steep ridges. If you need 2 trips to get your gear across each of those portages, you'll be walking nearly 20 miles on this journey—a challenge to most folks and downright rugged to some.

The only other drawback to this route is that the Canadian side of the border is outside the Wilderness. You may see and hear motorboats on any of the border lakes, and you may also hear chainsaws or motor vehicles on the Canadian shore. Motors not exceeding 10 horsepower are also allowed on the parts of North Fowl and Clearwater lakes that lie within the Wilderness.

If you enjoy long periods of paddling on big lakes surrounded by truly outstanding scenery, and you don't mind taking some long portages along the way, this route is sure to please. Anglers will have plenty of opportunities to catch walleyes, smallmouth bass and lake trout along the way.

Day 1 (9 miles): P. 8 rods, **Bearskin Lake,** p. 60 rods, **Daniels Lake,** p. 264 rods, **Rove Lake, Watap Lake,** p. 100 rods, **Mountain Lake.** (See comments for Day 1, Route #61-1.)

Day 2 (10 miles): Mountain Lake, p. 90 rods, **Fan Lake,** p. 40 rods, **Vaseux Lake,** p. 140 rods, **Moose Lake.** (See comments for Day 4, Route #58-2.)

Day 3 (10 miles): Moose Lake, p. 130 rods, **North Fowl Lake, Royal River,** p. 100 rods, **river, Royal Lake, Royal River,** p. 78 rods, **river, John Lake,** p. 200 rods, **East Pike Lake.** (See comments for Day 5, Route #58-2.)

Day 4 (11 miles): East Pike Lake, p. 177 rods, **West Pike Lake,** p. 214 rods, **Clearwater Lake,** p. 150 rods, **Caribou Lake.** (See comments for Day 6, paragraphs 1 and 2, Route #58-2.) Motorboats that don't exceed 10 horsepower are permitted in the BWCAW on Clearwater Lake. You won't see much of that pretty lake, however, since you cross only the easternmost tip of the lake en route to your final portage. The trail there passes over a high ridge separating Clearwater and Caribou lakes. You'll climb rather steeply during the first 30 rods; but most of the trail is downhill, including some steep parts as you approach Caribou Lake. The path is plagued with rocks and roots.

There are half a dozen campsites along the north shore of Caribou Lake. Eleven miles of travel will take you just beyond the center of the lake, across from a steep hillside that rises more than 250 feet above the water. Claim your campsite as early in the day as possible. Anglers may find largemouth bass, northern pike and walleyes in the lake.

Day 5 (8 miles): Caribou Lake, p. 50 rods, **Deer Lake,** p. 15 rods, **Moon Lake,** p. 115 rods, **Flour Lake,** p. 162 rods, **Hungry Jack Lake,** p. 8 rods. The 50-rod portage starts on a steep uphill slope from the shore of Caribou Lake. At the top of the ridge, after gaining 70 feet of elevation, the trail joins the good, level path of an old road that continues south (left) to the north shore of Deer Lake. (Note: if you turned right onto this old road you could hike northwest to Clearwater Lake. See the Sketch on opposite page.)

Note the tall, old white pines covering the hill adjacent to the 15-rod portage between Deer and Moon lakes. The 115-rod portage from the west end of Moon Lake gradually gains 90 feet of elevation on a well worn path that carries you out of the Wilderness.

The final 4½ miles of this route lie outside the BWCAW. You'll see private cabins and resorts along the shores of Flour and Hungry Jack lakes. The ½-mile portage from Flour to Hungry Jack Lake crosses 2 gravel roads and starts at the Flour Lake Campground. Be alert for traffic. After a short climb from the shore of Flour Lake, the trail gradually descends most of the way to Hungry Jack Lake.

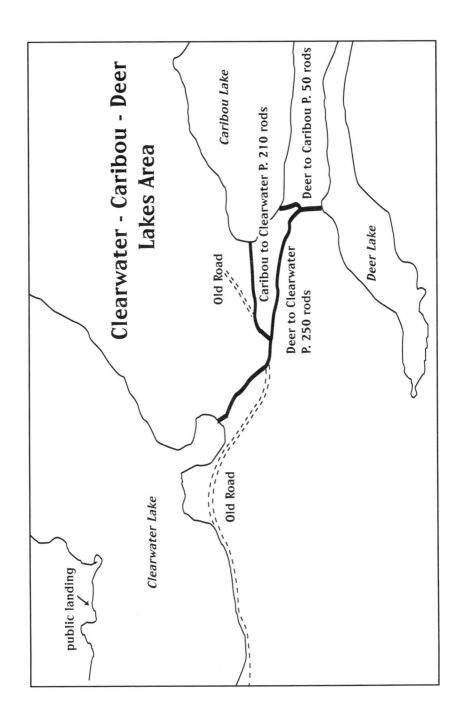

Clearwater - Caribou - Deer Lakes Area

Caribou Lake

Deer to Caribou P. 50 rods

Caribou to Clearwater P. 210 rods

Deer Lake

Old Road

Deer to Clearwater P. 250 rods

Clearwater Lake

Old Road

public landing

After completing the portage, take a few minutes for a side trip to Honeymoon Bluff. About 6 rods east of the entrance to the Flour Lake Campground, on the north side of County Road 66, is the start of a foot trail that winds its way north to the top of a bluff. There you'll be treated to a breathtaking view of Hungry Jack Lake, nearly 200 feet below, and Bearskin Lake in the distance. Near the top of your 5-minute climb, you'll also enjoy a panoramic view across Wampus Lake, south of County Road 66. The views are especially outstanding in autumn when the leaves have changed color.

The short final portage crosses County Road 65 and leads to the small parking lot from which this route started.

Entry Point 62—Clearwater Lake

SEASONAL PERMITS: 405

POPULARITY RANK: 20th

DAILY QUOTA: 4

LOCATION: Clearwater Lake is located 22 airline miles north of Grand Marais. From Highway 61 in Grand Marais, drive 27.1 miles to the junction of County Road 66. Turn right onto the "Clearwater Road" and drive 5¼ miles on this winding, hilly gravel road to the public boat landing at the road's end.

DESCRIPTION: There is a small parking lot that will accommodate 10-12 vehicles next to the public access. Except for an outhouse, there are no other facilities at the landing. Private cabins are adjacent to the landing, and much of the shoreline at the southwest end of Clearwater Lake is occupied by private cabins, lake homes, resorts and canoe trip outfitters.

Camping is not allowed at the access. The Flour Lake Campground is a good, convenient place to spend the night before your canoe trip. It is located just 3½ miles from the landing—½-mile east of County Road 66 via Forest Route 143. The campground is operated by a concessionaire, Golden Eagle Lodge, and a fee is charged to camp at any of the 35 sites. Make your reservation by calling the National Recreation Reservation Service (see Chapter 2). Or, if you'd rather not unpack your tent for the night before your canoe trip, you could stay in an inexpensive bunkhouse, tipi or screenhouse at Clearwater Lodge and Canoe Outfitters. It is located at the west end of Clearwater Lake, 1 mile from the public landing. There you can have a hot shower and breakfast on the morning of your departure. Complete and partial outfitting services are also available. Bed and breakfast rooms in the historic lodge are discounted for groups that are completely outfitted.

Clearwater is a lovely lake, with steep ridges rising as much as 350 feet from its south shoreline. A canoe trip from this entry point will take you into an area that many consider the most scenic part of the

BWCA Wilderness. Minnesota "mountains" tower above the dark green shores of these deep, crystal-clear lakes—a setting not found in the western parts of the Boundary Waters.

Clearwater Lake is the second most popular entry point for the Tip of the Arrowhead. In 1997, ⅔ of the available overnight camping permits were issued to visitors. If your trip will start on a weekend or during the peak of the canoeing season, it's a good idea to make a reservation for your permit. With 8 canoeing entry points and 4 hiking entry points all serving the same basic area, the Tip of the Arrowhead region is often saturated with visitors during the peak of the canoeing season. Get an early start every morning and try to claim your campsite early in the afternoon while there is still a choice to be made.

Motorboats not exceeding 10 horsepower are permitted on Clearwater Lake within the Wilderness. They may not travel beyond the lake itself, however. The interior parts of the BWCAW, away from the Canadian border, are strictly for paddling.

Fishing is usually quite good in many of the lakes in this area. Anglers may want to add to the suggested number of days, in order to avail themselves of the unlimited fishing opportunities around them.

ROUTE #62-1: The Pine Alder Loop

3 Days, 16 Miles, 9 Lakes, 10 Portages

DIFFICULTY: Challenging

FISHER MAP: F-14

INTRODUCTION: This short, scenic loop will take you to one of the prettiest spots in the eastern region of the BWCAW—Johnson Falls. From the public landing you'll paddle to the southeast end of Clearwater Lake and then portage to Caribou Lake. You will continue traveling east to Little Caribou and Pine lakes. After viewing Johnson Falls, then, you'll begin your return trip by crossing a rugged portage to Canoe Lake. From there you will paddle west through Alder Lake to East Bearskin Lake, where you'll veer north to Moon and Deer lakes. A long portage from the north shore of Deer Lake will return you to your origin at Clearwater Lake.

If you are not in good physical shape, choose a different route. Although the route covers only 16 miles, you'll be crossing one of the most exhausting portages in the BWCAW. A couple of others are not easy either. Fortunately, most of the carries are much shorter and easier. Spread over 3 full days, this route should provide enough challenge for most groups. And you should be able to make camp early in the afternoon, when there are still some campsites available. Strong trippers could surely complete the loop in just 2 days, with a night on Canoe Lake, but that would allow little time to explore Johnson Falls.

You may see and hear motorboats on Clearwater and East Bearskin lakes, but the rest of the route is "paddle only." Since 1999, motorboats are no longer permitted on Canoe and Alder lakes.

Anglers will find smallmouth bass along much of the route. Lake trout and walleyes also inhabit some of the water. Pine Lake, in particular, is prized for its fine walleye fishing.

Day 1 (7 miles): Clearwater Lake, p. 150 rods, **Caribou Lake,** p. 25 rods, **Little Caribou Lake.** The first 5½ miles of this route should be a very pleasant passage between the scenic shores of Clearwater Lake, if there is not a strong east wind against you. The portage at the east end of the lake passes over a high ridge separating Clearwater and Caribou lakes. You'll climb rather steeply during the first 30 rods; but most of the trail is downhill, including some steep parts as you approach Caribou Lake. The path is plagued with rocks and roots.

There is only 1 campsite on Little Caribou Lake—a very nice site that is in demand—so try to arrive there early in the afternoon. If it's occupied, you could proceed onward to Pine Lake, where there are several nice campsites along its north shore; but none is close to the portage. It might be more prudent to backtrack to Caribou Lake if you noticed that the campsite near its east end was vacant when you passed by earlier.

Day 2 (4 miles): Little Caribou Lake, p. 80 rods, **Pine Lake,** p. 380 rods, **Canoe Lake,** p. 22 rods, **Alder Lake.** This day is short for two reasons. First, it's not easy. Second, you should allow plenty of time to explore along the way.

The 80-rod trail from Little Caribou Lake is downhill for all but the first 5 rods, descending nearly 100 feet to Pine Lake. Near the beginning, the scenic trail dips down to cross a log bridge over the creek that drains Little Caribou Lake.

Before continuing onward to Canoe Lake, take time out for a hike to lovely Johnson Falls. The trail to it begins at the western tip of Pine Lake, on the south side of a shallow creek flowing into the lake. The well-worn path winds for ⅓-mile uphill to an elevation nearly 100 feet above Pine Lake. There you'll find yourself at the top of a 2-tier cascade. The upper cascade is the more spectacular of the 2 major falls. The hike takes only about 15 minutes (1-way) and is well worth the effort. Use caution on the steep, slippery trail, especially as you descend into the canyon at the base of the falls. Take your time. There aren't many places like this anywhere in the BWCA Wilderness.

The long portage to Canoe Lake is by far the worst you'll encounter. It is one of the most exhausting carries in the entire BWCA Wilderness. The trail surmounts 3 steep hills, gaining over 300 feet of elevation above Pine Lake before descending steeply over the final 40 rods to Canoe Lake. The only level parts of the trail are through marshy areas between the hills. There is a 3-rod boardwalk across the wettest spot, just west of Table Lake about 150 rods from Pine Lake. Fortunately, this portage has a good, well-worn path.

The final carry is across a pretty trail that passes through tall white pines. The campsites on Alder Lake are in great demand. If they are already occupied, or if you prefer to get off the "beaten path," you might consider portaging east to Pierz Lake. There you will find 3 more campsites along the north shore, all facing a steep ridge that borders the south shores of both Alder and Pierz lakes.

Day 3 (5 miles): Alder Lake, p. 70 rods, **East Bearskin Lake,** p. 115 rods, **Moon Lake,** p. 15 rods, **Deer Lake,** p. 250 rods, **Clearwater Lake.** This is the easiest segment of the 3-day route, with portages that are mostly level or downhill. You'll see some large, old red and white pines along the shore of Alder Lake and at some of the portages.

The 70-rod portage that connects Alder Lake with the north bay of East Bearskin Lake is on the shortest route to Moon Lake. A 48-rod portage to the south bay of East Bearskin Lake is easier than the 70-rod carry, but that route requires an extra 2 miles of paddling outside the BWCAW. It's your choice.

Near the start of the 115-rod portage, you may see some remains of the Hedstrom Lumber Company, which operated a sawmill there until 1948. The trail starts out fairly level, with a gradual incline for the first 90 rods. It then descends about 100 feet during the final 25-rod stretch to Moon Lake. The steep descent begins on a stairway with 21 steps.

The final portage is long but not difficult. (See the Sketch on page 231.) The trail follows the path of an old dirt road most of the way. The road continues all of the way to County Road 66, part of it across private land along the south shore of Clearwater Lake outside the BWCAW. Watch for the spur trail to Clearwater Lake, which veers off to the right (north) about 15 rods west of the intersection of the trail from Caribou Lake.

ROUTE #62-2: **The Moose, Caribou and Deer Loop**

6 Days, 46 Miles, 18 Lakes, 1 River, 19 Portages

DIFFICULTY: Challenging

FISHER MAP: F-14

INTRODUCTION: As with most routes in the Tip of the Arrowhead, this loop follows long, scenic lakes, separated by infrequent but fairly long portages. From the public landing you'll paddle to the southeast end of Clearwater Lake and then portage north to Mountain Lake. After following the Canadian border east to North Fowl Lake, you'll navigate the Royal River, which loops west to John Lake. From the west end of John Lake the Pike lakes will then carry you back to the east end of Clearwater Lake. At that point, you'll portage south to Caribou Lake and then follow a chain of smaller lakes that loops past scenic Johnson Falls before returning to your origin at the west end of Clearwater Lake.

Averaging only 7½ miles of travel with barely more than 3 portages per day, this route might warrant an "easier" rating were it not for the length and difficulty of several of the carries. Those portages will average about 1¼ miles per day—that's over 22 miles of walking if you need 2 trips to get your gear across each portage. Also, because of the size of the lakes and their east-west orientation, wind is always a potential threat that can slow your progress considerably if the wind is against you.

This loop can easily be shortened by 7 miles and 9 portages by eliminating all of Day 6 and part of Day 5 described below. Simply paddle from the east end of Clearwater Lake all the way back to the public landing at the west end instead of looping south first to view Johnson Falls. In so doing, however, you will be bypassing one of the most scenic cascades in the BWCA Wilderness.

Regardless of the ending that you choose, don't expect to totally escape from other people anywhere along this popular route. Also, since the Canadian side of the border lakes is not part of any protected wilderness, you may see or hear motorboats throughout the eastbound part of the journey. After leaving the border via the Royal River, however, the only lakes where motorboats are permitted in the BWCAW are East Bearskin and Clearwater.

Anglers will have opportunities to catch lake trout, smallmouth bass and walleyes along the route. If any members of your group would rather hike than fish, they'll have several opportunities to access the famed Border Route Trail from portages along the route.

Day 1 (8 miles): Clearwater Lake, p. 90 rods, **Mountain Lake.** This should be an easy day of paddling across 2 big, beautiful lakes that are absolutely stunning in autumn. The 8 miles of paddling are split evenly on the 2 lakes if you camp near the middle of Mountain Lake. Motorboats that don't exceed 10 horsepower are permitted in the BWCAW on Clearwater Lake, but not on Mountain Lake. Unfortunately, motorboats are allowed on the Canadian side of the border and there is road access to the north shore of Mountain Lake. So you could see or hear motors throughout this day. Nevertheless, the scenery more than compensates for the distraction of motorboats. You'll be flanked on the south by steep ridges towering as high as 350 feet above the water.

The only portage of the day will accelerate your heart, as you climb nearly 100 feet over a ridge separating the 2 lakes. At the crest of the hill is an intersection with the Border Route Trail. You can hike along the trail in either direction to the tops of cliffs that afford spectacular views across Mountain Lake. The overlook to the east is closer (about ¼-mile), but the vista from the cliff west of the portage (¾-mile hike) is more impressive.

Day 2 (7 miles): Mountain Lake, p. 90 rods, **Fan Lake,** p. 40 rods, **Vaseux Lake,** p. 140 rods, **Moose Lake.** (See comments for Day 4, paragraphs 2-3, Route #58-2.)

Day 3 (7 miles): Moose Lake, p. 130 rods, **North Fowl Lake, Royal River,** p. 100 rods, **river, Royal Lake, Royal River,** p. 78 rods, **river, John Lake.** (See comments for Day 5, paragraphs 1-4, Route #58-2.) There are 2 excellent campsites at the southeast end of John Lake. John Lake is a BWCAW entry point and both campsites are less than a mile from the end of the Arrowhead Trail (County Road 16).

Day 4 (8 miles): John Lake, p. 200 rods, **East Pike Lake,** p. 177 rods, **West Pike Lake.** This is another day of paddling across beautiful lakes that are absolutely stunning in autumn. All 3 lakes are bordered on the south by steep ridges towering 300 to 400 feet above the water, and rising as high as 500 feet at one point near the west end of West Pike Lake.

The first long portage of the day is the biggest challenge so far. The trail gradually gains nearly 120 feet elevation during the first 120 rods. At the end there is a short, steep descent to the shore of East Pike Lake. The second portage is fairly level, but quite rocky. Resist the temptation to put in at a small pond about midway across the portage. The trail veers away from the pond, so there is no place to take out at the other end of the pond.

For an 8-mile day of travel, plan to camp near the center of scenic West Pike Lake. It's a deep, very clear lake that harbors lake trout and smallmouth bass. If you are in the mood for hiking, rather than fishing, you can access the Border Route Trail from the portages at both ends of the lake.

Day 5 (9 miles): West Pike Lake, p. 214 rods, **Clearwater Lake,** p. 150 rods, **Caribou Lake,** p. 25 rods, **Little Caribou Lake,** p. 80 rods, **Pine Lake,** p. 380 rods, **Canoe Lake.** This day starts and ends with long portages. The first portage shares a path used by hikers on the Border Route Trail. It ascends nearly 100 feet during the first 75 rods from the shore of West Pike Lake and then levels off for the rest of the way to Clearwater Lake. The second portage passes over a high ridge separating Clearwater and Caribou lakes. You'll climb rather steeply during the first 30 rods; but most of the trail is downhill, including some steep parts as you approach Caribou Lake. The path is plagued with rocks and roots. (Also see comments for Day 2, paragraphs 2-4, Route #62-1.)

Because of the popularity of this area (sometimes more demand for campsites than there is supply of them), you might want to claim your campsite on Canoe Lake before exploring Johnson Falls. Then paddle back to the Pine Lake portage and cache your canoe off to the side where it doesn't block access for other paddlers. From there you can hike all the way to Johnson Falls. From the north end of the portage, a trail leads ¼-mile west along the south shore of Pine Lake to the start of the Johnson Falls Trail. You'll be hiking a little more than 3½ miles. Allow a couple of hours to fully explore and enjoy the cascade. Of course, don't forget to safely hang your food pack before leaving your campsite on Canoe Lake. Campsites that are popular with humans are often also popular with black bears.

(Note: If you are behind schedule at the start of this day, or if you simply prefer not to take the 2 difficult portages described above, you could paddle 5 miles directly back to the landing on Clearwater Lake after the portage from West Pike Lake. It's an 8-mile day of travel with only one portage—an easy ending to a delightful 5-day route.)

Day 6 (7 miles): Canoe Lake, p. 22 rods, **Alder Lake**, p. 48 rods, **East Bearskin Lake,** p. 115 rods, **Moon Lake,** p. 15 rods, **Deer Lake,** p. 250 rods, **Clearwater Lake.** (See comments for Day 3, paragraphs 2-4, Route # 62-1.)

Entry Point 64—East Bearskin Lake

SEASONAL PERMITS: 485

POPULARITY RANK: 15th

DAILY QUOTA: 5

LOCATION: East Bearskin Lake is 20 airline miles north of Grand Marais. From Highway 61, drive north on the Gunflint Trail for 26 miles to its junction with Forest Route 146. Turn right and drive 1 mile northeast on this good gravel road to a sign indicating "National Forest Campground." Turn right and drive ½-mile to the public boat landing adjacent to the campground.

DESCRIPTION: A parking lot next to the landing will accommodate up to 15 vehicles. The East Bearskin Campground is a very convenient place to spend the night prior to your canoe trip. Thirty-three campsites are available on a first-come-first-served basis and a fee is charged.

East Bearskin Lake is the most popular of the entry points serving the Tip of the Arrowhead region. The east end and much of the south shore of the lake lie in the BWCA Wilderness. At the west end is a popular resort, Bearskin Lodge. Along the north shore are many private cabins. Because most are well hidden, you may see only the docks from the lake.

Boats with up to 25 horsepower motors are permitted in the BWCAW on East Bearskin Lake. Since 1999, however, motorboats are no longer permitted on Alder and Canoe lakes, which lie to the east. Although the buzzing of motors should not plague your route from this entry point, you may find it hard to elude other canoeists. The outstanding scenery in this hilly region necessitates sharing. With 8 canoeing entry points and 4 hiking entry points all serving the same basic area, the "Tip of the Arrowhead" region is often saturated with visitors during the peak of the canoeing season. Get an early start every morning and try to claim your campsite early in the afternoon while there is still a choice to be made.

During the summer of 1997, 63% of the available overnight permits were actually issued to visitors. If your trip will start on a weekend or during the peak of the canoeing season, it's a good idea to make a reservation for your permit.

ROUTE #64-1: The Johnson Falls Loop

3 Days, 18 Miles, 8 Lakes, 8 Portages

DIFFICULTY: Challenging

FISHER MAPS: F-13, F-14

INTRODUCTION: This loop will take you through a popular chain of lakes that leads to a spectacular natural attraction. From the public landing near the west end of East Bearskin Lake, you will paddle east to Alder and Canoe lakes and then portage over a Minnesota "mountain" to Pine Lake. There you will leave your canoe for awhile and hike to one of nature's spectacles—Johnson Falls. Then you'll start your return trip from Pine Lake, first northwest through Little Caribou and Caribou lakes and then southwest through Deer and Moon lakes to your origin at East Bearskin Lake.

This short, scenic route would be classified "easier," were it not for one long, difficult portage in the middle. If you can transport all of your gear across portages in just one trip, and you're traveling with a group of strong paddlers, you could "easily" complete the loop in just 2 days, with a night on Pine Lake. Spreading it over 3 full days, however, will shorten each day enough to enable finding vacant campsites early in the afternoons.

Anglers will find smallmouth bass in these crystalline lakes, and the avid angler may even want to add an extra day to search the depths of Pine Lake for the tasty walleyes and elusive lake trout that inhabit that long, scenic lake.

Day 1 (6 miles): East Bearskin Lake, p. 48 rods, **Alder Lake,** p. 22 rods, **Canoe Lake.** This is an easy day, with portages that have good, well-worn and well-maintained paths. Tall white pines, cedars and birch trees border the lakes. And the portages pass through lovely stands of tall, old white pines and Norway pines. During the busiest summer season, there is a good chance that all the campsites along the route will be occupied early each day (maybe even by noon). So get an early start and claim your campsite as early as possible.

Johnson Falls

The campsites on Alder and Canoe lakes are in great demand. If they are already occupied, or if you prefer to get off the "beaten path," you might consider portaging east from Alder to Pierz Lake or from Canoe to Crystal Lake. You will find several more campsites along the north shores of both lakes. If you continue across the big portage to Pine Lake, you may have to paddle a considerably distance out of your way to find a vacant campsite on that long lake (which is an entry point from the east).

Day 2 (6 miles): Canoe Lake, p. 380 rods, **Pine Lake,** p. 80 rods, **Little Caribou Lake,** p. 25 rods, **Caribou Lake.** The long portage from Canoe Lake to Pine Lake starts with a steep uphill climb, gaining over 100 feet in the first 40 rods. After that climb, however, it is mostly downhill or level. Three steep downhill segments have a total drop of just over 300 feet. Two wet spots separate the downhill segments. The first one may be muddy; the second is a bog over which a 3-rod boardwalk passes. Be glad you're not portaging in the opposite direction.

Before continuing onward to Little Caribou Lake, take time out for a hike to lovely Johnson Falls. The trail to it begins at the western tip of Pine Lake, on the south side of a shallow creek flowing into the lake. The well-worn path winds for ⅓-mile uphill to an elevation nearly 100 feet above Pine Lake. There you'll find yourself at the top of a 2-tier cascade. The upper cascade is the more spectacular of the 2 major falls. The hike takes only about 15 minutes (1-way) and is well worth the effort. Use caution on the steep, slippery trail, especially as you descend into the canyon at the base of the falls. Take your time. There aren't many places like this anywhere in the BWCA Wilderness.

The 80-rod trail to Little Caribou Lake is uphill for all but the final 5 rods, gaining nearly 100 feet elevation from Pine Lake. Near the end, the scenic trail dips down to cross a log bridge over the creek that drains Little Caribou Lake.

Plan to camp at one of the 3 campsites at the west end of Caribou Lake for 6 miles of travel. Anglers with energy left at the end of this interesting day will have an opportunity to catch largemouth bass, northern pike and walleyes in the water nearby.

Day 3 (6 miles): Caribou Lake, p. 50 rods, **Deer Lake,** p. 15 rods, **Moon Lake,** p. 115 rods, **East Bearskin Lake.** The 50-rod portage starts on a steep uphill slope from the shore of Caribou Lake. At the top of the ridge, after gaining 70 feet of elevation, the trail joins the good, level path of an old road that continues south (left) to the north shore of Deer Lake. (Note: if you turned right onto this old road you could hike northwest to Clearwater Lake. See the Sketch on page 231.)

Note the tall, old white pines covering the hill adjacent to the 15-rod portage between Deer and Moon lakes. The 115-rod portage from the south shore of Moon Lake starts with a steep ascent, gaining about 100 feet during the first 25 rods. Near the top, there is a stairway with 21 steps to aid the climb. Beyond the stairs, the trail is fairly level, with a gradual decline over the final 90 rods. Near the end of the portage is the site of a former sawmill. You may still see some remains from the Hedstrom Lumber Company, which operated there until 1948.

ROUTE #64-2:	The Alder Moose Loop
	6 Days, 51 Miles, 18 Lakes, 1 River, 20 Portages
DIFFICULTY:	Challenging
FISHER MAPS:	F-13, F-14
INTRODUCTION:	This loop is an expansion of Route #64-1, adding several long and scenic lakes that are separated by infrequent but long portages. From the public landing near the west end of East Bearskin Lake, you will paddle east to Alder and Canoe lakes and then portage over a Minnesota "mountain" to Pine Lake. There you will leave your canoe to hike to Johnson Falls. Then, from Pine Lake you'll head northwest through Little Caribou and Caribou lakes to Clearwater Lake. From the east

end of that long lake, you'll paddle east on the Pike lakes and John Lake to the Royal River, which flows to North Fowl Lake. From that point, you will follow the Canadian border first north and then west to the west end of beautiful Mountain Lake. After portaging back to Clearwater Lake and then on to Caribou Lake, you'll veer southwest across a chain of smaller lakes and more frequent portages that lead back to your origin at East Bearskin Lake.

Averaging just over 8 miles of travel with 3 to 4 portages per day, this route might warrant an "easier" rating were it not for the length and difficulty of several of the carries. Those portages will average about 1¼ miles per day—that's over 22 miles of walking if you need 2 trips to get your gear across each portage. Also, because of the size of the lakes and their east-west orientation, wind is always a potential threat that can slow your progress considerably if the wind is against you.

Don't expect to totally escape from other people anywhere along this popular route. Since the Canadian side of the border lakes is not part of any protected wilderness, you may see or hear motorboats throughout the westbound part of the journey. South of the border, however, the only lakes where motorboats are permitted in the BWCAW are East Bearskin and Clearwater.

Anglers will have opportunities to catch lake trout, smallmouth bass and walleyes along the route. If any members of your group would rather hike than fish, they'll have several opportunities to access the famed Border Route Trail from portages along the route.

Day 1 (6 miles): East Bearskin Lake, p. 48 rods, **Alder Lake,** p. 22 rods, **Canoe Lake.** (See comments for Day 1, Route #64-1.)

Day 2 (9 miles): Canoe Lake, p. 380 rods, **Pine Lake,** p. 80 rods, **Little Caribou Lake,** p. 25 rods, **Caribou Lake,** p. 150 rods, **Clearwater Lake,** p. 214 rods, **West Pike Lake.** Get an early start. This is probably the most rugged day of the entire trip. (See comments for Day 2, paragraphs 1-3, Route #64-1.)

If you're already exhausted by the time you reach Caribou Lake, it might be wise to rest there awhile before continuing onward. The 150-rod portage climbs most of the way to Clearwater Lake, including some rather steep parts near the beginning, on a path plagued with rocks and roots. The final 30 rods are on a fairly steep downhill slope.

The final carry of the day is longer than the previous trek, but not as exhausting. It starts out on a fairly level path and then descends nearly 100 feet during the final 75 rods to West Pike Lake. The path is shared with hikers using the Border Route Trail.

Plan to camp near the center of West Pike Lake for a 9-mile day of travel. It's a deep, very clear lake that harbors lake trout and small-mouth bass.

Day 3 (8 miles): West Pike Lake, p. 177 rods, **East Pike Lake,** p. 200 rods, **John Lake.** You will be paddling this day across beautiful lakes that are absolutely stunning in autumn. Steep ridges tower 300 to 400 feet above the water, rising as high as 500 feet at one point near the west end of West Pike Lake.

The first long portage of the day is mostly level, but quite rocky. At the beginning of the second portage there is a short, steep ascent from the shore of East Pike Lake. The trail then gradually descends nearly 120 feet during the remaining 120 rods.

There are 2 excellent campsites at the southeast end of John Lake. John Lake is a BWCAW entry point and both campsites are less than a mile from the end of the Arrowhead Trail (County Road 16).

Day 4 (8 miles): John Lake, Royal River, p. 78 rods, **river, Royal Lake, Royal River,** p. 100 rods, **river, North Fowl Lake,** p. 130 rods, **Moose Lake.** Cliffs face the Royal River along the mile-long stretch leading southeast to Royal Lake, which may be clogged with reeds, weeds and cattails after mid-summer. Follow the narrow channel that is kept open by the river's current. A steep bluff rises more than 450 feet from the south shore of the little lake. At the end of the 100-rod portage, unless the Royal River is running high, you may have to bush-whack 15 to 20 more rods along the grassy edge of the river before you can put back into the river. The actual portage trail has a good, well-worn path.

North Fowl is another beautiful lake, with high cliffs on the Canadian shore and steep hills bordering the US shore. Unlike most other border lakes, it is neither deep nor clear. The maximum depth is only 10 feet, and most of the lake is even shallower. During late summer, you'll see parts of the lake full of weeds and wild rice. In fact, it may be hard to see the start of the 130-rod portage at the grassy northwest end of the lake. Expect to see and hear motorboats throughout the lake. There is a small resort (Ron's Lodge) located on the only part of North Fowl Lake's west shore that lies outside the BWCA Wilderness. The Canadian shore of the lake has road access.

You may see motorboats lined up on the Canadian shoreline at the west end of "Moose Portage" (130 rods). They serve guests staying at resorts on North Fowl Lake. The portage has a rocky path on a gradual uphill slope that tends to be muddy and wet early in the canoeing season.

Plan to camp near the northwest end of Moose Lake for a day with 8 miles of travel. Avoid the westernmost site, however—a poor site for

2 tents hidden in an aspen grove, marked by a tall rock cairn along the shore (in 1998). Like most of the border lakes in this region, Moose is a very pretty lake. It is also a deep lake that harbors walleyes, smallmouth bass and lake trout.

Day 5 (8 miles): Moose Lake, p. 140 rods, **Vaseux Lake,** p. 40 rods, **Fan Lake,** p. 90 rods, **Mountain Lake.** If you're not bucking a strong west wind, this should be another pleasant day of paddling along the scenic Canadian border—easier than the previous day, but not without some challenges.

The 3 portages through the "Lily Lakes" chain (Fan and Vaseux) are more difficult than most along the Canadian border. The paths are plagued with rocks, roots and muddy spots, and the landings at both ends of Fan Lake are poor. Also, the longest carry of the day (140 rods) is uphill and fairly steep near the west end, gaining nearly 150 feet of elevation.

Plan to camp near the west end of Mountain Lake. During the peak of the canoeing season, however, it might be prudent to claim the first vacant campsite you see on the south shore. Paddlers have easy access to this beautiful lake from Clearwater Lake, just 90 rods to the south. There is also primitive road access to the Canadian shoreline. If the anglers in your group have any energy at the end of this long day, they are likely to find lake trout and smallmouth bass nearby. Mountain is a very clear lake that reaches a maximum of 210 feet deep.

Day 6 (12 miles): Mountain Lake, p. 90 rods, **Clearwater Lake,** p. 150 rods, **Caribou Lake,** p. 50 rods, **Deer Lake,** p. 15 rods, **Moon Lake,** p. 115 rods, **East Bearskin Lake.** The first portage of the day will accelerate your heart, as you climb nearly 100 feet over a ridge separating the 2 lakes. At the crest of the hill is an intersection with the Border Route Trail. You can hike along the trail in either direction to the tops of cliffs that afford spectacular views across Mountain Lake. The overlook to the east is closer (about ¼-mile), but the vista from the cliff west of the portage (¾-mile hike) is more impressive.

Motorboats that don't exceed 10 horsepower are permitted in the BWCAW on Clearwater Lake. You won't see much of that pretty lake, however, since you cross only the easternmost tip of the lake en route to your final portage. The trail there passes over a high ridge separating Clearwater and Caribou lakes. You'll climb rather steeply during the first 30 rods; but most of the trail is downhill, including some steep parts as you approach Caribou Lake. The path is plagued with rocks and roots. (Also see comments for Day 3, Route #64-1.)

Entry Point 66—Crocodile River

SEASONAL PERMITS: 34

POPULARITY RANK: 57th

DAILY QUOTA: 1

LOCATION: The Crocodile River lies 19½ miles due north of Grand Marais, most easily accessible by boat from East Bearskin Lake. From Highway 61, drive north on the Gunflint Trail for 26 miles to its junction with Forest Route 146. Turn right and drive 1 mile northeast on this good gravel road to a sign indicating "National Forest Campground." Turn right and drive ½-mile to the public boat landing adjacent to the campground—the public access for both East Bearskin Lake (#64) and the Crocodile River.

DESCRIPTION: A parking lot next to the landing will accommodate up to 15 vehicles. The East Bearskin Campground is a very convenient place to spend the night prior to your canoe trip. Thirty-three campsites are available on a first-come-first-served basis and a fee is charged.

You can also access the Crocodile River from Forest Route 309 (the "Greenwood Lake Road") and Forest Route 313. That access, however, is hard to find and may be difficult to use, due to lack of maintenance and virtually no canoe traffic. Nevertheless, if you want to go where few others dare to venture, give it a try. From Highway 61 in Grand Marais, drive north for 16 miles to the Greenwood Lake Road. Turn right and drive 4 miles east on Forest Route 309 to its intersection with Forest Route 313. Turn left there and proceed north for 5 more miles to the "vegetable lakes" region. An unmarked, seldom-used 80-rod portage leads west from the road to South Bean Lake. The trail is hard to find, located just prior to a big bend where the road veers east. From South Bean a 75-rod portage leads to Parsnip Lake and then a 100-rod trail connects the northwest end of Parsnip with the Crocodile River. All portages are mostly downhill, descending a total of more than 250 feet during the 2-mile route from the road to the river. But don't expect easy treks across these trails. They are seldom used and may not be cleared of windfalls, and the paths are wet in places. Simply finding the portages may be the greatest challenge.

A 120-rod portage from the south shore of East Bearskin Lake is a much better access, but it requires a steep climb at the beginning. The good path gains nearly 100 feet of elevation during the first 30 rods. The trail starts and ends in cedar groves and passes through a nice stand of big aspen trees en route to Crocodile Lake.

You may see a fair amount of activity on East Bearskin Lake, the most popular of the entry points serving the Tip of the Arrowhead region. At the west end of the lake is a popular resort, Bearskin Lodge. Along the north shore are many private cabins. Boats with up to 25 horsepower motors are permitted in the BWCAW on East Bearskin Lake. Don't worry though—there is a good chance that none of the boat traffic you see is Crocodile-bound.

Crocodile Lake parallels the south shores of East Bearskin and Alder lakes, stretching west-to-east for nearly 4½ miles. It's debatable just where the lake ends and the Crocodile River begins. A 20-rod portage at the east end of Crocodile Lake, however, offers a good divider. From there it's just ⅔-mile to the 100-rod portage leading out of the Wilderness to Parsnip Lake.

There are no good "routes," per se, from this entry point. The entire route from the East Bearskin Lake landing through Crocodile Lake and the Crocodile River to Forest Route 313—thus in and out of the Wilderness—is just 8 miles long. Because the route leads to nowhere but out of the Wilderness, Crocodile Lake is a destination, not the beginning of a canoeing route. For that reason, there are basically just 2 reasons to go there: 1) to fish, or 2) to seek respite from the civilized world, as well as from crowds of other canoeists on busy weekends or holidays.

The entry point is used more by daytime visitors than by overnight campers. The visitors are probably attracted by the good walleye fishing there. Most of the lake is less than 10 feet deep and not very clear, with an abundance of small yellow perch. The perch aren't large enough to attract anglers, but they provide excellent forage for the walleye population. Walleyes of all sizes are abundant, and they have survived so well that a stocking program was discontinued in 1991. A few largemouth bass may also be found in the lake.

There are 2 campsites along the south shore of the lake near its west end and 2 more on the north shore toward the narrow east end. Don't worry about competition for the sites. Only 22% of the available overnight camping permits were issued to visitors in 1997. Of course, with a quota of only 1 permit per day, there is a possibility that the entry point could be filled up on the day when you want to enter. So, even though the Crocodile River is the least popular canoeing entry point in the BWCAW, you may still want to make a reservation—especially if your trip will start on a weekend or holiday.

Entry Point 68—Pine Lake

SEASONAL PERMITS: 107

POPULARITY RANK: 41st

DAILY QUOTA: 1

LOCATION: Pine Lake is accessed by boat from McFarland Lake, which is 24 airline miles northeast of Grand Marais. From Grand Marais, drive 20 miles east on Highway 61 to the tiny village of Hovland. Turn left onto County Road 12 and follow the "Arrowhead Trail" north for 18 miles to McFarland Lake. You'll see a spur road leading down to the shore of McFarland Lake just before arriving at the bridge crossing the creek that connects McFarland and Little John lakes.

DESCRIPTION: The McFarland Lake Camping Area, a small clearing adjacent to the public landing, is a convenient place to camp the night before your canoe trip. It allows a hasty departure by canoe the following morning. If those campsites are occupied, you'll find a much larger campground at Judge C.R. Magney State Park; along Highway 61, 5 miles southwest of Hovland. There are no National Forest campgrounds in this vicinity.

All 3 entry points accessible from the Arrowhead Trail (#'s 68, 69 and 70) receive roughly the same number of overnight visitors each summer. Because you must cross McFarland Lake to reach Pine Lake, however, you'll encounter a good deal more activity en route to the BWCAW at Pine Lake. McFarland, which lies entirely outside the Wilderness, is a lake populated with many private cabins along the north and southeast shorelines. The crystal-clear water of both McFarland and Pine lakes harbors good populations of walleyed pike and smallmouth bass. Pine Lake also contains lake trout. There are no restrictions on the use of motorboats on McFarland, but motorists may not enter the Boundary Waters at Pine Lake. Pine entertains far more BWCAW day-use visitors than the other 2 nearby entry points combined.

With a quota of only 1 overnight camping permit issued each day, a reservation is strongly advised. In 1997, Pine Lake ranked second among all BWCAW entry points filled the greatest number of days. Don't wait until the last minute to make your reservation. This entry point fills up early.

With 8 canoeing entry points and 4 hiking entry points all serving the same basic area, the "Tip of the Arrowhead" region is often saturated with visitors during the peak of the canoeing season. Get an early start every morning and try to claim your campsite early in the afternoon while there is still a choice.

Pine Lake affords easy access to the south-central interior of the beautiful Tip of the Arrowhead region. At 7½ miles long and averaging nearly ½-mile in width, Pine is one of the largest lakes in this part of the Wilderness. Because of its east-west orientation and the fact that there is not a single island on the lake, this wide-open expanse is highly susceptible to the effects of a strong wind. Be cautious and paddle close to the shore, especially if a storm is brewing.

ROUTE #68-1:	The Pike Lakes Loop
	3 Days, 25 Miles, 9 Lakes, 8 Portages
DIFFICULTY:	Challenging
FISHER MAP:	F-14
INTRODUCTION:	This route loops through the heart of the scenic Tip of the Arrowhead region. From the boat landing on McFarland Lake you will paddle west across the full lengths of McFarland and Pine lakes. After a side trip on foot to view spectacular Johnson Falls, you will then loop north through Little Caribou and Caribou lakes to the east end of Clearwater Lake. From there the route leads east across the Pike lakes to John Lake. You'll exit the BWCAW from the southeast end of John Lake and then return to your origin via Little John Lake.

This route consists of mostly big, long lakes, bordered by high hills and separated by long portages. Wind could be a problem on most of the lakes, and the constant paddling might approach tedium if it were not for the magnificent scenery of the Tip of the Arrowhead. For paddlers who dread portages, this route may deserve a "most rugged" rating. There are only 8 portages (2 of which will probably not be necessary) but, if you need 2 trips to get your gear across them, you'll be walking a total of more than 7½ miles. Spread over 3 full days, however, strong trippers should find the route relatively easy.

During the summer months, don't expect to have this route all to yourself. You'll probably see plenty of other people, especially on the westbound part of the loop. Try to break camp early each day and claim your campsite as early in the afternoon as possible. The supply of campsites in this region is sometimes not as large as the demand for them. Motorboats are permitted on McFarland, Clearwater and Little John lakes.

Anglers will have good opportunities to catch some tasty meals. Lake trout inhabit the clear, deep waters of Pine, Clearwater and West Pike lakes. Most of the lakes harbor smallmouth bass and walleyes. The smaller lakes also contain all sizes of northern pike and perch.

Day 1 (8 miles): McFarland Lake, p. 2 rods, **Pine Lake.** You can pack away your portage boots this morning. This will be the easiest day of your journey, unless you are paddling into a strong west wind. The short portage can be avoided by paddling, walking or lining your canoe up through the shallow rapids separating McFarland and Pine lakes. With a light tail wind or no wind at all, you might easily paddle all the way to the west end of Pine Lake by early afternoon. Resist the temptation to continue onward. This is a very popular area and the campsites may fill up early in the afternoon. Claim one of the campsites along the north shore of Pine Lake toward its west end. Then, if there is plenty of daylight remaining, consider visiting Johnson Falls at the end of this day (see Day 2 for details).

Day 2 (8 miles): Pine Lake, p. 80 rods, **Little Caribou Lake,** p. 25 rods, **Caribou Lake,** p. 150 rods, **Clearwater Lake,** p. 214 rods, **West Pike Lake.** Contrary to the first day, this will be the most challenging day of your expedition—but every bit as rewarding as it is tiring. Before portaging to Little Caribou Lake, take time out for a hike to Johnson Falls. The trail to it begins at the west tip of Pine Lake, on the south side of a shallow creek flowing into the lake. The well-worn path winds for ⅓-mile uphill to an elevation nearly 100 feet above Pine Lake. There you'll find yourself at the top of a 2-tier cascade. The upper cascade is the more spectacular of the 2 major falls. The hike takes only about 15 minutes (1-way) and is well worth the effort. Use caution on the steep, slippery trail, especially as you descend into the canyon at the base of the falls. Take your time. There aren't many places like this anywhere in the BWCA Wilderness.

Now get ready for the challenges. The 80-rod trail to Little Caribou Lake is uphill for all but the final 5 rods, gaining nearly 100 feet of elevation from Pine Lake. Near the end, the scenic trail dips down to cross a log bridge over the creek that drains Little Caribou Lake. After a short and easy trek on the good path between Little Caribou and Caribou lakes, you'll approach the most exhausting carry on this route. The 150-rod portage surmounts a steep ridge between Caribou and Clearwater lakes. The trail climbs most of the way, including some rather steep parts near the beginning, on a path plagued with rocks and roots. The final 30 rods are on a fairly steep downhill slope.

You might see or hear motorboats on Clearwater Lake. The west end of the lake lies outside the Wilderness, where it is populated with summer homes, resorts and outfitters. Motorboats that don't exceed 10 horsepower are permitted on the part of the lake within the BWCAW. It's one of the prettiest lakes in the North Country, bordered by steep ridges and some cliffs along the south shore. Unfortunately, you won't see the most scenic central part of the lake.

The final carry of the day is longer than the previous one, but not as exhausting. It starts out on a fairly level path and then descends nearly 100 feet during the final 75 rods to West Pike Lake. The path is shared with hikers using the Border Route Trail.

Plan to camp near the center of West Pike Lake for an 8-mile day of travel. It's a deep, very clear lake that harbors lake trout and smallmouth bass.

Day 3 (9 miles): West Pike Lake, p. 177 rods, **East Pike Lake,** p. 200 rods, **John Lake,** p. 10 rods, **Little John Lake.** Again this day you will be paddling across beautiful lakes that are absolutely stunning in autumn. Steep ridges tower 300 to 400 feet above the water, rising as high as 500 feet at one point near the west end of West Pike Lake.

The first long portage of the day is mostly level, but quite rocky. At the beginning of the second portage there is a short, steep ascent from the shore of East Pike Lake. The trail then gradually descends nearly 120 feet during the remaining 120 rods. Normally the 10-rod carry from John to Little John Lake will not be necessary. The shallow rapids can easily be shot when the water level is high, and walked or lined when the water is low.

From the boat landing for Little John Lake, it is a short walk (16 rods) across the road and through the woods to the parking lot for McFarland Lake.

ROUTE #68-2: The Pine Mountain Loop

4 Days, 33 Miles, 13 Lakes, 1 River, 12 Portages

DIFFICULTY: Challenging

FISHER MAP: F-14

INTRODUCTION: This interesting route consists mostly of big, long lakes separated by long, sometimes steep portages. From the boat landing on McFarland Lake you will paddle west across the full lengths of McFarland and Pine lakes. After a side trip on foot to view Johnson Falls, you will then loop north through Little Caribou and Caribou lakes to the east end of Clearwater Lake. At the portage to Mountain Lake, you'll have an opportunity to explore some panoramic overlooks. Then you'll begin the eastbound part of the route by following the Canadian border through Mountain, Moose and North Fowl lakes to the mouth of the Royal River. That river will carry you northwest to John Lake. From there you will exit the BWCAW and paddle south across Little John Lake to your origin.

As in most of the Tip of the Arrowhead region, steep ridges that tower from 300 to 500 feet above the lakes they border characterize this area. It's a beautiful setting any time of the year and absolutely stunning in autumn.

Canoe traffic is likely to be moderate throughout most of the route but heavier on the westbound part of the loop. Motorboats that do not exceed 10 horsepower are permitted on Clearwater and North Fowl lakes within the Wilderness. And, although motors are not allowed on the US side of the Canadian border, there are no motor restrictions on the Canadian side of those lakes. There is also road access to the Canadian shores of North Fowl and Mountain lakes. So don't expect total peace and solitude anywhere along this popular route.

Nevertheless, if seeing outstanding scenery is high on your list of canoe trip priorities and you don't mind a few tough portages to achieve that goal, you are bound to enjoy this loop. Most groups of competent paddlers should have no problem completing the loop in 4 days—and still have time for a couple of side trips on foot along the way. Avid anglers and novice paddlers, however, might want to expand their trip to 5 days. On big, wind-swept lakes like these, it's always a good idea to be prepared for a wind-bound layover day.

Anglers should be delighted with the fishing opportunities. Lake trout inhabit the deep waters of Pine, Mountain and Moose lakes. Walleyes, northern pike and smallmouth bass are also found in most of the lakes.

Day 1 (8 miles): McFarland Lake, p. 2 rods, **Pine Lake.** (See comments for Day 1, Route #68-1.)

Day 2 (7 miles): Pine Lake, p. 80 rods, **Little Caribou Lake,** p. 25 rods, **Caribou Lake,** p. 150 rods, **Clearwater Lake,** p. 90 rods, **Mountain Lake.** (See comments for Day 2, paragraphs 1-3, Route #68-1.) The final portage of the day will also take your breath away, as you climb nearly 100 feet over a ridge separating Clearwater and Mountain lakes. At the crest of the hill is an intersection with the Border Route Trail. You can hike along the trail in either direction to the tops of cliffs that afford spectacular views across Mountain Lake. The overlook to the east is closer (about ¼-mile), but the vista from the cliff west of the portage (¾-mile hike) is more impressive.

During the peak of the canoeing season, you would be wise to claim the first vacant campsite you see at the west end of the lake (on US soil). There is primitive road access to the Canadian shoreline and motorboats are permitted on Canadian water. So don't be alarmed if you hear the faint drone of motors off in the distance. If the anglers in your group have any energy left at the end of this long day, they are likely to find lake trout and smallmouth bass nearby. Mountain is a very clear lake that reaches a maximum depth of 210 feet.

Day 3 (10 miles): **Mountain Lake,** p. 90 rods, **Fan Lake,** p. 40 rods, **Vaseux Lake,** p. 140 rods, **Moose Lake.** (See comments for Day 4, paragraphs 2-3, Route #58-2.)

Day 4 (8 miles): Moose Lake, p. 130 rods, **North Fowl Lake, Royal River,** p. 100 rods, **river, Royal Lake, Royal River,** p. 78 rods, **river, John Lake,** p. 10 rods, **Little John Lake.** (See comments for Day 5, paragraphs 1-4, Route #58-2.) Normally the 10-rod carry from John to Little John Lake will not be necessary. The shallow rapids can easily be shot when the water level is high, and walked or lined when the water is low.

From the boat landing for Little John Lake, it is a short walk (16 rods) across the road and through the woods to the parking lot for McFarland Lake.

Entry Point 69—John Lake

SEASONAL PERMITS: 109

POPULARITY RANK: 39th

DAILY QUOTA: 1

LOCATION: John Lake is accessed by boat from Little John Lake, which is 25 airline miles northeast of Grand Marais. From Grand Marais, drive 20 miles east on Highway 61 to the tiny village of Hovland. Turn left onto County Road 12 and follow the "Arrowhead Trail" north for 18 miles. As you approach the end of the Arrowhead Trail, you'll pass a spur road that leads left to the public landing for McFarland Lake. Just beyond it is the landing for Little John Lake (right side). You'll see it just before arriving at the bridge crossing the creek that connects McFarland and Little John lakes. John Lake is one small lake and one short portage (⅔-mile) north of the road.

DESCRIPTION: A small parking lot 10 rods east of the boat landing on the north side of the road holds about a dozen vehicles. Don't worry if the lot is crowded with other vehicles. It serves not only 2 BWCAW canoeing entry points (#69 and #70), but also the easternmost trailhead for the famed Border Route Trail, a backpacker's path to Paradise.

The McFarland Lake Camping Area, a small clearing adjacent to the McFarland Lake public landing, is a convenient place to camp the night before your canoe trip. It affords a hasty departure by canoe the following morning. If those campsites are occupied, you'll find a much larger campground at Judge C.R. Magney State Park.R. Magney State Park; along Highway 61, 5 miles southwest of Hovland. There are no National Forest campgrounds in this vicinity.

All 3 entry points accessible from the Arrowhead Trail (#'s 68, 69 and 70) receive roughly the same number of overnight visitors each summer. Unlike at the other 2 neighboring entry points, however, you'll see few, if any, other people from the public landing to the entry point. This is, by far, the quietest of the 3 ways into the Wilderness. While motorboats are permitted on Little John Lake, you aren't likely to see or hear any there, and motorists are not allowed into the Wilderness at John Lake.

With a quota of only 1 overnight camping permit issued each day, a reservation is strongly advised. In 1997, John Lake ranked fourth among all BWCAW entry points filled the greatest number of days. Don't wait until the last minute to make your reservation. This entry point fills up early. With 8 canoeing entry points and 4 hiking entry points all serving the same basic area, the "Tip of the Arrowhead" region is often saturated with visitors during the peak of the canoeing season. Get an early start every morning and try to claim your campsite early in the afternoon while there is still a choice.

John Lake provides a lovely access to the quietest interior part of the Tip of the Arrowhead region. Long, deep lakes are bordered by steep ridges that hold the path of the Border Route Trail. Access to the trail is possible at some of the portages along the canoe route.

ROUTE #69-1:	The Clearwater Lake Route
	2 Days, 17 Miles, 5 Lakes, 4 Portages
DIFFICULTY:	Challenging
FISHER MAP:	F-14
INTRODUCTION:	This short route slices right through the center of the Tip of the Arrowhead. From the boat landing on Little John Lake you'll first paddle north to John Lake. Then you'll steer west and cross the Pike lakes en route to Clearwater Lake. The route ends at the public landing near the west end of Clearwater Lake, 70 miles by road from your origin (see Entry Point 62).

This short route offers a brief but delightful introduction to the BWCAW. If you can transport all of your gear across the portages in just one trip and you have no aversion to long carries, this could surely be rated an "easier" route. On the other hand, if you need 2 trips to get your gear across the portages, you'll be walking over 5½ miles during these 2 days. The route may then seem "most rugged" to those with heavy gear and little experience carrying it. If so, you might want to spread the route over 3 full days, with your 2 nights on East Pike and West Pike lakes, thus requiring only one long portage each day.

Anglers will find lake trout in the cool, deep, crystal-clear waters of West Pike and Clearwater lakes. Smallmouth bass are also found there, as well as in East Pike Lake. For those in your group who would rather hike than fish, they can access the spectacular Border Route Trail from the portages at both ends of West Pike Lake, as well as at the beginning and end of this route.

Perhaps the only drawback to this scenic canoe route is the long drive between starting and ending points. If this is your first visit to the Tip of the Arrowhead, however, you might actually appreciate the opportunity to view much of it from roads before and after your canoe outing. It's a lovely drive along Lake Superior's North Shore and the Gunflint Trail which, unlike the Arrowhead Trail, is blacktop most of the way to Clearwater Lake. If you have only one vehicle, make prior arrangements with an outfitter on Clearwater Lake to leave your car there and have the outfitter shuttle you to Little John Lake. Allow at least 2 full hours for the drive.

A wonderful alternative for hiking enthusiasts is to return to your car on foot via the Border Route Trail. Allow 3 days for the hike back to Little John Lake. This is a spectacular way to enjoy this rugged part of the BWCA Wilderness—first on the lakes looking up at the bordering ridges, and then high atop those ridges looking down at the sky-blue lakes. In autumn, you won't find a more satisfying journey through the Wilderness.

Day 1 (8 miles): Little John Lake, p. 10 rods, **John Lake,** p. 200 rods, **East Pike Lake,** p. 177 rods, **West Pike Lake.** Normally the 10-rod carry from Little John to John Lake should not be necessary—if you don't mind wet feet. The shallow rapids can easily be walked or lined when the water is low. When the water is high, you might be able to paddle right through the narrow channel.

The first long portage of the day is also the biggest challenge. The trail gradually gains nearly 120 feet of elevation during the first 120 rods. At the end there is a short, steep descent to the shore of East Pike Lake. The second long portage is fairly level, but quite rocky. Resist the temptation to put in at a small pond about midway across the portage. The trail veers away from the pond, so there is no place to take out at the other end of the pond.

For an 8-mile day of travel, plan to camp near the center of scenic West Pike Lake. It's a deep, very clear lake that harbors lake trout and smallmouth bass. If you are in the mood for hiking, rather than fishing, you can access the Border Route Trail from the portages at both ends of the lake.

Day 2 (9 miles): West Pike Lake, p. 214 rods, **Clearwater Lake.** This is another long day of paddling across beautiful lakes that are absolutely stunning in autumn. You'll be flanked on the south by steep ridges towering 300 to 400 feet above the water, and rising as high as 500 feet at one point near the west end of West Pike Lake.

The only portage shares a path used by hikers on the Border Route Trail. It ascends nearly 100 feet during the first 75 rods from the shore of West Pike Lake and then levels off for the rest of the way to Clearwater Lake.

After reaching Clearwater Lake, you will still have over 5 miles to paddle. Motorboats that don't exceed 10 horsepower are permitted in the BWCAW on this deep, very clear lake. If there is a brisk west wind, you might want to rest during the afternoon at one of the campsites near the lake's east end, then paddle to the public landing later in the evening after the wind (hopefully) dies.

One great way to kill time while waiting for the wind to subside is a side trip to a scenic overlook. The 90-rod portage from the north shore of Clearwater Lake to Mountain Lake passes over a 100-foot ridge separating the 2 lakes. At the crest of the hill is an intersection with the Border Route Trail. You can hike along the trail in either direction to the tops of cliffs that afford panoramic views across Mountain Lake. The overlook to the east is closer (about ¼-mile), but the vista from the cliff west of the portage (¾-mile hike) is more impressive.

ROUTE #69-2: The John Deer Loop

4 Days, 33 Miles, 13 Lakes, 12 Portages

DIFFICULTY: Challenging

FISHER MAP: F-14

INTRODUCTION: This loop is a fine choice for anyone who appreciates outstanding scenery and paddling on long, narrow lakes separated by relatively few portages. From the boat landing on Little John Lake you'll first paddle north to John Lake. Then you'll steer west and cross the Pike lakes en route to Clearwater Lake. From there you will portage south to Caribou Lake and then continue westbound to the end of that pretty lake. From that point, you'll head across a chain of smaller lakes and shorter portages leading southeast to Canoe Lake. After crossing the longest portage of the route and visiting scenic Johnson Falls, you will return to your origin via Pine and McFarland lakes.

Along the way you will enjoy some truly spectacular scenery, including pine-covered ridges that tower as much as 500 feet above your canoe, and the impressive cascades of Johnson Falls. Most of the route consists of large lakes with an east-west orientation where wind could be a problem. The constant paddling might approach tedium if it were not for the magnificent scenery in the Tip of the Arrowhead.

For those who dread portages, this route might deserve a "most rugged" rating. Six portages each exceed half a mile in length, including 3 measuring at least 200 rods. Some require significant climbs, too. If you need 2 trips to get your gear across the portages, you'll be hiking more than 13 miles during these 4 days—not including your side trip to Johnson Falls or any optional side trips on the Border Route Trail. Nevertheless, the long carries are distributed fairly evenly throughout the route with plenty of time between them to rest your weary shoulders.

Anglers will have good opportunities to catch some tasty meals. Lake trout occupy the depths of several lakes along the route. Smallmouth bass are found in many of the lakes, and walleyes and northern pike inhabit some. If fishing is your primary objective, you may want to add an extra day to your itinerary. A scheduled layover day is not a bad idea, regardless, when you are traveling on large lakes that are highly susceptible to the effects of wind.

Day 1 (8 miles): Little John Lake, p. 10 rods, John Lake, p. 200 rods, **East Pike Lake,** p. 177 rods, **West Pike Lake.** (See comments for Day 1, Route #69-1.)

Day 2 (8 miles): West Pike Lake, p. 214 rods, **Clearwater Lake,** p. 150 rods, **Caribou Lake.** The first long portage shares a path used by hikers on the Border Route Trail. It ascends nearly 100 feet during the first 75 rods from the shore of West Pike Lake and then levels off for the rest of the way to Clearwater Lake.

Motorboats that don't exceed 10 horsepower are permitted in the BWCAW on Clearwater Lake. You won't see much of that pretty lake, however, as you cross only the easternmost tip of the lake en route to your final portage. The trail there passes over a high ridge separating Clearwater and Caribou lakes. You'll climb rather steeply during the first 30 rods; but most of the trail is downhill, including some steep parts as you approach Caribou Lake. The path is plagued with rocks and roots.

There are half a dozen campsites along the north shore of Caribou Lake. Eight miles of travel will take you to the west end of the lake. Claim your campsite as early in the day as possible. Anglers may find largemouth bass, northern pike and walleyes in the lake.

Lunch break at an Alder Lake campsite

Day 3 (5 miles): Caribou Lake, p. 50 rods, **Deer Lake,** p. 15 rods, **Moon Lake,** p. 115 rods, **East Bearskin Lake,** p. 70 rods, **Alder Lake,** p. 22 rods, **Canoe Lake.** (See comments for Days 3 and 1, Route #64-1.) This day is short for two reasons. First, it will afford you the opportunity to find a good campsite while there are still some vacant choices available. Second, after making camp, you should have plenty of time to visit Johnson Falls during the afternoon.

Paddle to the Pine Lake portage and cache your canoe off to the side where it doesn't block access for other paddlers. From there you can hike all the way to Johnson Falls. At the north end of the long portage to Pine Lake a trail leads ¼-mile west to the start of the Johnson Falls Trail at the west tip of the lake. The well-worn path winds for ⅓-mile uphill to an elevation nearly 100 feet above Pine Lake. There you'll find yourself at the top of a 2-tier cascade. The upper cascade is the more spectacular of the 2 major falls. Use caution on the steep, slippery trail, especially as you descend into the canyon at the base of the falls. Take your time. There aren't many places like this anywhere in the BWCA Wilderness. This afternoon hike is a little more than 3½ miles round-trip. Allow a couple of hours to fully explore and enjoy the cascade. Of course, don't forget to safely hang your food pack while you're away from the campsite. Campsites that are popular with humans are often also popular with black bears.

Day 4 (12 miles): Canoe Lake, p. 380 rods, **Pine Lake,** p. 2 rods, **McFarland Lake.** The long portage from Canoe Lake to Pine Lake starts with a steep uphill climb, gaining over 100 feet in the first 40 rods. After that climb, however, it is mostly downhill or level. Three steep downhill segments have a total drop of just over 300 feet. Two wet spots separate the downhill segments. The first one may be muddy; the second is a bog over which a 3-rod boardwalk passes. Be glad you're not portaging in the opposite direction.

After the long portage, you can pack your portage boots away for the rest of this day. The 2-rod portage can be avoided by running, walking or lining your canoe through the shallow rapids separating Pine and McFarland lakes.

You will see many cabins and lake homes along the southeast and north shores of McFarland Lake. But there is very little development along the steep ridge bordering the southwest shoreline. Motorboats are permitted throughout the lake, which lies entirely outside the BWCA Wilderness.

Entry Point 70—North Fowl Lake

SEASONAL PERMITS: 104

POPULARITY RANK: 42nd

DAILY QUOTA: 2

LOCATION: North Fowl Lake is the easternmost of all BWCAW entry points. It is accessed by boat from Little John Lake, which is 25 airline miles northeast of Grand Marais. From Grand Marais, drive 20 miles east on Highway 61 to the tiny village of Hovland. Turn left onto County Road 12 and follow the "Arrowhead Trail" north for 18 miles. As you approach the end of the Arrowhead Trail, you'll pass a spur road that leads left to the public landing for McFarland Lake. Just beyond it is the landing for Little John Lake (right side). You'll see it just before arriving at the bridge crossing the creek that connects McFarland and Little John lakes. North Fowl Lake lies about 3 miles east of the landing via Little John and John lakes and the Royal River.

DESCRIPTION: A small parking lot 10 rods east of the boat landing on the north side of the road holds about a dozen vehicles. Don't worry if the lot is crowded with other vehicles. It serves not only 2 BWCAW canoeing entry points (#69 and #70), but also the easternmost trailhead for the famed Border Route Trail, a backpacker's path to Paradise.

The McFarland Lake Camping Area, a small clearing adjacent to the McFarland Lake public landing, is a convenient place to camp the night before your canoe trip. It affords a hasty departure by canoe the following morning. If those campsites are occupied, you'll find a much larger campground at Judge C.R. Magney State Park.R. Magney State Park; along Highway 61, 5 miles southwest of Hovland. There are no National Forest campgrounds in this vicinity.

North Fowl Lake is unique among BWCAW entry points. To get there, you must first paddle through part of another entry point—John

Lake—and the scenic Royal River, both of which are free of motor-boats. The boundary between Canada and the United States runs through the middle of North Fowl Lake. Motorboats not exceeding 10 horsepower are permitted on the US side of the lake, and motorboats without restriction are allowed on the Canadian side of the border. Furthermore, not all of the US shore of the lake is actually inside the Wilderness. A small resort (Ron's Lodge) is located on the west shore, about a mile north of the mouth of the Royal River. There is road access to the Canadian side of the lake. Consequently, you should expect to see and hear motorboats throughout the lake, as well as far more day-use visitors than USFS statistics might suggest.

North Fowl is a beautiful lake, with high cliffs on the Canadian shore and steep hills bordering the US shore. Unlike most other border lakes, it is neither deep nor clear. With a maximum depth of only 10 feet, most of the lake is even shallower. During late summer, you'll see parts of the lake clogged with weeds and wild rice. In spite of the activity on the lake, it provides a wonderful access for paddlers to the scenic Canadian border route, where deep, crystal-clear lakes are rimmed by lovely "mountainous" terrain.

All 3 entry points accessible from the Arrowhead Trail (#'s 68, 69 and 70) receive roughly the same number of overnight visitors each summer. With a quota of 2 overnight camping permits per day, how-ever, North Fowl is by far the easiest of the three for which to get a per-mit. Only ⅓ of the available permits were actually issued to visitors during the summer of 1997. While advanced reservation are strongly recommended for the other 2 entry points (68 and 69), you may not need one for North Fowl Lake. It's always a good idea, however, to make a reservation if your trip will start on a weekend or holiday.

With 8 canoeing entry points and 4 hiking entry points all serving the same basic area, the "Tip of the Arrowhead" region is often satu-rated with visitors during the peak of the canoeing season. Get an early start every morning and try to claim your campsite early in the after-noon while there is still a choice to be made.

ROUTE #70-1:   The Lily Lakes Loop

    4 Days, 32 Miles, 11 Lakes, 1 River, 12 Portages

DIFFICULTY: Challenging

FISHER MAP: F-14

INTRODUCTION: This lovely loop is a wonderful introduction to the Minnesota Arrowhead region. High ridges, sheer cliffs and crystal-clear lakes are the rule, not the exception. From the public landing on Little John Lake, you will first paddle north to enter the BWCAW at John Lake. The Royal River will then carry you southeast to North Fowl Lake. From there you will follow the Canadian border northwest through Moose and the "Lily Lakes" to Mountain Lake. At the west end of that big, beautiful lake, you will portage south to Clearwater Lake. An eastbound course from there will take you across the Pike lakes and back to John and Little John lakes.

When finished you will have visited some of the most scenic lakes in the entire BWCA Wilderness, having paddled on several long, deep lakes that are bordered on the south by ridges rising as high as 500 feet above the water. The portages are few in number, averaging only 3 per day, but they tend to be long and a few are steep. For strong groups that need only one trip to transport all gear across the portages, this is probably an "easier" route. Indeed, experienced paddlers traveling lightly could surely complete it in just 3 days. If you need 2 trips to get your gear across the portages, however, you'll be walking a total of 12 miles—8 miles with gear. That is a challenge to most groups. Some might even consider it "most rugged."

Anglers should have plenty of time and opportunities to catch all types of game fish. Lake trout dwell in the cool waters of the largest and deepest lakes. Smallmouth bass are also abundant in most of the lakes, and 2 are known to harbor good populations of walleyed and northern pike. With 4 full days to ply these waters, you'll surely catch enough tasty meals to satisfy your entire party.

Day 1 (8 miles): Little John Lake, p. 10 rods, **John Lake, Royal River,** p. 78 rods, **river, Royal Lake, Royal River,** p. 100 rods, **river, North Fowl Lake,** p. 130 rods, **Moose Lake.** Normally the 10-rod carry from Little John to John Lake should not be necessary—if you don't mind wet feet. The shallow rapids can easily be walked or lined when the water is low. When the water is high, you might be able to paddle up through the narrow channel. (Also see comments for Day 4, Route #64-2.)

Day 2 (8 miles): Moose Lake, p. 140 rods, **Vaseux Lake,** p. 40 rods, **Fan Lake,** p. 90 rods, **Mountain Lake.** (See comments for Day 5, Route #64-2.)

Day 3 (7 miles): Mountain Lake, p. 90 rods, **Clearwater Lake,** p. 214 rods, **West Pike Lake.** The first portage of the day will accelerate your heart, as you climb nearly 100 feet over a ridge separating the 2 lakes. At the crest of the hill is an intersection with the Border Route Trail. You can hike along the trail in either direction to the tops of cliffs that afford spectacular views across Mountain Lake. The overlook to the east is closer (about ¼-mile), but the vista from the cliff west of the portage (¾-mile hike) is more impressive.

The final carry of the day is longer than the previous trek, but not as exhausting. It starts out on a fairly level path and then descends nearly 100 feet during the final 75 rods to West Pike Lake. The path is shared with hikers using the Border Route Trail.

Plan to camp near the center of West Pike Lake for a 7-mile day of travel. It's a deep, very clear lake that harbors lake trout and small-mouth bass.

Day 4 (9 miles): West Pike Lake, p. 177 rods, **East Pike Lake,** p. 200 rods, **John Lake,** p. 10 rods, **Little John Lake.** (See comments for Day 3, paragraphs 1-2, Route #64-2.)

ROUTE #70-2:	The Mountain Pine Loop
	5 Days, 41 Miles, 17 Lakes, 1 River, 16 Portages
DIFFICULTY:	Challenging
FISHER MAP:	F-14
INTRODUCTION:	This beautiful route is a good way to see much of the scenic Tip of the Arrowhead region. From the public landing on Little John Lake, you will first paddle north to enter the BWCAW at John Lake. The Royal River will then carry you southeast to North Fowl Lake. From there you will follow the Canadian border northwest through Moose and the "Lily Lakes" to Mountain Lake. At the west end of that big, beautiful lake, you will portage south to Clearwater Lake and then south again to Caribou Lake. Then you'll swing through a chain of smaller lakes that skirts the south edge of the Wilderness en route to Canoe Lake. Finally, after a visit to one of the prettiest waterfalls in the area, you'll paddle across Pine and McFarland lakes and return to your origin.

With more carries than most routes in the Tip of the Arrowhead, this outstanding loop may be a challenge for paddlers with no propensity for portaging. Although you will never have more than 5 portages on the same day (usually fewer), the carries tend to be longer than the

North Fowl Lake

BWCAW norm. And some pass over steep ridges. Since the carries are distributed fairly evenly throughout this route, however, most groups should have no trouble completing the loop in 5 days. Nevertheless, since wind could slow your progress on the big lakes, it might be a good idea to add a sixth day to your itinerary.

In addition to seeing some of the most attractive lakes in the Wilderness, you will also have an opportunity to visit Johnson Falls— one of the most scenic cascades in the Boundary Waters. Don't expect total solitude anywhere along the route. This popular region entertains many visitors. You also may see or hear motorboats on much of the loop. They are permitted on the Canadian side of all the border lakes and, with motors up to 10 horsepower, on Clearwater and North Fowl lakes in the BWCAW. Of course, they are also permitted at the beginning and end of the loop on lakes outside the Wilderness. Don't let that discourage you. This beautiful area is worth sharing—even with motorboats.

Anglers will have good opportunities to catch all of the game fish that are common to the BWCAW. Lake trout dwell in the cool waters of the largest and deepest lakes. Smallmouth bass are abundant in most of the lakes. Good populations of walleyed pike and northern pike may also be found in several lakes—the smaller bodies of water, in particular.

Day 1 (8 miles): Little John Lake, p. 10 rods, **John Lake, Royal River,** p. 78 rods, **river, Royal Lake, Royal River,** p. 100 rods, **river,**

North Fowl Lake, p. 130 rods, **Moose Lake.** (See comments for Day 1, Route #70-1.)

Day 2 (8 miles): Moose Lake, p. 140 rods, **Vaseux Lake,** p. 40 rods, **Fan Lake,** p. 90 rods, **Mountain Lake.** (See comments for Day 5, Route #64-2.)

Day 3 (8 miles): Mountain Lake, p. 90 rods, **Clearwater Lake,** p. 150 rods, **Caribou Lake,** p. 50 rods, **Deer Lake,** p. 15 rods, **Moon Lake.** The first portage of the day will accelerate your heart, as you climb nearly 100 feet over a ridge separating the 2 lakes. At the crest of the hill is an intersection with the Border Route Trail. You can hike along the trail in either direction to the tops of cliffs that afford spectacular views across Mountain Lake. The overlook to the east is closer (about ¼-mile), but the vista from the cliff west of the portage (¾-mile hike) is more impressive.

Motorboats that don't exceed 10 horsepower are permitted in the BWCAW on Clearwater Lake. You won't see much of that pretty lake, however, since you cross only the easternmost tip of the lake en route to your final portage. The trail there passes over a high ridge separating Clearwater and Caribou lakes. You'll climb rather steeply during the first 30 rods; but most of the trail is downhill, including some steep parts as you approach Caribou Lake. The path is plagued with rocks and roots.

The 50-rod portage starts on a steep uphill slope from the shore of Caribou Lake. At the top of the ridge, after gaining 70 feet of elevation, the trail joins the good, level path of an old road that continues south (left) to the north shore of Deer Lake. (Note: if you turned right onto this old road you could hike northwest to Clearwater Lake. See the Sketch on page 231.)

You will see tall, old white pines covering the hill adjacent to the 15-rod portage between Deer and Moon lakes. Three campsites are situated along the north shore of Moon Lake. Try to claim yours as early as possible. Moon is just one portage away from the popular East Bearskin Lake entry point.

Day 4 (5 miles): Moon Lake, p. 115 rods, **East Bearskin Lake,** p. 70 rods, **Alder Lake,** p. 22 rods, **Canoe Lake.** The 115-rod portage from the south shore of Moon Lake starts with a steep ascent, gaining about 100 feet during the first 25 rods. Near the top, there is a stairway with 21 steps to aid the climb. Beyond the stairs, the trail is fairly level, with a gradual decline over the final 90 rods. Near the end of the portage is the site of a former sawmill. You may still see some remains from the Hedstrom Lumber Company, which operated there until 1948.

This day is short for two reasons. First, it affords you the opportunity to find a good campsite while there are still some vacant choices.

Second, after making camp, you will have plenty of time to visit Johnson Falls during the afternoon.

After setting up camp on Canoe Lake, paddle to the Pine Lake portage and cache your canoe off to the side where it doesn't block access for other paddlers. From there you can hike all the way to Johnson Falls. From the north end of the long portage to Pine Lake a trail leads ¼-mile west to the start of the Johnson Falls Trail at the west tip of the lake. The well-worn path winds for ⅓-mile uphill to an elevation nearly 100 feet above Pine Lake. There you'll find yourself at the top of a 2-tier cascade. The upper cascade is the more spectacular of the 2 major falls. Use caution on the steep, slippery trail, especially as you descend into the canyon at the base of the falls. Take your time. There aren't many places like this anywhere in the BWCA Wilderness. This afternoon hike is a little more than 3½ miles round-trip. Allow a couple of hours to fully explore and enjoy the cascade. Of course, don't forget to safely hang your food pack before leaving your campsite on Canoe Lake. Campsites that are popular with humans are often also popular with black bears.

Day 5 (12 miles): Canoe Lake, p. 380 rods, **Pine Lake,** p. 2 rods, **McFarland Lake.** (See comments for Day 4, Route #69-2.)

Appendix I

Routes Categorized by Difficulty and Duration

Duration	Rte #	Name of Route	Entry Point Name (and #)
10 Easier Routes:			
2 days	39-1	Weird Brule Route	Baker Lake (#39)
2 days	40-1	June Lake Loop	Homer Lake (#40)
2 days	55-1	Red Rock Lake Loop	Saganaga Lake (#55)
2 days	58-1	Historic Border Route	South Lake (#58)
3 days	36-1	Perent River Route	Hog Creek (#36)
3 days	54-1	Eddy Falls Loop	Seagull Lake (#54)
3 days	80-1	Devil's Elbow Route	Larch Creek (#80)
4 days	57-1	Granite River Route	Magnetic Lake (#57)
5 days	80-2	Ester Lake Route	Larch Creek (#80)
7 days	55-2	Knife & Hatchet Loop	Saganaga Lake (#55)
34 Challenging Routes:			
2 days	41-1	Mulligan Cliff Loop	Brule Lake (#41)
2 days	45-1	Vista Swallow Route	Morgan Lake (#45)
2 days	48-1	Hensen Horseshoe Loop	Meeds Lake (#48)
2 days	50-1	Snipe Tuscarora Loop	Cross Bay Lake (#50)
2 days	60-1	Rose Lake Loop	Duncan Lake (#60)
2 days	61-1	Mountain Lake Loop	Daniels Lake (#61)
2 days	69-1	Clearwater Lake Route	John Lake (#69)
3 days	37-1	Lady Lakes Route	Kawishiwi Lake (#37)
3 days	38-1	Temperance River Loop	Sawbill Lake (#38)
3 days	43-1	Lily Horseshoe Route	Bower Trout (#43)

Duration	Rte #	Name of Route	Entry Point Name (and #)

34 Challenging Routes (continued):

3 days	47-1	Horseshoe Hensen Loop	Lizz Lake (#47)
3 days	62-1	Pine Alder Loop	Clearwater Lake (#62)
3 days	64-1	Johnson Falls Loop	East Bearskin Lake (#64)
3 days	68-1	Pike Lakes Loop	Pine Lake (#68)
4 days	68-2	Pine Mountain Loop	Pine Lake (#68)
4 days	69-2	John Deer Loop	John Lake (#69)
4 days	70-1	Lily Lakes Loop	North Fowl Lake (#70)
5 days	43-2	Cherokee Vista Loop	Bower Trout (#43)
5 days	44-2	Winchell Swan Loop	Ram Lake (#44)
5 days	45-2	Cherokee Swan Route	Morgan Lake (#45)
5 days	60-2	Rose Mt. Moose Loop	Duncan Lake (#60)
5 days	61-2	Royal Caribou Loop	Daniels Lake (#61)
5 days	70-2	Mountain Pine Loop	North Fowl Lake (#70)
6 days	47-2	Cliff & Muskeg Loop	Lizz Lake (#47)
6 days	58-2	Canadian Border Route	South Lake (#58)
6 days	62-2	Moose-Caribou-Deer Loop	Clearwater Lake (#62)
6 days	64-2	Alder Moose Loop	East Bearskin Lake (#64)
7 days	38-2	Copper Pan Loop	Sawbill Lake (#38)
7 days	48-2	Frost River Route	Meeds Lake (#48)
7 days	50-2	Cherokee Pan Loop	Cross Bay Lake (#50)
7 days	52-2	Kekekabic Beaver Loop	Brant Lake (#52)
7 days	54-2	Adams Knife Loop	Seagull Lake (#54)
8 days	36-2	Long Rivers Route	Hog Creek (#36)
8 days	57-2	Thunder Point Route	Magnetic Lake (#57)

10 Most Rugged Routes:

2 days	44-1	Misquah Hills Route	Ram Lake (#44)
2 days	51-1	Crooked Bat Loop	Missing Link Lake (#51)
3 days	49-1	Cave Swallow Loop	Skipper Lake (#49)
3 days	52-1	Flying Seahorse Loop	Brant Lake (#52)
5 days	40-2	Frost Duck Route	Homer Lake (#40)
6 days	37-2	Louse River Loop	Kawishiwi Lake (#37)
6 days	41-2	Long Island Flame Loop	Brule Lake (#41)
7 days	49-2	Banadad Duck Loop	Skipper Lake (#49)
7 days	51-2	Louse River Knight Loop	Missing Link Lake (#51)
8 days	39-2	Jack Frost Loop	Baker Lake (#39)

Appendix II

BWCAW Travel Permit Data* for ALL ENTRY POINTS

EP#	Entry Pt. Name	Daily Quota	Total Permits	Overall Rank	Quota % Full	Summer Day Use	Motor** Usage
1	Trout Lake	14	880	11th	41%	17	894
3	Pine Lake Trail	None	0	69th (T)	n/d	0	No
4	Crab Lake	4	375	21st (T)	61%	56	No
6	Slim Lake	2	150	36th	49%	150	No
7	From Big Lake	2	75	51st	25%	70	No
8	Moose River So.	1	74	52nd (T)	48%	29	No
9	Little Indian Sioux R. South***	1/2	26	60th (T)	34%	11	No
10	Norway Trail	None	0	69th (T)	n/d	n/d	No
11	Blandin Trail	None	1	68th	n/d	6	No
12	Little Vermillion Lake	14	483	16th	23%	53	150
13	Herriman Lake Trail	None	8	66th	n/d	19	No
14	Little Indian Sioux R. North	6	670	14th	73%	84	No
15	Devil's Cascade Trail	None	18	63rd (T)	n/d	29	No
16	Moose & Portage Rivers***	7	856	12th	80%	19	No
19	Stuart River	1	98	45th (T)	61%	26	No

EP# Entry Pt. Name	Daily Quota	Total Permits	Overall Rank	Quota % Full	Summer Day Use	Motor** Usage
20 Angleworm Lake	2	145	37th	47%	9	No
21 Angleworm Trail	2	60	54th	20%	103	No
23 Mudro Lake (and 22)***	8	984	9th	80%	68	No
24 Fall Lake	14	1,384	5th	65%	233	1653
25 Moose Lake	27	3,060	1st	74%	381	2059
26 Wood Lake	2	204	33rd	67%	69	No
27 Snowbank Lake (and 28)***	9	1,000	8th	73%	135	263
29 N. Kawishiwi River***	1	108	40th	71%	63	No
30 Lake One***	18	2168	2nd	79%	617	No
31 From Farm Lake	3	328	25th	71%	175	104
32 S. Kawishiwi River***	2	225	30th	74%	92	No
33 Little Gabbro Lake***	2	254	29th	83%	133	No
34 Island River	3	267	28th	58%	39	No
35 Isabella Lake	3	326	26th	71%	71	No
36 Hog Creek	5	422	18th	55%	32	No
37 Kawishiwi Lake	9	959	10th	70%	86	No
38 Sawbill Lake	14	1,717	3rd	80%	453	No
39 Baker Lake	3	350	23rd	76%	109	No
40 Homer Lake	2	208	31st	68%	58	No
41 Brule Lake (with 41A)	10	1,032	7th	67%	122	No
43 Bower Trout Lake***	1	98	45th (T)	64%	27	No
44 Ram Lake***	1	102	43rd	67%	14	No
45 Morgan Lake	1	74	52nd (T)	48%	0	No
47 Lizz, Swamp & Meeds lakes	7	685	13th	64%	80	No
49 Skipper & Portage lakes	2	121	38th	40%	22	No
50 Cross Bay Lake***	3	337	24th	73%	77	No
51 Missing Link Lake	5	429	17th	56%	36	No
52 Brant Lake	4	420	19th	69%	12	No

EP# Entry Pt. Name	Daily Quota	Total Permits	Overall Rank	Quota % Full	Summer Day Use	Motor** Usage
54 Seagull Lake (with 54A)	13	1311	6th	66%	208	354
55 Saganaga Lake (with 55A)	20	1651	4th	54%	161	1964
56 Kekekabic Trail – East End	2	37	56th	n/d	138	No
57 Magnetic Lake	3	302	27th	66%	108	No
58 South Lake	3	159	35th	35%	32	No
59 Partridge Lake Trail	1	12	65th	8%	1	No
60 Duncan Lake	4	375	21st (T)	61%	314	No
61 Daniels Lake	1	89	49th	58%	76	No
62 Clearwater Lake	4	405	20th	66%	149	56
64 East Bearskin Lake	5	485	15th	63%	122	62
66 Crocodile River	1	34	57th	22%	44	No
67 Bog Lake	2	49	55th	16%	9	No
68 Pine Lake***	1	107	41st	70%	53	No
69 John Lake***	1	109	39th	71%	30	No
70 North Fowl Lake	2	104	42nd	34%	3	No
71 From Canada	3	189	34th	41%	112	No
74 Snowbank Trail & Kekekabic Trail - West	4	100	44th	16%	57	No
75 Little Isabella R.	1	98	45th (T)	64%	9	No
76 Big Moose Lake Trail	None	3	67th	n/d	8	No
77 South Hegman Lake***	2	205	32nd	67%	483	No
79 Eagle Mountain Trail	2	28	58th (T)	9%	642	No
80 Larch Creek	1	87	50th	57%	38	No
81 Border Route Trail – West	1	18	63rd (T)	12%	12	No
82 Border Route Trail – Central	2	28	58th (T)	9%	4	No
83 Border Route Trail – East	3	23	62nd	5%	n/d	No
84 Snake River	1	98	45th (T)	64%	12	No
86 Pow Wow Trail	None	26	60th (T)	n/d	12	No

* Based on USFS 1997 Year End Report, the most recent information available at the time this book was written.

Note: Meeds Lake (#48) was not designated as a separate entry point until 1999. Thus there is no data available for 1997.

Total Permits: Total number of overnight permits issued during the quota season (May 1–September 30).

Overall Rank: Based on the total number of overnight permits issued during the quota season for 70 entry points listed above. (T) = tie.

Quota % Full: Based on the total number of overnight permits issued as a percent of the total number of overnight permits available during the quota season (entry point quota per day x 153 days during the quota season).

Summer Day Use: Total number of non-quota permits (day use) from May 1 through September 30, 1996.

Motor Usage: Total number of permits issued for motorized entry, including overnight use & day use.

** Does not include towboat use or exempt permits.

*** Among the top 15 entry points filled the greatest number of days (70% or more days full in 1997). Note: Mudro Lake Entry Points 22 & 23 each exceeded 70%.

Appendix III

Commercial Canoe Trip Outfitters

Canoe trip outfitters provide a valuable service for the first-time visitor to the Boundary Waters Canoe Area Wilderness. For a reasonable fee, an outfitter will provide you with *everything* needed for a wilderness canoe trip. All you must do is show up with your personal items. The outfitter will take care of the rest.

Not all people are "cut out" for wilderness tripping. If you are not sure of yourself, it is foolish to invest hundreds of dollars in your own gear and outdoor clothing. After you have tried it, if it seems likely that you will return to the BWCAW at least once every year, *then* you may want to own your own gear, to save money in the long run.

To obtain current brochures from the outfitters in the Eastern Region of the BWCAW, contact either of the agencies listed below for the names, addresses, phone numbers and Internet web sites of the outfitters they serve.

Serving entry points along the Gunflint Trail:

The Gunflint Trail Association
PO Box 205
Grand Marais, MN 55604
(800) 338-6932
http://www.gunflint-trail.com/

Serving entry points accessible from the Sawbill Trail:

The Lutsen-Tofte Tourism Association
PO Box 2248
Tofte, MN 55615
(888) 616-6784 or (218) 663-7804
http://www.61north.com/recreation/

Appendix IV

Lake Index for Fishing

This appendix includes the 242 lakes that lie on the routes described in this book. It does *not* include every lake in the BWCA Wilderness. The appendix supplies useful information of interest to anglers, including the general location, the overall size of the lake, the amount of shallow water in the lake (where most fish are found), the maximum depth, and the fish species that are known to inhabit the lake. When two lakes share the same name, neighboring lakes of each are included in parentheses to identify the one meant. Data for this index was compiled from the Minnesota DNR database (accessible via the Internet at www.dnr.state.mn.us), as well as from personal observations by the author. There may be other fish species in the lakes that were neither found by DNR test netting nor observed by the author.

KEY
W = walleye, **NP** = northern pike, **LT** = lake trout, **SB** = smallmouth bass, **LB** = largemouth bass, **BT** = brook trout, **BG** = bluegill, **CR** = black crappie, **MU** = muskellunge, **n/d** = no DNR data available, **none** = no game fish reported. **Boldface** indicates the predominate species. **(Year)** indicates last known year that the species was stocked by the DNR. **Acres** = lake's total surface area. **Littoral** = acreage of lake less than 15' deep. The littoral zone is where the majority of aquatic plants are found and is a primary area used by young fish. This part of the lake also provides the essential spawning habitat for most warm-water fish (e.g., walleyes, bass, and pan fish). **Depth** = maximum depth.

OTHER FISH SPECIES that could be found in lakes but are not included in this chart as "game fish" include yellow perch, sunfish, rock bass and white sucker.

LAKE NAME	COUNTY	ACRES	LITT	DEPTH	FISH SPECIES
Ada	Cook	22	22	13'	NP
Adams	Lake	448	116	84'	**NP**, W, BG
Afton	Cook	n/d	n/d	n/d	n/d
Agamok	Lake	n/d	n/d	n/d	n/d
Ahmakose	Lake	38	9	68'	n/d
Alder	Cook	506	132	72'	**W, LT** (84), SB, NP
Alice	Lake	1,566	438	53'	**NP, W**, BG
Allen	Cook	n/d	n/d	n/d	n/d
Alpine	Cook	839	403	65'	**W, NP**, LT, SB
Alton	Cook	1,039	320	72'	**NP, SB, W**, LT
Anit	Lake	12	9	19'	NP
Annie	Lake	18	16	16'	**NP**
Ashdick	Lake	100	63	50'	**NP**, LB
Ashigan	Lake	189	9	59'	**SB**
Baker	Cook	24	24	19'	NP, W
Bald Eagle	Lake	1,238	929	36'	**W, NP, CR**, BG
Banadad	Cook	168	89	45'	NP
Bat	Cook	80	19	110'	**LT** (91)
Beaver	Lake	237	95	76'	**NP, W**, BG
Beth	Cook	182	n/d	22'	**NP, SB**
Bingshick	Cook	44	22	37'	**BT** (97)
Birch	Lake	711	342	34'	**W** (93), **NP, SB**, LB, BG
Boga	Lake	n/d	n/d	n/d	n/d
Bonnie	Lake	71	71	11'	**NP**
Boulder	Lake	236	109	54'	**NP**
Bower Trout	Cook	149	149	6'	**W**, NP, SB
Boze	Lake	n/d	n/d	n/d	n/d
Brant	Cook	104	66	80'	**NP**
Brule	Cook	4,617	1,431	78'	**W, NP**, SB
Bug	Cook	n/d	n/d	n/d	n/d
Burnt	Cook	327	222	23'	**NP**, W
Cam	Cook	60	29	57'	**NP**
Canoe	Cook	n/d	n/d	n/d	n/d
Cap	Lake	n/d	n/d	n/d	n/d
Caribou (Lizz)	Cook	255	204	26'	**W**, NP
Caribou (Deer)	Cook	452	n/d	n/d	**LB**, NP, W (96)
Carl	Cook	59	53	22'	**NP**

LAKE NAME	COUNTY	ACRES	LITT	DEPTH	FISH SPECIES
Carp	Lake	n/d	n/d	n/d	**LT, NP, SB, W**
Cattyman	Lake	17	17	9'	**NP**, W
Cave	Cook	n/d	n/d	n/d	n/d
Chase	Cook	n/d	n/d	n/d	n/d
Chaser	Cook	n/d	n/d	n/d	n/d
Cherokee	Cook	753	87	142'	NP, LT
Clearwater	Cook	1,325	260	130'	**LT** (93), **SB**
Cliff	Cook	n/d	n/d	n/d	n/d
Clove	Cook	172	n/d	n/d	**W, NP, SB**
Confusion	Lake	n/d	n/d	n/d	n/d
Copper	Cook	34	24	52'	NP
Crocodile	Cook	272	247	17'	**W** (91), LB
Crooked	Cook	233	109	66'	**LT**, NP
Cross Bay	Cook	n/d	n/d	n/d	n/d
Crystal	Cook	218	n/d	n/d	**W, LT**, NP
Daniels	Cook	489	86	90'	**LT** (96), **SB**
Deer	Cook	71	n/d	n/d	**NP, W**
Dent	Cook	n/d	n/d	n/d	n/d
Devil's Elbow	Cook	48	n/d	n/d	**W, SB**, NP
Duck	Cook	n/d	n/d	n/d	n/d
Dugout	Cook	25	25	8'	**NP, W**
Duncan	Cook	481	148	130'	**LT, SB**
East Bearskin	Cook	441	146	66'	**W** (95), **NP,** LT (97)
East Pike	Cook	496	124	40'	**SB**, NP, MU
Eddy	Lake	122	45	95'	**NP**, LB
Edith	Cook	10	n/d	n/d	**NP**
Ella	Cook	53	53	6'	**NP**
Elton	Lake	123	84	53'	**NP**
Ensign	Lake	1,408	605	30'	**W, SB**, NP
Ester	Lake	388	155	110'	**LT**
Fan	Cook	6	6	3'	none
Fay	Cook	66	15	62'	BT, LT
Fente	Cook	n/d	n/d	n/d	n/d
Flame	Cook	55	n/d	n/d	**NP**
Flying	Cook	n/d	n/d	n/d	n/d
Four	Lake	655	511	25'	**W, NP**, BLG
Fraser	Lake	811	n/d	n/d	**W**, NP, LT
French	Cook	112	17	130'	LT

LAKE NAME	COUNTY	ACRES	LITT	DEPTH	FISH SPECIES
Frog	Lake	n/d	n/d	n/d	n/d
Frond	Lake	n/d	n/d	n/d	n/d
Frost	Cook	236	61	88'	**LT**, NP
Gabbro	Lake	896	457	50'	**W, NP**, CR, BG
Gabimichigami	Cook	1,198	149	209'	**LT, NP**
Gasket	Cook	n/d	n/d	n/d	n/d
Gaskin	Cook	346	104	82'	W, SB, NP, LT
Gerund	Lake	98	27	85'	NP
Gibson	Lake	34	24	24'	**W, NP**
Gillis	Cook	570	88	180'	**LT**, NP
Glee	Cook	49	49	8'	none
Gneiss	Cook	59	n/d	n/d	**W, NP**, SB, LT
Gordon	Cook	139	64	95'	**NP**, LT
Gotter	Cook	n/d	n/d	n/d	n/d
Grace	Cook	391	297	16'	**W, NP**
Granite	Cook	20	n/d	n/d	**W**, NP, SB
Green	Cook	40	7	75'	none
Hanson	Lake	284	43	100'	**LT**, NP
Hatchet	Lake	126	107	40'	**W**, NP
Hazel	Lake	98	98	7'	**NP**
Hensen	Cook	n/d	n/d	n/d	n/d
Homer	Cook	443	400	22'	**W** (93), **NP**
Horseshoe	Cook	202	200	26'	**W**, NP, SB
Hub	Cook	98	98	7'	**NP**
Hubbub	Cook	n/d	n/d	n/d	n/d
Hudson	Lake	381	225	35'	**W, NP, BG**
Hug	Cook	n/d	n/d	n/d	n/d
Ima	Lake	772	208	116'	**LT, NP**, W, BL
Insula	Lake	2,957	1,183	63'	**W, NP**, BG
Isabella	Lake	1,516	1,165	19'	**W, NP**
Jack	Cook	101	101	10'	**W, NP**
Jake	Cook	28	22	26'	**NP**, BT
Jasper	Cook	239	86	125'	**W, SB, LT**
Jenny	Lake	102	53	93'	NP
John	Cook	169	168	20'	**NP**, W
Jordan	Lake	136	60	66'	W, NP
Juno	Cook	248	233	23'	**W**, NP

LAKE NAME	COUNTY	ACRES	LITT	DEPTH	FISH SPECIES
Karl	Cook	105	70	70'	**NP**, LT
Kawasachong	Lake	162	162	11'	**W, NP**
Kawishiwi	Lake	400	400	12'	**W, NP**
Kekekabic	Lake	1,620	97	195'	**LT**
Kelly	Cook	152	152	13'	**W**, SB, NP
Kelso	Cook	97	95	16'	**NP**
Kingfisher	Cook	35	n/d	n/d	W, LT
Kiskadinna	Cook	n/d	n/d	n/d	n/d
Kivaniva	Lake	38	30	49'	BG, NP, W
Knife	Lake	5,254	1,037	179'	**W, NP, LT**, SB
Knight	Cook	99	99	6'	**NP**
Koma	Lake	260	260	14'	**W, NP**, BG
Kroft	Cook	22	22	12'	n/d
Larch	Cook	131	131	14'	W (87), NP
Lily	Cook	22	n/d	n/d	NP
Little Caribou	Cook	58	49	18'	**W, NP, SB**
Little Gabbro	Lake	154	117	26'	W, NP
Little Rush	Cook	n/d	n/d	n/d	n/d
Little Saganaga	Cook	1,575	428	150'	**NP**, LT
Little Trout	Cook	123	n/d	n/d	**LT**
Lizz	Cook	30	21	30'	**BT** (97)
Long Island	Cook	864	310	85'	**LT**, NP
Lower George	Cook	n/d	n/d	n/d	n/d
Lujenida	Cook	n/d	n/d	n/d	n/d
Lux	Cook	47	41	21'	**NP**, BT (88)
Magnetic	Cook	431	95	90	**LT**, W, SB
Makwa	Lake	143	49	76'	**LT**, NP
Malberg	Lake	404	n/d	37'	**W**, NP, BG
Maraboeuf	Cook	398	n/d	n/d	**W, SB**, NP
Marshall	Cook	51	50	16'	**W**, NP, SB
Meeds	Cook	337	142	41'	**W**, NP
Melon	Lake	n/d	n/d	n/d	n/d
Mesaba	Cook	201	n/d	n/d	**NP**, LT
Middle Cone	Cook	73	37	30'	NP, **SB**, W
Misquah	Cook	60	15	60'	**LT**, BT (97)
Missing Link	Cook	40	25	25'	**BT** (97)
Moon	Cook	145	n/d	n/d	**W, NP, SB**
Moose	Cook	1,005	146	113'	**W, SB**, LT
Mora	Cook	205	n/d	n/d	**NP**
Morgan	Cook	82	40	46'	**NP**, BT (89)

LAKE NAME	COUNTY	ACRES	LITT	DEPTH	FISH SPECIES
Mountain	Cook	2,088	497	210'	**LT, SB**
Mueller	Lake	n/d	n/d	n/d	n/d
Mulligan	Cook	30	12	62'	**BT** (96)
Muskeg	Cook	n/d	n/d	n/d	n/d
North	Cook	2,695	477	125'	**LT, W, SB, NP**
North Cone	Cook	86	25	55'	**W**, NP, SB
North Fowl	Cook	1,020	1,020	10'	**W, NP, SB**
N. Temperance	Cook	178	84	50'	**W, NP**
Octopus	Cook	n/s	n/d	n/d	n/d
Ogishkemuncie	Lake	701	294	75'	**W**, LT
Omega	Cook	n/d	n/d	n/d	n/d
One	Lake	876	456	57'	**NP, BG, W**
Ottertrack	Lake	1,146	251	116'	**W, NP**, LT
Owl	Cook	81	30	70'	LT
Pan	Lake	100	47	59'	**W, NP**, BG
Panhandle	Lake	8	7	22'	**NP**, W, BG
Pencil	Cook	n/d	n/d	n/d	n/d
Perent	Lake	1,800	1,368	28'	**W**, NP
Peter	Cook	259	70	120'	**LT**
Peterson	Cook	88	88	15'	W, NP, SB
Phoebe	Cook	625	388	25'	**W, NP**
Pickle	Lake	n/d	n/d	n/d	n/d
Pierz	Cook	88	51	28'	none
Pillsbery	Cook	n/d	n/d	n/d	n/d
Pine	Cook	2,257	366	113'	**LT** (94), **W, SB**, NP
Polly	Lake	513	410	21'	**W**, NP
Powell	Cook	51	21	75'	**LT**
Ram	Cook	67	28	40'	**RT** (96), **LT** (97)
Rat	Cook	56	56	5'	**SB**
Rattle	Cook	45	28	30'	**NP**
Red Rock	Cook	353	145	59'	W, SB, NP
Rib	Cook	n/d	n/d	n/d	n/d
Rice	Lake	n/d	n/d	n/d	n/d
River	Lake	n/d	n/d	n/d	n/d
Roe	Lake	70	70	7'	none
Rose	Cook	1,315	408	90'	**LT, SB, W**
Ross	Cook	n/d	n/d	n/d	n/d
Rove	Cook	78	55	30'	**SB**, W

LAKE NAME	COUNTY	ACRES	LITT	DEPTH	FISH SPECIES
Royal	Cook	n/d	n/d	n/d	n/d
Rum	Cook	n/d	n/d	n/d	n/d
Rush	Cook	274	137	54'	**NP**
Saganaga	Cook	17,593	n/d	n/d	**W, NP, SB**, LT
Sagus	Lake	172	107	37'	**W**, NP
Sawbill	Cook	765	445	45'	**W**, NP, SB
Sea Gull	Cook	4,032	942	145'	**W, NP, SB**, LT
Sebeka	Cook	n/d	n/d	n/d	n/d
Seed	Lake	n/d	n/d	n/d	n/d
Shepo	Lake	52	43	17'	NP, W
Sitka	Cook	n/d	n/d	n/d	n/d
Skidway	Cook	18	18	8'	**NP**, W
Skipper	Cook	108	40	30'	**W, NP**
Skoop	Cook	n/d	n/d	n/d	n/d
Smoke	Cook	158	130	20'	**W, NP**
Snipe	Cook	112	88	90'	LT (93)
South	Cook	1,190	167	140'	**LT, SB**
South Cone	Cook	67	58	21'	**SB**, W, NP
S. Temperance	Cook	204	151	24'	**SB, W**, NP
Spoon	Lake	223	87	85'	NP
Square	Lake	127	127	7'	**W, NP**
Strup	Lake	n/d	n/d	n/d	n/d
Swallow	Cook	n/d	n/d	n/d	n/d
Swamp	Cook/Lake	n/d	n/d	n/d	n/d
Swan	Cook	180	49	108'	**W, SB**, NP, LT (97)
Tarry	Cook	n/d	n/d	n/d	n/d
Thomas	Lake	1,471	441	110'	**LT**, W, NP, BL
Three	Lake	881	388	37'	**W, NP**, BG
Town	Cook	79	25	72'	LT
Townline	Lake	n/d	n/d	n/d	n/d
Trail	Lake	n/d	n/d	n/d	n/d
Trapline	Lake	n/d	n/d	n/d	n/d
Trident	Lake	n/d	n/d	n/d	n/d
Tuscarora	Cook	833	200	130'	**LT**
Two	Lake	481	158	35'	**NP**, W, BG
Unload	Cook	n/d	n/d	n/d	n/d
Vaseux	Cook	10	10	10'	none

LAKE NAME	COUNTY	ACRES	LITT	DEPTH	FISH SPECIES
Vern	Cook	142	92	42'	**NP**, W
Vernon	Cook	233	70	83'	**SB**, W, LT (97)
Vesper	Cook	n/d	n/d	n/d	n/d
Virgin	Cook	n/d	n/d	n/d	n/d
Vista	Cook	222	202	47'	**W**, NP
Wanihigan	Cook	n/d	n/d	n/d	n/d
Warclub	Cook	n/d	n/d	n/d	n/d
Watap	Cook	202	n/d	n/d	**SB, W** (88)
Weird	Cook	33	33	6'	**NP**, W
West Fern	Cook	75	16	60'	**LT**
West Pike	Cook	715	224	120'	**LT, SB**
Whipped	Cook	n/d	n/d	n/d	n/d
Winchell	Cook	826	223	160'	**LT, NP**
Wisini	Lake	n/d	n/d	n/d	n/d
Zenith	Cook	n/d	n/d	n/d	n/d

Appendix V

BWCAW Hiking Trails in the Eastern Region

In addition to the 28 canoeing entry points detailed in this book, there are also 6 entry points for designated hiking trails in the eastern part of the Boundary Waters. Although the BWCA Wilderness is renowned for its canoeing opportunities, it also offers some of the most outstanding hiking trails in the Midwest. They include both short trails for day trips and long trails for overnight backpack outings. The lengths shown below are one-way. None of the trails makes a loop. The shorter trails are out-and-back. The longer trails each start at one point and end at another, which requires shuttling vehicles or making arrangements for a drop-off at the trailhead. This appendix briefly summarizes the hiking trails in the eastern region of the Wilderness. For more details, contact the Superior National Forest headquarters in Duluth or one of the Ranger District offices listed in Chapter 2.

EP #	Trail Name	Length	Loop?	Difficulty
56	**Kekekabic Trail (East)**	38 mi.	1-way	Rugged
Highlights—Mueller Falls, wildlife habitat				
59	**Partridge Lake Trail**	4 mi.	1-way	Moderate
Highlights—Partridge and South lakes, old growth pines				
79	**Eagle Mountain Trail**	3.5 mi.	1-way	Moderate
Highlights—Panoramic overlook from the highest point in Minnesota				

EP #	Trail Name	Length	Loop?	Difficulty
81	**Border Route Trail-West**	70 mi.	1-way	Moderate

Highlights–Spectacular views from many scenic overlooks, towering
and cliffs, virgin pine forests, moderate to rugged terrain

EP #	Trail Name	Length	Loop?	Difficulty
82	**Border Route Trail-Center**	70 mi.	1-way	Moderate
	and Caribou Rock Trail	3.5 mi.	1-way	Rugged

Highlights–Spectacular views from many scenic overlooks, towering
and cliffs, virgin pine forests, moderate to rugged terrain

EP #	Trail Name	Length	Loop?	Difficulty
83	**Border Route Trail-East**	70 mi.	1-way	Moderate

Highlights–Spectacular views from many scenic overlooks, towering
and cliffs, virgin pine forests, moderate to rugged terrain

INDEX